BABA YAGA

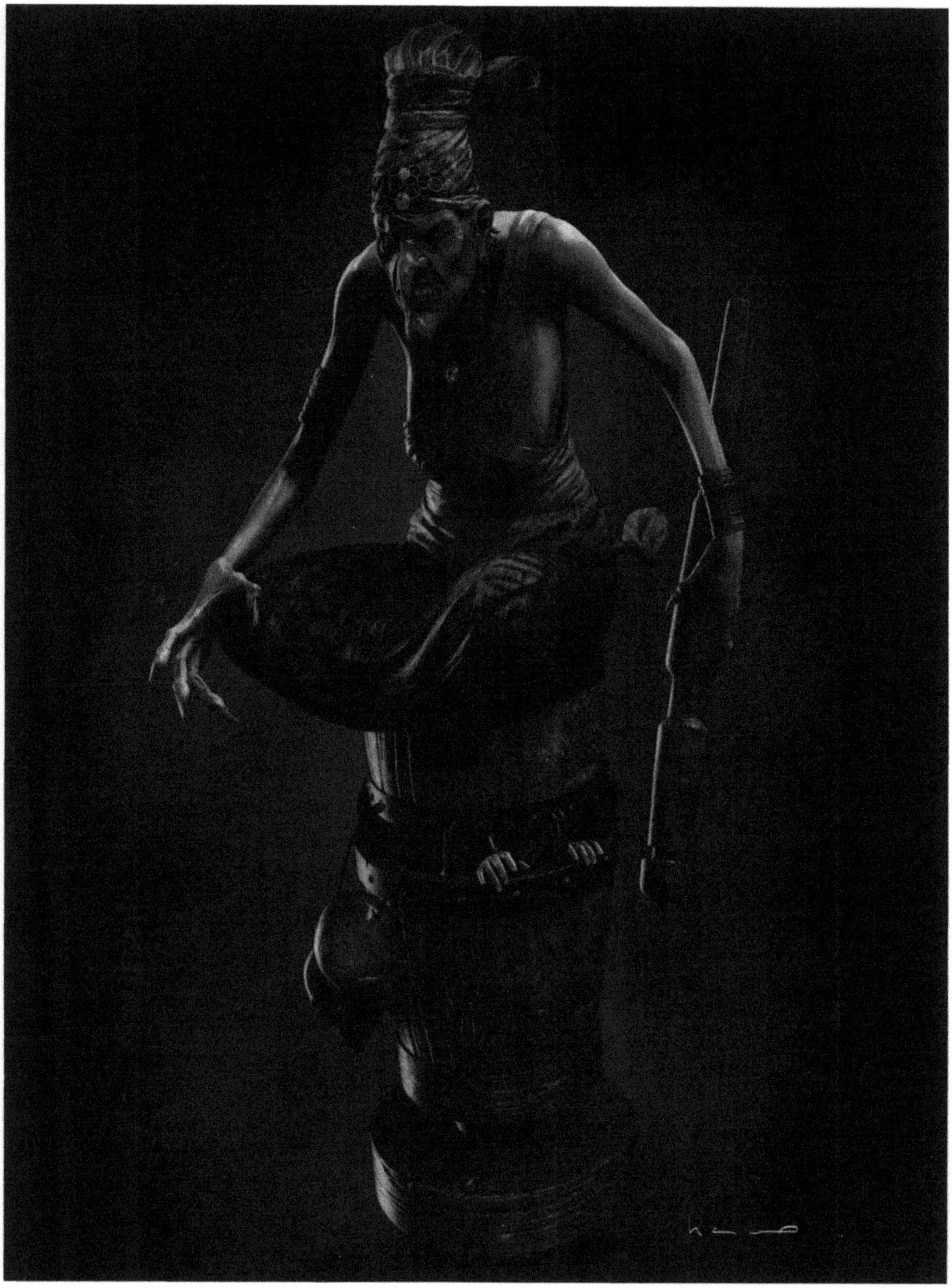

Baba Yaga by Fabiano Mello de Lima. A digital sculpture by the storyboard artist Fabiano Mello de Lima that desexes Baba Yaga. An original feature is the pair of small hands protruding from the aperture in the vehicular mortar on which she is seated, presumably belonging to a captured child who will become Baba Yaga's meal and end up as a skull to be added either to Baga Yaga's fence or to those dangling from the mortar. Illustration by Fabiano Mello de Lima, Fabiano Lima <biano3d@yahoo.com>.

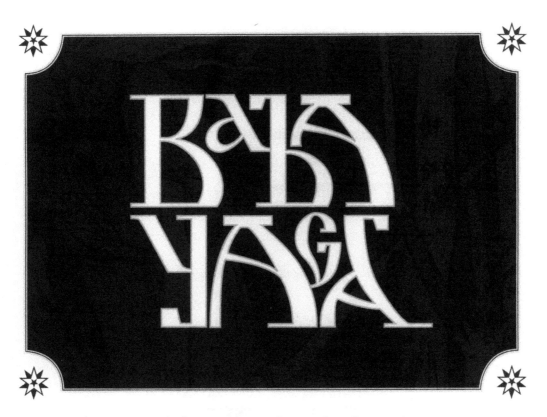

BABA YAGA

The Wild Witch of the East in Russian Fairy Tales

Introduction and Translations by Sibelan Forrester

Captions to Images by Helena Goscilo

Selection of Images by Martin Skoro and Helena Goscilo

Edited by Sibelan Forrester, Helena Goscilo, and Martin Skoro

Foreword by Jack Zipes

UNIVERSITY PRESS OF MISSISSIPPI ✵ JACKSON

www.upress.state.ms.us

The University Press of Mississippi is a member of the Association of American University Presses.

With Support and Assistance from The Museum of Russian Art, 5500 Stevens Ave. S., Minneapolis, MN 55419, http://tmora.org

First printing 2013

Library of Congress Cataloging-in-Publication Data

Baba Yaga : the wild witch of the East in Russian fairy tales / introduction and translations by Sibelan Forrester ; captions to images by Helena Goscilo ; selection of images by Martin Skoro and Helena Goscilo ; edited by Sibelan Forrester, Helena Goscilo, and Martin Skoro ; foreword by Jack Zipes.
pages : illustrations ; cm
Includes bibliographical references.
ISBN 978-1-61703-596-8 (cloth paper) — ISBN 978-1-61703-778-8 (ebook)
1. Baba Yaga (Legendary character) 2. Tales—Russia. I. Forrester, Sibelan E. S. (Sibelan Elizabeth S.), translator, editor of compilation. II. Goscilo, Helena, 1945–, editor of compilation. III. Skoro, Martin, editor of compilation. IV. Zipes, Jack, 1937–, writer of added commentary.
GR75.B22B22 2013
398.20947—dc23 2013003373

British Library Cataloging-in-Publication Data available

CONTENTS

Tales of Baba Yaga

Illustration by Ivan Bilibin (1876–1942).

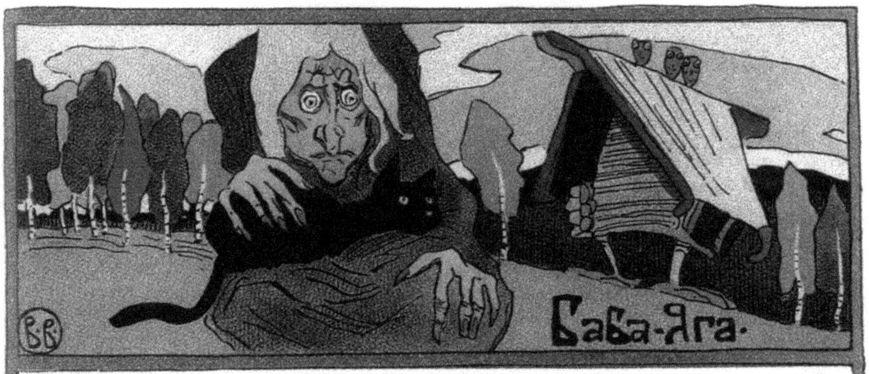

FOREWORD

Unfathomable Baba Yagas

JACK ZIPES

In *Baba Yaga: The Ambiguous Mother and Witch of the Russian Folktale*, the most thorough study of Baba Yaga to date, Andreas Johns demonstrates that Baba Yaga has appeared in hundreds if not thousands of folktales in Russia, Ukraine, and Belarus since the eighteenth century, if not earlier. She is not just a dangerous witch but also a maternal benefactress, probably related to a pagan goddess. Many other Russian scholars such as Joanna Hubbs in *Mother Russia: The Feminine Myth in Russian Culture*, Linda Ivanits in *Russian Folk Belief*, and Cherry Gilchrist in *Russian Magic: Living Folk Traditions of an Enchanted Landscape* have confirmed this: Baba Yaga transcends definition because she is an amalgamation of deities mixed with a dose of sorcery. Though it is difficult to trace the historical evolution of this mysterious figure with exactitude, it is apparent that Baba Yaga was created by many voices and hands from the pre-Christian era in Russia up through the eighteenth century when she finally became "fleshed out," so to speak, in the abundant Russian and other Slavic tales collected in the nineteenth century. These Russian and Slavic folktales were the ones that formed an indelible and unfathomable image of what a Baba Yaga is. I say "a Baba Yaga," because in many tales there are three Baba Yagas, often sisters, and in some tales a Baba Yaga is killed only to rise again. And no Baba Yaga is exactly like another.

Illustration by Viktor Vasnetsov (1848–1926).

A Baba Yaga is inscrutable and so powerful that she does not owe allegiance to the Devil or God or even to her storytellers. In fact, she opposes all Judeo-Christian and Muslim deities and beliefs. She is her own woman, a parthogenetic mother, and she decides on a case-by-case basis whether she will help or kill the people who come to her hut that rotates on chicken legs. She shows very few characteristics and tendencies of western witches, who were demonized by the Christian church, and who often tend to be beautiful and seductive, cruel and vicious. Baba Yaga sprawls herself out in her hut and has ghastly features—drooping breasts, a hideous long nose, and sharp iron teeth. In particular, she thrives on Russian blood and is cannibalistic. Her major prey consists of children and young women, but she will occasionally threaten to devour a man. She kidnaps in the form of a Whirlwind or other guises. She murders at will. Though we never learn how she does this, she has conceived daughters, who generally do her bidding. She lives in the forest, which is her domain. Animals venerate her, and she protects the forest as a mother-earth figure. The only times she leaves it, she travels in a mortar wielding a pestle as a club or rudder and a broom to sweep away the tracks behind her. At times, she can also be generous with her advice, but her counsel and help do not come cheaply, for a Baba Yaga is always testing the people who come to her hut by chance or by choice. A Baba Yaga may at times be killed, but there are others who take her place. Baba Yaga holds the secret to the water of life and may even be Mother Earth herself. This is why Baba Yaga is very much alive today, and not only in Mother Russia, but also throughout the world.

While a Baba Yaga is still a uniquely Russian folk character, she has now become an international legendary figure and will probably never die. Stories about her dreadful and glorious deeds circulate throughout the world in translation. Fabulous book illustrations, paintings, and colorful designs imprinted, painted, or carved on all kinds of artifacts have flourished in the twentieth and twenty-first centuries. She is often the star figure in children's picture books, even though she functions primarily as a witch. Films, animated cartoons, and digital images have portrayed a Baba Yaga as omnipotent, dreadful, and comical. In many of the images, she is shown flying about in her mortar and wielding her pestle as in the illustrations by Viktor Bibikov, Dimitri Mitrokhin, and Viktor Vasnetsov. She seems always obsessed and vicious. Some artists such as Aleksandr Nanitchkov and Rima Staines are fond of showing her in weird types of huts on chicken legs. No matter how she is portrayed, there are always hints of her Russian heritage in the images. The emphasis on traditional dress and nineteenth-century styles are especially evident in the famous illustrations for *Vasilisa the Beautiful* by Ivan Bilibin and the gouache paintings by Boris Zvorykin for *Vasilisa the Fair*. In particular, Bilibin's watercolors have had a profound influence on how Baba Yaga and other characters were to be imagined. That is, he set a high artistic standard at the beginning of the twentieth century. Yet, no matter how Baba Yaga is portrayed, it is her strange Russian otherness that paradoxically strikes a common chord in readers of her tales. This strange commonality can be viewed in a wide array of illustrations, designs, and artifacts created by artists of different nations, many which have been carefully selected by Martin Skoro for this volume.

While Skoro's colorful selection of images reveals the breadth and depth of numerous artists inspired by Baba Yaga tales, the superb translation of the Russian tales by Sibelan Forrester provides an unusual opportunity to appreciate the cultural significance of Baba Yaga in the nineteenth century. Forrester has carefully selected tales in which Baba Yaga plays a key role from Aleksandr Nikolaevich Afanas'ev's *Russian Folk Tales* (1855–1866) and Ivan Aleksandrovich Khudiakov's *Great Russian Tales* (1860–1862), two of the pioneer collections of Russian folktales. As Jack Haney has pointed out in his significant study, *An Introduction to the Russian Folktale*, Afanas'ev and Khudiakov were not alone during this period when many writers and scholars began collecting folktales, but their collections are generally considered the richest and most interesting, especially with regard to the oral wonder tales that feature Baba Yaga. Afanas'ev did not collect most of his tales himself but relied on the archives of the Geographical Society in Moscow and on tales sent to him by friends and colleagues. As for Khudiakov, he actually went into the countryside to collect his tales, and he had a keen eye for satirical stories.

It was not easy for either Afanas'ev or Khudiakov to publish their tales because of the strict censorship in the Russian Empire during the nineteenth century, and any work that appeared to be anticlerical, politically questionable, or scatological was often denied permission for publication. Or, the texts were heavily edited and changed. In general, tales largely told by peasants, which might reinforce belief in ancient rituals, beliefs, witches, wizards, and supernatural animals, were looked upon with great suspicion by the governmental authorities, the church, and the upper classes. Nevertheless, it had been impossible before and still was in the nineteenth century for the church and state to prevent the oral dissemination of wonder tales that were deeply rooted in pagan traditions. By the nineteenth century their appeal to intellectuals grew. Indeed, the national and cultural interest in historical Russian folklore had grown stronger among the literate classes so that social conditions in the latter part of the nineteenth century favored the publication of all kinds of tales. Finally, we must bear in mind, as Haney has suggested, that Russians, especially the peasants, continued to believe deeply in the meanings of the tales for their lives and in such figures as Baba Yaga, Russalka, Kolschei the Deathless, fierce dragons, and bears with magical powers. What may seem fiction and superstition to us today was fact and faith in the nineteenth century.

The Baba Yaga tales chosen for this volume by Forrester are vivid depictions of how Baba Yaga functioned and figured in different tale types of the mid-nineteenth century and lent a distinct Russian aura to the stories. But it is important first to bear in mind the commonalities of the tales that were widespread in Europe and the Middle East during the nineteenth century. For instance, "Again the Stepmother and the Stepmother's Daughter" is similar to numerous western European tales in which a wise woman in an underground world bestows gifts on an industrious young girl and punishes a lazy, arrogant girl. "Vasilisa the Beautiful" belongs to the great Indo-European tradition of "Cinderella" tales. The motif of incest in "Prince Danila-Govorila" was a significant one in numerous medieval romances and tales in Europe. "Finist the Bright Falcon" is related to the numerous beast bridegroom tales that were disseminated throughout Europe. Other motifs such as the magic tablecloth, the invisible cloak, the flying carpet, the stick that hits by itself, and the donkey that spews gold were common in Europe and the Middle East. "The Three Kingdoms—Copper, Silver, and Gold" recalls numerous Italian and Arab tales, distinguished by plots in which a youngest brother is sent down a well by his two older brothers to rescue three princesses, only to be abandoned by them in the well after he is successful. The only way the youngest brother can return to his father's kingdom and claim that he was the true rescuer is by riding a magic eagle that eats some of his flesh. Almost every tale in the collection translated by Forrester can be found in other European or Middle Eastern collections of tales in the nineteenth century that speak to the amazing oral and print dissemination of wonder tales and say something about the universal appeal of these tales.

Yet, there are differences that reflect cultural particularities, and the most distinguishable feature of Russian wonder tales, in my opinion, is Baba Yaga. No matter what a tale type or how common it may be in the Indo-European tradition, she will emerge in the story as the decisive figure and turn the plot in favor of or against the protagonist. Moreover, I know of no other witch/wise woman character in European folklore who is so amply described and given such unusual paraphernalia as Baba Yaga. Most important, she clearly announces how enmeshed she is with Russia whenever she senses Russian blood is near. No one has ever fully explained why it is that she is always so eager to spill and devour Russian blood and not the blood of some other nation. One would think that, as a protector of Russian soil, she might always be helpful when Russians appear at her hut. Yet, she is most severe with Russians and seems strangely to be protecting Russian soil from the Russians. She also demands the most from Russians and shows no mercy if they fail to listen to her. A Baba Yaga is the ultimate tester and judge, the desacralized omnipotent goddess, who defends deep-rooted Russian pagan values and wisdom and demands that young women and men demonstrate that they deserve her help. But what Baba Yaga also defends in the nineteenth-century tales collected in this volume are qualities that the protagonists need to adapt and survive in difficult situations such as perseverance, kindness, obedience, integrity, and courage. If we bear in mind that these tales reflect the actual living conditions of the Russian people in the mid-nineteenth century to a large degree, and that they were listened to and read at face value, they are very profound "documents" about the struggles of ordinary Russians and their faith in extraordinary creatures to help them in times of need. They are also dreams of compensation for their helplessness. Stories of hope. The tales are filled with sibling rivalry, bitter conflicts between stepchildren and stepmothers, incest, class struggle, disputes about true heirs, ritual initiations, the pursuit of immortality, and so on. Though the tales may take place in another time and realm, they are always brought down to earth by the storyteller at the end, for what may happen metaphorically to the characters in the tales is very close to the conditions experienced by the listeners. In all the tales Baba Yaga is compelling and dreaded, because she forces the protagonists to test themselves and not to delude themselves that there is an easy way to reconcile conflicts. This is also why Baba Yaga transcends Russia and has become woven in other cultures, to be sure, in ways that are much different from the nineteenth-century tales in this collection.

The intercultural weaving of witches and wise women is a fascinating aspect of all folklore throughout the world. Indeed, when we begin to study the otherness of such characters as Baba Yaga, we learn a great deal about our own culture by noting differences, while, at the same time, we can make startling comparisons that show why Baba Yaga may be connected to other folk traditions of folk sorcery throughout the world. In a fascinating study of recorded stories of Sicilian fairies and witches from the sixteenth to the nineteenth centuries, Gustav Henningsen writes: "Like southern Spain, Sicily was a region in which sorcery and black magic thrived, but where popular notions of witchcraft were absent. However, in contrast to Spain, Sicily could boast of a particular type of charismatic healer, who was a specialist in curing diseases caused by the fairies: these healers were women and sometimes men, too, who claimed to possess 'sweet blood' (*sangre dulce*), and who therefore each Tuesday, Thursday, and Saturday night were obliged to rush out in spirit (*in espíritu*) and take part in the meetings and nocturnal journeyings of 'the company.'"[1] Henningsen explains that numerous Sicilian women from the sixteenth through the nineteenth centuries asserted they were healers, *donas di fuora* (ladies from outside), and that they often combined the qualities of a witch and a fairy to perform healing acts to offset the evil of some other fairies or supernatural creatures. In other words, the *donas di fuora* were very similar to the Baba Yagas of Russian tradition; they belonged to a dualistic system of widespread belief and could cause harm or do good. Even if fairy-witches caused harm, there were ways through offerings or expiation to repair damage. Henningsen believes that the fairy cult was, to a certain extent, compensation for the hopeless poverty of daily life throughout Sicily. More important, he explains that the fairy cult is "a variant of a widely extended and therefore presumably old and deep-rooted Mediterranean and east European complex of shamanistic beliefs." In Sicily, the belief in fairies and sorceresses led to the creation of a character called La Mamma-dràa (Mamma-draga the Ogress) by the nineteenth century. She appears in numerous Sicilian wonder tales and is connected to the "ladies from the outside." Though this figure (sometimes a male) is never amply described in the tales, she functions like a Baba Yaga, dangerous and benevolent, a cannibal and a wise counselor.

It is not necessary, I believe, to draw "exact" parallels between the Sicilian fairy cult and the shamanistic Baba Yaga cult in Russia. There is enough evidence to indicate that there were strongly held beliefs in pagan goddesses in Sicily and Russia that were transformed into tales that enabled peasants in both countries to contend with their suffering and to offer some hope for a better life. It is perhaps strange to conclude that Baba Yaga may be a symbol of hope because she is so ambiguous, as often frightening as benevolent. But hope may be best generated when a wise woman does not mince her words, and a true Baba Yaga is never one to mince her words.

PREFACE, ACKNOWLEDGMENTS, AND TRANSLATOR'S NOTE

What could be more intriguing than a book about a famous witch? This collection offers twenty-nine fairy tales featuring Baba Yaga, along with images that show how artists have imagined her for over more than two centuries. We love Baba Yaga and want to present her here in all her richness and complexity.

This book is meant for many kinds of readers. Those with a Russian background will find familiar tales, an introduction that presents a variety of ways to understand Baba Yaga, images from a variety of sources, and some recommendations for further reading. Specialists in Russian culture and in folklore will reach for the volume to learn more about Baba Yaga or perhaps will assign it to students in courses on Russian folklore or fairy tales. The book will also appeal to readers who are simply curious about this colorful folkloric figure.

The brief bibliography (pages liii–lv) includes many of the sources mentioned in the introduction, along with a filmography and the sources for images. The tales are taken from two famous nineteenth-century collections: the 1855–1863 compilation of Aleksandr Afanas'ev, the best-known and most often translated in the West (*Narodnye russkie skazki*), and the tales collected by Ivan Khudiakov, first published in 1861–1862 (*Velikorusskie skazki*).[1] Afanas'ev was an editor more than a collector, though his well-developed sense of what constituted "real" folklore led him to exclude versions that had been spoiled by the educated collectors who had written them down. Some of the tales in Afanas'ev's editions had appeared in earlier printed

Illustration by Ivan Bilibin (1876–1942).

version, making them even further removed from the oral originals than the handwritten recordings he worked with in the archives of the Russian Geographical Society. His versions tend in general to be longer, more poetic, and less conversational than Khudiakov's; many though not all of them have something of a literary finish. Khudiakov recorded most of his tales from the tellers themselves, often identifying the place and teller in brief notes that we have included after the tales taken from his collection; his versions are less stylistically elegant or elaborate than Afanas'ev's. Juxtaposing Afanas'ev's and Khudiakov's versions makes for interesting differences, especially when the plots overlap. We might compare the pleasure of reading variants of the same tale to that of hearing a familiar song performed by a new singer, and sometimes the voices of individual tellers come strongly through the layers of time and translation. Where the tales include variants (different versions of the same plot, perhaps told by different individuals at different times), these are included in the notes that follow the tales. The variants are interesting to general readers as well as to folklorists, and including them was something of an innovation in Afanas'ev's collection.

Martin Skoro conceived the idea for this book some years ago. He gathered images of Baba Yaga and found information about her in numerous books and on the Web. Sibelan Forrester selected and translated a group of folktales that feature Baba Yaga and was primarily responsible for writing the introduction to the book. Helena Goscilo brought striking images of Baba Yaga from her own collection and added incisive analysis of the images, along with valuable comments on the introduction and translations. We are grateful to have the foreword from Jack Zipes, a folklorist and scholar we tremendously admire. His comments and suggestions also contributed significantly to the introduction and the translations.

ACKNOWLEDGMENTS

Thanks to the Slavic Collection of the Library of the University of Illinois in Urbana-Champaign, whose shelves hold nineteenth-century editions of Afanas'ev and Khudiakov. Thanks also to McCabe Library at Swarthmore College and to the magical powers of Inter-Library Loan. Swarthmore College supported this project with research funding (a James A. Michener Faculty fellowship) and the opportunity for me (SF) to teach a course on Russian Folktales; I owe particular thanks to Provost Tom Stephenson for

Kak Muzhik u Vsex v Dolgu ostalsia i kak [How the Peasant Man Wound up in Debt to Everyone and How] by Vasilii Lebedev, 1923. Reproduced courtesy of the Cotsen Children's Library, Princeton University Library.

support of the edition. I am grateful to Robert Chandler, one of the foremost translators from Russian in the world today, for comments on the introduction and some of the translations, and for including a briefer version of the introduction as an appendix in his edition, *Russian Magic Tales from Pushkin to Platonov*.[2] It has been a great pleasure working with Craig Gill at the University Press of Mississippi, and the other thoughtful and talented workers at the Press. Jack Zipes has proved yet again to be a true prince, and I am eternally grateful to N.B., as well as to my collaborators in this venture, Marty and Helena. (SF)

My gratitude to the hundreds of magic-loving students at the University of Pittsburgh enrolled in Russian Fairy Tales, the course I originated there many moons ago, and to David Birnbaum, who proved not only a fellow image-maven, but also a benevolent stepfather when he adopted the course and, in quintessential fairy-tale mode, transformed it into a different beast—a veritable hydra with numerous teaching heads. (HG)

I'm grateful to so many friends, family members, and business professionals for their interest, encouragement, and help in seeing this book come to fruition.

The synthesis that produces a book is an exciting experience to behold. It's humbling to witness like-minded individuals bringing diverse expertise to bear with such grace. I'm truly grateful that the swirl of fate brought me to encounter renowned literary scholar Jack Zipes, that Jack took me under his wing to guide and mentor me, and that he connected me to Professor Sibelan Forrester, who in turn brought to the project Professor Helena Goscilo. All three are remarkable scholars in the field of literary scholarship. Another suggestion from Jack directed me to the University Press of Mississippi, whose assistant director and editor in chief, Craig Gill, was a most gracious, patient, and broad-minded steward.

I thank Jack for generously providing the foreword for the book; Sibelan for her counsel, the enormous work and expertise on the translations and the writing of the introduction, the preface, and the index; Helena for contributing her time, advice, the writing of the wonderful image captions and guidance on image use and placement; Craig for his creative administration and problem-solving of many quandaries along the way. John Langston and Pete Halverson, also of the Press, were saving graces with their design expertise, and patience.

To the organizations and individuals that were gracious in their help and granting usage of images I am deeply appreciative. Andrea Immel, AnnaLee Pauls, and Charles E. Greene at the Princeton Cotsen Children's Library were very helpful and encouraging. Jennifer Chang Rowley at Random House, Inc., and Lia Ribacchi at Dark Horse Comics, Inc., all were generous and well-wishing. I thank, too, for their indispensable help, friends Sam Ross, Tony Santucci, Tom McGrail, and in spirit, Doug Sharp.

I also would like to acknowledge those individual artists who have graciously permitted use of their art. Specific artists who did artwork for the book or worked hard to update or polish their work are Rima Staines of England; Alexander Nanitchkov of Bulgaria; Cindy Furguson and Forest Rogers of the United States; Sergei Tyukanov and Waldemar Kazak of Russia; and Fabiano Mello de Lima of Brazil.

I have many friends to thank also for their interest and generous monetary contributions that have helped to make possible the printing of the book in full color. I am deeply indebted. Thank you.

The seed of the desire to see this book realized grew from a deep love of stories, folktales, and mysteries cultivated by my father and mother, who loved books and all the knowledge and wisdom within them. They provided a loving atmosphere of adventure and wonder.

Kak Muzhik u Vsex v Dolgu ostalsia i kak by Vasilii Lebedev, 1923. Reproduced courtesy of the Cotsen Children's Library, Princeton University Library.

My life companion, partner, and wife, Ross (Roselyn), has been a blessing throughout my life and my best friend. She has been ever patient and gracious for understanding my want to see this book completed. (MS)

TRANSLATOR'S NOTE

As Roman Jakobson and Pëtr Bogatyrev noted in the 1920s, folklore is a special kind of creativity. Folktale plots do exist in a kind of ideal, potential state, but they are encountered only in real-time oral performance (or, secondarily, in written recordings drawn from spoken performances). Usually a single person tells a tale, but even if he or she is the best teller in the region, with the biggest repertoire of stories, the audience will "edit" a tale in the course of its performance. If listeners are at loose ends and the tale grabs their attention, their appreciation may encourage the teller to go into more detail. Perhaps they will even offer the teller something to wet his or her whistle; many of the tales end with a ritual hint that the teller would indeed like a drink, if not two. If the audience is in a hurry, the tale will be short; if the audience gets bored, it will not request that tale or teller again. Listeners feel no compunction about shouting down an unappealing teller or tale. Thanks to such collective "censorship," these tales are the property of

A *lubok* (popular woodcut print) showing Baba Yaga dancing to bagpipes played by a bearded, balding peasant. Early eighteenth century, anonymous. Some commentators view this scene as a positive depiction of the domestic relations between Peter the Great and his wife, Catherine, the first woman to rule Russia, though briefly (1725–1727).

a whole community and a whole culture. Thus, we can assume that people liked Baba Yaga and appreciated her role in the tales, since she shows up in many of the most popular and widely attested Russian tales.

In the late 1920s, when Jakobson and Bogatyrev were writing about the distinctions between folklore and literature, folktales were still a living phenomenon in the villages around Moscow—and not only as children's amusement or unofficial form of cultural education. They also offered adults a way to pass the time as they worked, or to while away a long night, when in winter it was too dark to work and in summer perhaps too light to sleep. Like folk songs, dances, and fortune-telling, tales could form part of seasonal rituals. Variation among versions of the tales is not just typical, but inevitable, since, again, the tales were told under different circumstances. We today might similarly reorder and "improve" a story we heard from a friend or adapt a joke to suit different audiences. In order to convey something of this aspect of "live" folklore, we include not just a variety of Baba Yaga tales, but also several variants of tale plots. The reader will see that some tales with different titles overlap considerably in the structure of their plots (as do "The Brother" and "The Geese and Swans"), while others have the same title but significant differences in plot (compare the two versions of "The Three Kingdoms"). Baba Yaga's popularity in Russia fairy tales means that a book of tales involving her is also a rich introduction to this part of the

Russian folk heritage, including one or another version of many of the best-known and best-loved tales.

Folktales are everyone's property, and they have always crossed linguistic and ethnic boundaries just as people migrate in time and space. Baba Yaga is a Russian witch who will sound somewhat different transported into American English. Some of the original sources include dialect words from the regions of Russia where they were recorded, but I have tried to make the language fairly neutral, emphasizing the story more than the narrator's linguistic idiosyncrasies. The overall style aims to be comfortable for reading aloud. Where the original Russian includes a particularly enjoyable or unusual word, it is mentioned in a note to the text. At the same time, this is a translation rather than a retelling by a folk teller who performs in a different language, and so I have endeavored to preserve some of the foreignness of these texts. The introduction below will dwell on a few forms of this foreignness.

Some parts of the tales are difficult to render in English, such as the unusual names (beginning with Baba Yaga, whose name in Russian is rarely written with upper-case letters and often refers not to a single person, but to a figure that can show up three times in one tale), titles (like the *tsar*, whose title comes from "Caesar" by way of Byzantine Greek), or objects from everyday traditional life in Russia, including Baba Yaga's own hut and accoutrements. These aspects convey a wonderful strangeness, an imprint of Russian traditional culture quite distinct from other national traditions. Some of the details that might catch the reader's interest are also glossed briefly in in notes.

Reading aloud may be the closest that most of us will come to the original *spoken* performance of folktales. For better or worse, we live in a literate culture, where most people can no longer produce a long narrative without memorizing it, though we probably all know people who have an unusual talent for telling stories. We do continue to practice folklore, but today it tends to be in different genres: ghost stories, jokes, rumors, or the various urban legends that shade into popular culture.

Nevertheless, perhaps the reader of the tales in this book will be inspired to tell them to someone—and bring Baba Yaga back to life.

Sibelan Forrester
Swarthmore, Pennsylvania
August 2012

B is for Baba Yaga, from *Picture Alphabet* by Alexandre Benois (1904). A frequently reproduced image from the children's alphabet book conceived and illustrated by Benois—B is for Baba Yaga. Interrupted at gathering mushrooms, the older of two potential victims stares in awed terror at the Frequent Flyer old crone overhead. Benois's choice implies that Russian children learned about Baba Yaga at a very early age and possibly derived some pleasure from fear. Illustration by Alexandre Benois (1870–1960).

INTRODUCTION

Baba Yaga: The Wild Witch of the East

Who is this wild witch, and why is she riding in a *mortar*?

As the classic Russian fairy-tale witch, Baba Yaga has elicited fascination, trepidation, and wonder in generations of Russian children and adults. This book offers twenty-nine stories and even more images; the tales are from Russia, while the illustrations come both from Russia and from the wider world. Our introduction is meant to put Baba Yaga in context and perhaps to answer questions that arise during or after reading. We hope this collection will appeal to many kinds of readers, whether they have a special personal or scholarly interest in Russia, are students of folklore or popular culture, are curious about the psychological resonance of folktales, or are simply following their instinct for pleasure.

THE HISTORY OF THE WORDS

Though only a few of the tales say it in so many words, most Russians would agree that Baba Yaga is a witch. The Russian word for witch is *ved'ma*. The word root *ved-* means 'to know,' and related words in Modern Russian mean 'news' (as in the title of *Pravda*'s one-time competitor, the Soviet newspaper *Izvestiia*), as well as information or consultation, and the particle *ved'* means

Illustration by Ivan Bilibin (1876–1942).

'indeed' (as if commanding one's listener "know this!"). The word *witch* in English has a similar linguistic history: the root of witch is *wit*. That verb still shows up in English "to wit," "unwitting," the old-fashioned phrase "God wot," and of course in keeping one's *wits* about one. Feminists and Wiccans have worked to reclaim the word witch in its sense of "wise woman" or "woman who knows," but in both Russian and English the words as commonly used suggest age and ugliness first, power second. Over the centuries, words that name women and girls have often slipped in meaning from ordinary or even admiring terms into insults, much as some neutral terms for ethnic, racial, or religious groups have come to be used as insults (which then requires invention of a new, neutral word that may feel clumsy at first). "Wench" was once a neutral term for a girl, and the Russian word *devka*, which suggests a prostitute as the word is used in many literary works, was the neutral term for an unmarried peasant girl—a member of the group most likely to be sexually exploited by upper-class Russian men. Language neatly shows the social standing of different groups, and its development can reveal historical changes in social relationships.

Even if we call her a witch, what does Baba Yaga's name mean? The first half is easy: *baba* in traditional Russian culture meant a married peasant woman, one at least old enough to have children. (In Russian now, *baba* is an insulting word for a woman: it suggests low class, slovenliness, lack of emotional restraint, or sexual availability of an aging or otherwise unattractive kind.) When Russians build a snowman, they call it not a man, but a snow *baba*. Suffixes bring out different shades of the basic meanings of Russian nouns: *babka* is a midwife (usually, an older woman with experience around pregnancy and childbirth); *babushka* is an affectionate term for 'grandmother' (and, in the West, the headscarf old women in Russia traditionally wore); on another note, *babochka* is a butterfly, or else the visually similar bow tie. The word *babochka* is related to an ancient belief that, when a person died, the soul left the body in the form of a bird or a butterfly (compare the Greek *psyche*, which meant both 'soul' and 'butterfly'). If a butterfly fluttered by, it was the soul of a little grandmother, presumably en route to a better place. Thus, *baba* can mean 'old woman,' though it does not always; the word *starukha* (more affectionately, *starushka*), 'old woman,' makes a woman's age clear. Age is described in Russian folktales in a way that might surprise us today, too. The "old man" and "old woman" in a tale are old enough to have children of marriageable age, but they may be just barely old enough—perhaps in their late thirties. Baba Yaga is far older than that.

The second part of her name, *yaga*, is harder to define. Scholars do not know exactly what it means, though they point to similar words as a comparison. One school of thought relates the word to verbs for riding—and it does sound rather like the Russian verb *ekhat'* 'to ride,' or the German word *Jaeger* 'huntsman.' Another theory is that *yaga* originally meant 'horrible,' 'horrifying,' and should be compared to the words *jeza* 'shiver' or *jezivo* 'chilling, horrifying' in some of the South Slavic languages (Bosnian, Croatian, Serbian). If Baba Yaga originally played a role in a secret corpus of myths or initiation rituals, a taboo might have discouraged people from saying her name in other contexts. (In another example, the original Russian word for *bear* is lost; most Slavic languages use a euphemism, like the Russian *medved'*. That word came from roots meaning 'honey-eater,' but now it looks like 'honey-knower,' with the same root, *ved-*, that appears in the word *ved'ma*. As contemporary political cartoons show, the bear is still a central figure in Russian culture.) Maks Fasmer's monumental *Etymological Dictionary of the Russian Language*[1] has a longish entry for "yaga," pointing out cognate words in other Slavic languages and arguing against several theories of the word's origins and original meaning. The amount of space Fasmer devotes to dismantling other theories suggests that we will never know the real origin of the word 'yaga.' Figures very much like Baba Yaga appear in West Slavic (Czech and Polish) tales; the rich reference work *Mify narodov mira*, 'Myths of the Peoples of the World,' mentions the Polish *jędza* and Czech *jezinka*, 'forest *baba*.' Baba Yaga is well known in Ukrainian and Belarusian tales, though we have limited our translations to Russian tales here.[2]

In Russian, Baba Yaga's name is not capitalized. Indeed, it is not a name at all, but a description—"old lady yaga" or perhaps "scary old woman." There is often more than one Baba Yaga in a story, and thus we should really say "a Baba Yaga," "the Baba Yaga." We do so in these tales when a story would otherwise be confusing. We have continued the western tradition of capitalizing Baba Yaga, since the words cannot be translated and have no other meaning in English (aside perhaps from the pleasant associations of a rum baba). There is no graceful way to put the name in the plural in English, and in Russian tales multiple iterations of Baba Yaga never appear at the same time, only in sequence: Baba Yaga sisters or cousins talk about one another, or send travelers along to one another, but they do not live together. The first-person pronoun "I" in Russian, '*ia*,' is also uncapitalized. In some tales our witch is called only "Yaga." A few tales refer to her as "Yagishna," a patronymic form suggesting that she is Yaga's daughter rather than Yaga herself.

(That in turn suggests that Baba Yaga reproduces parthenogenetically, and some scholars agree that she does.) The lack of capitalization in every published Russian folktale also hints at Baba Yaga's status as a type rather than an individual, a paradigmatic mean or frightening old woman. This description in place of a name, too, could suggest that it was once a euphemism for another name or term, too holy or frightening to be spoken, and therefore now long forgotten.

OTHER NAMES IN THE TALES

Many Russian personal names are recognizable in English, since they are related to familiar biblical or western names. Mar'ia is the folk form of Maria, though it is pronounced "MAR-ya." We have left the prime mark (') in Mar'ia Morevna's name in the eponymous tale to remind the reader of that difference. The second part of Mar'ia Morevna's name is a patronymic, formed from her father's name. It means "Daughter of the Sea"—quite unusual parentage. They suggest that she, like Baba Yaga, descends from some very old sources.[3] *Belaia lebed',* 'White Swan' Zakhar'evna, in the second version of "The Young Man and the Apples of Youth" here, has a more ordinary patronymic: her father's name was Zakharii (= Zacharias). Vasilii and Vasilisa are forms of the name Basil (which does not produce a woman's name in English). Ivan is the most common name for a Russian fairy-tale hero, whether he starts out as a prince or as a fool. Ivan is the same name as John; the relationship is easier to see if one compares the medieval Russian form, Ioann, to the German form of John, Johannes. Hans (short for Johannes) is generally the name of the common hero in German folktales, while Jack (a nickname for John) is the hero in many folktales from Great Britain and America. In the tales translated here, the word *tsar* is left as 'tsar' (a fairy tale is no place for a revolution!), rather than translated as "king," but the tsar's son *tsarevich* and daughter *tsarevna* are rendered as "prince" and "princess," more or less their equivalents in western terms. When a character has a "talking name" (such as Zlatokos, "Goldilocks"), we have glossed it in a note. Many of the heroines, especially, have no personal name in the tales. But even in "Vasilisa the Beautiful," Baba Yaga plays such a significant role that Pyotr Simonov (in his *Essential Russian Mythology*) adds her name to the tale's title: "Vasilisa the Beautiful and Baba Yaga."

Two characters besides Baba Yaga have uncommon names in these tales. One is the invisible magic helper and I-know-not-what, Shmat-Razum,

Baba Yaga, Karbel.Cotsen 26249 Lutoshen'ka, Moscow Karbel (circa 1910) illustration to the story "Lutoshen'ka," Moscow. Atypically traveling on foot, the appropriately long-nosed Baba Yaga as kidnapper carries on her back a sack with the meal she anticipates cooking in her stove at home. Her dish of choice is customarily male, as evident in tales describing her attempts to shove the boy-hero into the oven. Curiously, despite Baba Yaga's reputation for cannibalism, her guests normally thwart her attempts to roast and consume them, as in "Baba Yaga and the Kid" (Afanas'ev, no. 106). Reproduced courtesy of the Cotsen Children's Library, Princeton University Library.

who appears here in a single tale. *Shmat* means a scrap or fragment, and *razum* means 'sense,' so that one might translate it (him?) as "Rag-Reason," albeit with a loss of phonetic punch. The other, more common folktale character is *Koshchei* or *Kashchei bessmertnyi*, 'Koshchei the Deathless.' His proper name sounds as if it comes from the word *kost'*, 'bone,' and he is often drawn as a skeletal old man. Unlike Baba Yaga, Kashchei is always a villain, though he does possess a certain sense of honor: in "Mar'ia Morevna," he spares the life of Prince Ivan three times because Ivan once (unintentionally) set him free, by restoring his monstrous strength with three bucket-sized drinks of water. Koshchei is known as an abductor of young maidens. Both parts of his name—"bones" and "deathless"—suggest a tie with death, in spite of his libidinous-seeming behavior.

It turns out, of course, that the epithet "deathless" does not mean that he can't be killed, only that his death is outside him, in another place: it is the tip of a needle in an egg, in a duck, in a hare, in a trunk, and so forth, all located across the sea or in a distant forest. If I can tell you this, then the hero can find out, too. He journeys to the tree, unearths or unpacks the alienated death, and can then slay Koshchei to release the maiden. With Koshchei as well as Baba Yaga, the references to bones are ambiguous. Bones are the leftovers of a body after death, but they are also a repository of life force, a link between two incarnations. The Frog Princess hides leftover swan bones in her sleeve and makes them come to life as swimming and flying birds. In "Mar'ia Morevna," Koshchei must be burned after Ivan kills him, and his ashes must be scattered to all the winds to ensure he will never come back. Baba Yaga's epithet "bony leg" has been taken to mean that one of her legs is literally made of bone—or just that she is old and skinny in a culture that valued plumpness. Her fence of human bones, topped with skulls, shows another connection with Koshchei, and in some tales he has a *bogatyr* horse he won from her: they are allies in fairy-tale villainy.

Besides names, many of the characters are identified by fixed epithets: "fair maiden," "fine" or "goodly" young man. The tales often give no descriptions or specifics of character other than this, leaving the listener (or reader) to fill in whatever standard image of beauty or goodliness we prefer. The *bogatyr* is a traditional Russian hero, featured in epic songs but sometimes making a kind of guest appearance in folktales as well. These translations retain the Russian term *bogatyr*, since it is not quite the same as "hero"—especially when it is Baba Yaga who gives a *bogatyr* whistle.

Storehouse. Displayed in Stockholm, this Sami storehouse on stilts made of tree stumps with spreading roots recalls Baba Yaga's domicile. Research shows that a construction similar to it housed nomadic hunters in Siberia intent on preserving supplies from foraging animals during their absence. http://www.lesjones.com/2009/02/20/word-of-the-day-baba-yaga-mythology/.

THE OBJECTS AROUND BABA YAGA

In the majority of tales where she appears, Baba Yaga lives in an unusual house: it usually stands on chicken legs, or sometimes on just one chicken leg. Some scholars suggest that this underlines her connections with birds—though the eagle, or the geese and swans, that serve her in other stories are much more impressive than a chicken, that most domesticated fowl. At the same time, chicken legs might suggest that her dwelling, alive and mobile, cannot fly and probably never moves too fast or too far. One of our students recently returned from study abroad in Sweden, where she visited a swamp with houses built atop tree stumps standing in the water. With their gnarled roots, she said, the stumps looked surprisingly like chicken feet. Some of the tales specify instead that Baba Yaga's house stands on spindle heels. Given the importance of the spindle in women's traditional crafts, and in other parts of the tales (Prince Ivan may have to snap a spindle to free and recover his princess), this too seems to come from the culture's deep past. Often Baba Yaga's house turns around, as if to imitate the spinning of the earth. The word 'time' in Russian, *vremia*, comes from the same *vr-* root of turning and returning as the word for spindle, *vereteno*. A spindle holding up a rotating house where a frightening old woman tests her visitors and dispenses wisdom suggests a deep ritual past.

In Russian, Baba Yaga's home is most often called an *izba*. The *izba* is a house made of hewn logs, a kind of construction common all over northern Russia and Scandinavia. (Immigrants brought it to the United States in the form of that superlatively American presidential birthplace, the log cabin.) The word *izba* is often translated as 'hut,' but it does not signify a

Baba Yaga, a lacquer box by contemporary artist Antonina Medvedeva. The image depicts Baba Yaga and a cornucopia of elements that define her (forest, hut, skulls, mortar and broom, black cat) and those not part of her fairy-tale repertoire: owl, crosses, the steaming "witch's pot over a fire," with Baba Yaga concocting a magic potion presumably of toads, rats, snakes, and the standard witch ingredients. That brew sooner belongs to the three witches in Shakespeare's Macbeth than to Russian fairy tales, and its inclusion here demonstrates the Russian handicraft industry's profit-driven catering to Western traditions and tastes. Artist: A. Medvedeva. From the village of Mstera, http://www.russianlacquerart.com/gallery/Mstera/0000/001000.

shoddy piece of housing or necessarily a small one, as we see with the large, multistoried houses in the museum of Russian wooden architecture on the northern island of Kizhi. What does it tell us that Baba Yaga's house is an *izba?* It is a folk house built in vernacular architecture, a traditional peasant house, a house in the country (not the city), made of wood, and most often situated near a forest (from whose trees it was built). When the hut or house is turning around, the questing hero or heroine must order it to stop turning with a rhymed charm. Intriguingly, everyone in the tales knows what to say to make the house stop turning—even the first sisters or servant girls in tales like "The Brother," who fail to retrieve the kidnapped baby from Baba Yaga. In "The Frog Princess," the prince says, "Little house, little house! Stand in the old way, as your mother set you—with your face to me, your back to the sea." In "The Young Man and the Apples of Youth" the saying is shorter, though it suggests the same source: "Little house, little house! Turn your back to the forest, your front to me." Baba Yaga's house can be in the forest, in an empty field, or on the seashore. These locations all signify the same thing: they are far from the original home of the hero or heroine, on the border of another world.

When Baba Yaga goes out, she often rides in a mortar, rowing or punting herself along with a pestle, perhaps sweeping her tracks away after her with a broom. Her power lets her travel by means of these everyday house-

Mike Mignola, *Hellboy, Vol. 3: The Chained Coffin and Others* (2004). Dark Horse; 2nd edition, page 41. Hellboy: The Chained Coffin and Others™ © 2011 Mike Mignola.

keeping implements, much as western Europeans believed that witches rode on flying brooms. Her mortar and pestle may themselves be magic objects like the fairy-tale flying carpets and invisibility hats, but she never gives or even loans them to other characters. For many centuries the mortar and pestle were crucial parts of a woman's tool set, used to prepare herbs for cooking or medicine, or to break grain for porridge or baking. Old photographs of Russian peasant households show large, deep mortars that could have held a substantial measure of grain, though they could hardly have accommodated an adult. Ivan Bilibin's famous picture of Baba Yaga in flight (page 176) is in harmony with the old photographs: the pestle is a tall, relatively narrow tube, not shallow like a bowl. The food-related mortar and pestle rightly hint that Baba Yaga's house is stuffed with edible riches—the golden apples a child plays with until his rescuer finds him, or the stocks of grain, meat, and drink listed in "Vasilisa the Beautiful," nourishing raw materials to transform into the good things of Russian peasant life: linen, wheat, poppy seed.

Baba Yaga's house may be surrounded with a fence of bones, perhaps topped with skulls (or with one pole still untopped, waiting threateningly for the hero's "wild head"), but even if she has an ordinary fence and gate they play important roles in the story. While Baba Yaga is sharpening her teeth to eat the nameless heroine, the girl pours oil on the hinges of the

Ransome by Dmitrii Mitrokhin from *Old Peter's Russian Tales.* A transfixed dog gazes up at Mitrokhin's fully equipped Baba Yaga in flight. The female-gendered mortar and male-gendered pestle advert to her personified image as contradictory all-embracing nature, which explains why she sweeps away all traces of her passage with the broom. Reproduced courtesy of the Cotsen Children's Library, Princeton University Library.

gate and manages to escape. Baba Yaga scolds the gate for not slamming on the girl, and the gate responds to her with human words. Baba Yaga is also associated with the bathhouse, which in Russia resembles a sauna. In some tales she asks the heroine to stoke the fire in the bathhouse (sometimes with bones for fuel rather than firewood), to bathe her children (frogs, reptiles, and other vermin), or to steam Baba Yaga herself. Many of the tales mention Baba Yaga's stove. The traditional Russian stove is a large construction of brick and plaster (in a fancier house, it would be covered with ornamental tile), the size of a small room and certainly the dominant object in any room it occupies. Some stoves were built so that they heated, and took up parts of, more than one room. The stove would incorporate shelves, ovens, and hobs, nooks, or hooks for storing cookware. Such a stove would hold the fire's heat, gently diffusing it into the house. This made it a favorite place for sleeping. The upper shelves, high above the fire and safely far away from vermin or cold drafts on the floor, would stay warm through the night. The stove is also associated with the womb, and not only in Russian: the English expression "one in the oven" also connects baking with the rising belly of a pregnant woman. Joanna Hubbs writes that the stove is moreover a repository of dead souls, the ancestors.[4] Even more than an ordinary peasant stove, Baba Yaga's is a conduit from death to rebirth.

To escape from Baba Yaga, characters in the tales may themselves employ very ordinary objects—sometimes stolen from Yaga's own house—and these too recur from one tale to another. Thrown behind as a character flees, a comb or brush turns into thick forest, as if the wood from which they were carved came back to life. A mirror, already magical in its ability to show the gazer his or her own face, turns into a wide, deep sea. Throwing a kerchief or towel will create an impassable river, often a river of fire. Embroidered handkerchiefs or towels may become or summon bridges over impassable waters, or they may convey secret messages: the wife's mother and sisters in "Go I Don't Know Where . . ." recognize the hero as her husband when he dries his face with a towel she made. Towels in the Russian village bore beautiful ritual embroidery and were used in traditional ceremonies (such as the hospitable welcome with bread and salt). To find the house of Baba Yaga, the hero or heroine may receive a ball of thread (once known as a *clue* in English), like the one that took Theseus in to the Minotaur. Baba Yaga lives (or rather, every Baba Yaga lives) in the heart of the labyrinth, and the hero or heroine enters there to face his or her worst fears and vanquish them. The tales include many other magical objects: in wonder tales musical pipes or rings may contain magical helpers, and in "The Three Kingdoms" each kingdom is wrapped up into a ring made of the matching metal to be conveyed back to the prince's own kingdom.

One final traditional element in the tales deserves explanation: that is, searching for lice. Several tales mention searching for lice, or just "searching" in a character's hair. On the one hand, this must have been a useful grooming practice; on the other hand, it feels good to have someone riffle through one's hair and touch one's scalp—especially if the hair is worn in long shaggy braids, like Baba Yaga's. Lice were surely common in old Russia, as they were in Western Europe at the time, but the reader should be assured that "searching for lice" can also mean playing with someone's hair in a pleasant, affectionate way.

BABA YAGA IN THE RUSSIAN PANTHEON

How is Baba Yaga related to other female figures in Russian lore, especially in the most archaic remnants of East Slavic culture? The female figures best known today in Russian lore are *rusalki*, sometimes translated as "mermaids" though they do not live in the sea. They are said to be the spirits of girls who committed suicide out of disappointed love, or the spirits of babies who died unbaptized (victims of infanticide?), and they are described lolling in the branches of trees or beside streams, combing their long hair, sometimes reportedly green in color. They tempt men off the path, intending to drown them, or they may tickle children to death. *Rusalki* are most often represented as young and lovely (though the green hair recalls water-weeds, and their connection with nature). At the same time, their traits and activities largely parallel Baba Yaga's: they are like younger, lovelier dangerous females, tickling children to death instead of eating them. If we see Baba Yaga as the Crone face of the triune goddess (maiden, mother, crone), as Joanna Hubbs suggests in *Mother Russia*, then *rusalki* embody the maiden face. In many ways the *rusalka* resembles the South Slavic *vila*; some western readers already know of vilas, thanks to their role as mascots for the Bulgarian quidditch team in J. K. Rowling's Harry Potter novels.

Further in the past are the shadowy figures of the *beregini*, nameless plural female divinities whose title could come from *bereg*, 'river bank,' or from the verb root *bereg-*, 'to keep, conserve' or 'to preserve, economize.' Even now, in Russian, an *obereg* is an amulet, worn on the person or hung in a house, to ward off evil. Boris Rybakov[5] suggests that the *beregini* spring from a hunting culture, guaranteeing rich animal life but also protecting the hunter from the dangers of the woods. They are connected to Baba Yaga in her role as queen of the animals; we see echoes of this in the tales where old women summon all the birds of the air, animals of the earth, or fish of the sea in order to ask where a certain thing or person may be found.

Thanks to the list of the Kievan pagan pantheon recorded in the historical chronicles of old Rus', the name of one goddess has come down to us from the East Slavic past: *Mokosh*. Her name suggests wetness—in Russian the root *mok-* means 'wet' or 'soak'—and hence she may be linked with Moist (or Raw) Mother Earth, *Mat' syra zemlya*, mentioned in songs and traditional proverbs that concern planting or burial. This image of the earth invokes both the damp, chilly soil that is planted in the spring, and the earth as a mother's body to which the dead return—a cold, clammy body, unlike the body of the human mother. The Slavic pagan underworld was called *preispodn'ia*, 'close-under-place.' That suggests a world or afterworld in the near underground, like the one described in "The Three Kingdoms," into which the hero is lowered on leather straps. Though Baba Yaga is most often found in the forest, her role in the mysteries of death and rebirth also gives her a connection with the harvest and the space underground where grain germinates.

Scholars note that Mokosh is connected to the Christian Saint Paraskeva, called *Paraskeva-Piatnita* by Russian peasants, or 'Paraskeva-Friday.' Friday was traditionally the day of the goddess in European paganism, as we see in linguistic survivals. English *Friday* is named for Frigg or Freya, the Anglo-Scandinavian goddess of love, approximately the same as Venus, source of the French Friday, *vendredi*. Paraskeva in Russian folk religious belief was a special patron of women. She protected them in childbirth, but she also demanded that Orthodox Christians respect her by refraining from "women's" tasks, especially spinning, on Fridays. Paraskeva's day was celebrated on October 28, according to the Julian calendar. Her day is so close to Halloween and the Day of the Dead, the old cross-quarter day of November 1 that marked the beginning of winter,[6] that the date suggests Mokosh, who very probably underlies Paraskeva, is like Baba Yaga: a queen of gathering food and eventually of harvest but also of death, guarding the mysteries of winter and old age, the unprepossessing dry seeds that hold life until the following season. As Moist Mother Earth "eats" the bodies of the dead, so Baba Yaga eats human beings. Paraskeva's role of guarding women in childbirth also ties into some of Baba Yaga's concerns. Images of Paraskeva on Russian icons may show her holding a spindle—the same tool that, again, may sometimes hold up Baba Yaga's rotating hut. Folk narratives about Paraskeva mention that women who spin on Fridays make her dirty, and the "dirty" saint's tangled hair recalls Baba Yaga's gray braids.

Another, more occulted possibility is that Baba Yaga is "the devil's grandmother," who shows up in a Russian saying approximately equivalent to "*go to hell*": *Idi k chertovoi babushke*, "Go the devil's grandmother." There is no way to prove or trace this now, but it does suggest an interesting cosmogony.

Many of the tales involve a single Baba Yaga (especially those where she tests a daughter sent away by her stepmother, or where she or her avian minions kidnap children), but many others include three Baba Yagas, usually sisters or cousins,[7] whose houses serve as way stations for a hero or heroine in quest of a lost or distant beloved. Baba Yaga's trinity is not a Mozartian threeness, where hearing a motif twice lulls listeners into expecting the same result a third time, only to surprise them with something different. Baba Yaga's threeness is an exact, folkloric trebling, with ritual answers that are repeated the same way each time. As mentioned above, the triune Baba Yaga suggests connections with the triune goddess,[8] with the figures of the three Fates, et cetera.[9]

DEEPER MEANINGS OF BABA YAGA

Baba Yaga is a wonderfully rich figure: some of her appearances in the tales are quite specific, and we do not wish to blur her outlines by generalizing too much. Andreas Johns points out, in his thorough and valuable book *Baba Yaga, The Ambiguous Mother and Witch of the Russian Folktale*, "Baba Yaga's particular combination of traits and functions makes her unique among witches and witch-like characters in world folklore" (2). Like the Indian goddess Kali, Baba Yaga is terrifying because of her relationship to death. She mediates the boundary of death so that living human beings may cross it and return, alive but in possession of new wisdom, or "reborn" into a new status. Her central role in the fairy-tale process explains why she appears in so many wonder tales.[10]

Like most witches in folklore, Baba Yaga is striking in appearance. She is unusually tall (stretching diagonally across her room when she lies down); she has a huge nose that may stick up to the ceiling, a bony leg (or, sometimes, a golden or otherwise unusual leg), and iron teeth that she sharpens in anticipation of a tasty human snack. In some tales the descriptions are demeaning or disgusting—in one example, her tits (*tit'ki*) are slung up over a rail. Here Baba Yaga's aging female body incarnates the grotesque after-

Baba Yaga by Viktor Vasnetsov (1917). Having abducted a petrified little girl, Baba Yaga speeds home for supper, clutching the tender, as yet uncooked morsel. Illustration by Viktor Vasnetsov (1848–1926).

math of female fertility. The amount of detail devoted to her description in some of the tales is quite atypical for a wonder tale, where characters may have golden hair or starry foreheads, but not many other explicit features—and she is quite unlike the young beauties a listener may imagine, though she may have a lovely daughter. The vivid verbal picture of Baba Yaga has attracted many illustrators, as the reader shall see.

Among the functions that Vladimir Propp lists in his study of the wonder tale, Baba Yaga is most often a tester and donor. She grudgingly hands over riches, a horse or a large bird for transportation, or necessary weapons or tools, and she points out the path to the desired goal—most often, leading to or advising on how to recover a missing partner. She is both a cannibal and a kind of innkeeper, a woman who threatens but also often rewards. She is a goddess of death, but she also gives access to maturity and fertility. She dwells at the border of the other realm, not in *Rus'*.[11] Sometimes she helps the hero or heroine evade pursuit, while at other times she is the one who pursues. She may sneak into Rus' herself, mastering the path there and back; other times she is unable to cross and must stop pursuing the hero or heroine at the border. In a few tales she gives the hero and heroine a magic carpet (*kover-samolët*, or 'self-flying carpet') to carry them back home from the thrice-tenth kingdom.

Each tale in this collection is different, though many of them share common features and some are variants of the same plot. Baba Yaga appears in many different guises. Clearly folktale tellers did not expect her to be the same every time she appeared. Nevertheless, her various hypostases or stable images would remain in the back of a listener's mind even if a tale stressed another of her roles. If she is being pleasant and helpful, a listener would still feel some tension: what if she suddenly started sharpening her teeth? She may be a helpful if off-putting old woman, who lives in a peculiar house and, when someone arrives from Rus', comments on the smell with a "Foo, foo, foo!"—not unlike the western fairy-tale ogre's "Fee, fie, fo, fum!" A male hero gets the best treatment if he interrupts her questions and comments with a demand to be fed, given a drink, and put to bed before he will begin to tell her his news. She often asks, "Are you doing a deed or fleeing a deed?" and she may give the hero a ball of string that will lead to the next necessary place, perhaps the home of her own sister, another Baba Yaga. In this benign form, a trio of Baba Yaga sisters may be replaced by ordinary old women, but their "true identity" is revealed by their role in the tale as they send the questing character from one to the next, usually youngest to oldest.[12] Second, Baba Yaga can be a frightening witch who is nonetheless fair, a donor who rewards Vasilisa or the (step)daughter who serves her well, while punishing the evil stepmother and/or stepdaughter. She may give the good daughter dresses and other kinds of wealth, or, less fulsomely, "reward" her by knocking off the stepmother and/or stepsister(s)—or merely by not killing her as the stepmother had expected she would. Third, she can also be a frightening witch who is not a donor, or who is an inadvertent donor; in "Mar'ia Morevna," she plans to eat Prince Ivan even though he has fulfilled his part of the bargain to earn a wonderful horse, and he has to steal a mangy colt from her stable. Fourth, she is a thief of children and apparently also a cannibal. In one group of tales, her bird or birds steal a baby, who must be rescued by a servant or an older sister. In others, she is tricked into eating her own child or children by a boy she stole, who is old enough to figure out his own escape from her house.

These are not entirely stable versions of Baba Yaga, as her roles may blend into one another. There is always the threat that she will eat someone who fails her tests, and even when she is being fair or pleasant to a character, the listener must recall the possibility that she will suddenly change her mind. When she tears apart the bad stepsister after treating the good one fairly, nothing remains but bones; the tale does not specify where the flesh went, and perhaps it does not need to. At the same time, when we see her stealing babies (most often a little boy), the babies do not seem to be in immediate danger. The sister in "The Geese and Swans" discovers her brother playing with golden apples, which resonate with the apples of youth in other tales, and the brother in "The Brother" is discovered sitting on a chair (not

Baba Yaga, Tears of Joy Theatre 2012 Season. Nancy Aldrich, creative director, http://tinyurl.com/c8qb5hz, photo by Ithica Tell.

the cold, dirty floor) while the cat Yeremei tells him tales. In both these tales, servant birds stole the children, not Baba Yaga herself. The kid who tricks Baba Yaga into eating her own daughters is not so distant from the young hero who peremptorily orders her to bring him food and drink, thus compelling her to treat him well instead of eating him. I will return to Baba Yaga's role as a child-stealer below.

We see Baba Yaga traveling with her mortar and pestle, stealing children and wreaking havoc, but we also see her at the loom. Weaving, making the cloth for clothing, is not just a traditional "female" craft that follows after spinning; it is another link with the "women's" saint Paraskeva (and her Friday prohibitions), as well as with images of the Fates as spinners or weavers. Baba Yaga is sometimes alone in her hut; in other tales she has a variety of helpers or companions, the three pairs of disembodied hands Vasilisa sees but wisely does not ask about. These recall the hands that wait on Beauty in the palace of the Beast. In "Vasilisa the Beautiful," Baba Yaga also commands three riders: a white rider on a white horse, who represents dawn,[13] a red rider on a red horse representing the sun,[14] and a black rider on a black horse, for night. In some tales, such as "Prince Ivan and Beloy Polyanin," Baba Yaga has armies and servants who magically create soldiers for these armies. Finally, she often has a daughter or daughters.[15] The daughters can vary considerably: sometimes they are stupid girls, like their mother tending to come in threes, who obediently follow Yaga's orders only to be baked in her oven and eaten by their own mother, as in "Baba Yaga and the Kid." Even a mean, stupid Baba Yaga never wants to eat her own children, and she becomes viciously angry after she is tricked into doing it. In other tales, Baba Yaga has a single daughter, a great beauty, who aids the hero or heroine and is rewarded for this by escape from Baba Yaga into the ordinary world and marriage to a hero or a prince, as in "Prince Ivan and Beloy Polyanin" or "Prince Danila Govorila." Helping the hero or heroine puts the daughter in danger: aiding them, and thus betraying her mother, makes her a stranger to Baba Yaga, an enemy—and so herself liable to be caught and devoured. For all these daughters no father is visible; some of the negative ones are called *Yagishna*, 'daughter of Yaga,' using the Russian patronymic form that is otherwise always based on the *father*'s name, never the mother's. Being the mother of a magical beauty connects Yaga to other magical parents in Russian wonder tales, such as the Sea King.[16]

In some tales, Baba Yaga seems to be involved because the mother is missing, even if the tale is about a stepmother. In "Prince Danila Govorila," the mother is dead and the heroine in peril, but Baba Yaga's kind and lovely daughter turns out to look just like the heroine, and the magic ring that caused all the trouble presumably fits her too (so she can marry the brother, saving him and Katerina from the sin of incest). In "Vasilisa the Beautiful," the heroine's doll, a deathbed gift from her mother, keeps her safe in Baba Yaga's house. Baba Yaga grumbles and tells her to leave (albeit with the gift of fire, contained in a fire-eyed skull) once she learns that Vasilisa is protected by her mother's blessing. Vasilisa is as clever as she is beautiful: she mentions the blessing but not the doll. Baba Yaga tests girls not only by requesting impossible tasks, such as sorting poppy seeds from dirt, or by demanding completion of so many tasks that only a magical doll or help from the local mice can accomplish them in the allotted time. She also makes the girls show that they are proficient at the essential feminine tasks: cooking, washing, stoking the fires in stove and bathhouse. Even in a tale where she plans to eat the girl, Baba Yaga tells her to sit down and weave in her place while she goes to sharpen her teeth. This does in part reflect traditional *realia*, the cruel fact that a peasant girl who did not know how to weave or cook or stoke the bathhouse would not bring good fortune to her family. In a time and place where the margins for survival could be slim, these skills not only made a girl marriageable but could be a matter of life and death for her and her family. Baba Yaga is often kinder, or at least more fair, than the stepmother who sends her unloved stepdaughter to the witch in hopes that she will be eaten or destroyed.

Indeed, Baba Yaga tests peasant virtues: knowledge of the skills of husbandry and housekeeping, patience, persistence, kindness, generosity, and the capacity for hard work, Some scholars suggest that tales of Baba Yaga helped young people accept and understand their place in a traditional culture, even after the earlier initiation rituals where she played a role were abandoned. For young village women especially, marriage meant entering a new household and adapting to new household organization, under the authority of the mother-in-law. In Russian wonder tales, even royalty may need to know basic men's and women's skills, and even a tsar's wife may change her fate once she is tempted by a golden spindle that spins gold thread or a silver needle that embroiders by itself. Besides that, heroes and heroines of the tales must know how to handle Baba Yaga: when to tell the truth or to lie, to demand food and drink or to obey her meekly, to steal what they need or to stay with her until they have earned it.

So Baba Yaga appears as an initiatrix, a vestigial goddess, a forest power, and a mistress of birds or animals. In a hunting culture, like that of old Russia, all that made her a very important figure.[17] We even see, in one version of the tale "Go I Don't Know Where and Bring I Don't Know What," a place where Baba Yaga's evolving nature may have let one instance of her crowd out another: because the lustful general goes to a backstreet Baba Yaga for advice, identifying her as both evil and urban, the three old women our hero visits on his way cannot also be figures of the Baba Yaga. The reader will notice, though, how similar they are to the triple Baba Yaga in other tales. The tales evolve over time, as they are told and retold—another reason for the variations in the nature of this character.

Baba Yaga's link to death is less unsettling if we remember the constant place of death in peasant society. Russian peasant girls would tell fortunes each spring by making garlands of flowers and tossing them into a stream.

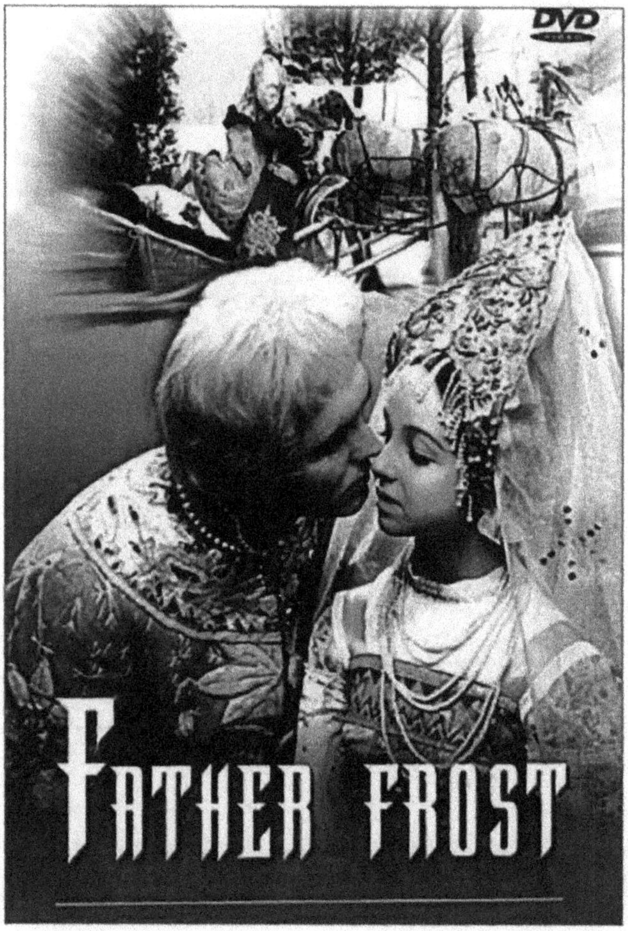

Father Frost, by Aleksandr Rou. Cover of the DVD, released in 2001, of Aleksandr Rou's *Father Frost* aka *Jack Frost* (Morozko, 1964), loosely based on several versions of the fairy tales narrating the ultimate triumph of a spineless man's Cinderella-like sweet, pure daughter over her nasty stepmother, imbecilic stepsister, and the malevolent Baba Yaga (Afanas'ev's Jack Frost [no. 95 and no. 96], Baba Yaga [no. 102 and no. 103], Daughter and Stepdaughter [no. 98]). Abandoned in the snow-laden forest by her henpecked sire, the heroine, Nasten'ka, is saved by Father Frost and the initially vain but finally matured Ivan. Georgii Milliar's reprisal of his role as Baba Yaga contains slapstick moments intended to defang the lethal nature of "her" evil machinations. The film contains miles of snow, the black cat as Baba Yaga's magic helper, the heroine's loyal dog, a wise old anthropomorphic mushroom, a visually captivating spell, and a bravura performance by the impressive actress Inna Churikova as the stunningly crude, greedy stepsister.

If her garland floated away, the girl would marry that year; if it stuck on a branch or rock, she would have to wait out that season. If her garland sank in the water, it meant that the girl would die. Yaga's role as a frightening tester in stories of initiation seems clear enough, and the element of testing is strong in many of the tales where a young man or woman finds his or her way to Baba Yaga's hut. In many of the tales, Baba Yaga (or another character who fulfills some of her functions) asks the new arrivals whether they have come of their own will or by compulsion. The question could very well be part of an initiation ritual, though the correct answer varies from tale to tale. Propp and others believe that tales about Baba Yaga are indeed remnants of initiation rituals for adolescents. This helps to explain why so many of the stories end with marriage or with the once separated, now matured spouses reunited. Marriage was a crucial moment in traditional society, marking the newlyweds as adults, producers of a new generation, and setting up or bolstering the economic unit of the family, in which many traditional tasks were gendered and therefore dependent on the character and preparation of the wife or husband. Moreover, the tradition of wedding laments suggests that for a young woman marriage could be tantamount to death,[18] even if some brides performed the ritual lamentation more as a way of keeping off the Evil Eye, to avoid tempting fate by seeming happy about the wedding arrangements. Given the strong possibility that she played a role in stories of initiation, it is no surprise that today Baba Yaga is used by Jungian therapists as a figure of dark, occult knowledge, and her hut to symbolize a stage on a difficult path. Even now she teaches readers or listeners how to win treasure or understanding out of loss, fear, and pain. One could argue that in the modern world people pass through many more roles and stages and face many tests besides those that prove traditional readiness for marriage. Modern encounters with Baba Yaga and what she represents still reaffirm our strength, cleverness, and worthiness as adults using stories in therapy.

I would argue, though, that the tales show a second important traditional role for Baba Yaga. She is important not only at the phase of adolescent initiation, when a young hero or heroine has reached marriageable age and must become a fully functioning member of the community, a member of the child-bearing generation. Recall that Paraskeva, the saint whose day is celebrated just before the end of the old traditional autumn, is a protector of women in childbirth. Her precursor Baba Yaga, in her role as a thief and presumably devourer of children, may serve to address fears of infant and child mortality.

There is no record of anything like an initiation ceremony for a woman in childbirth, perhaps because the event was already hedged round with a huge number of superstitions, spells, and careful practices meant to keep the child (and, to a lesser extent, the mother) from harm. Russian peasant women traditionally gave birth in the bathhouse—a sensible choice, since it was warm, relatively clean, and private, but it was also a place associated with Baba Yaga. In times of high infant and child mortality, the goddess of the borders of death would necessarily play a part here, too. Indeed, Baba Yaga's role in both types of tales, the "testing" and the "devouring," is formally similar. The child's passage into adulthood symbolically means the death of the child (and a girl's marriage, in particular, meant leaving her home and entering that of her husband's family, where the mother-in-law could be as ill-disposed and unwelcoming as a fairy-tale stepmother). If adulthood meant the death of the child, and marriage meant the death of the maiden,

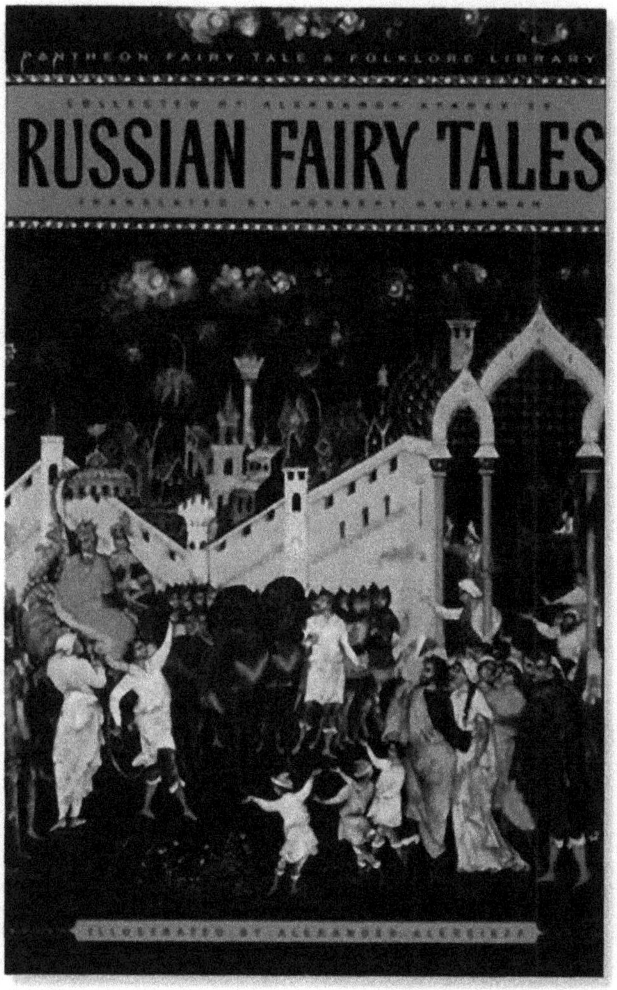

Russian Fairy Tales, showing the cover of the 1976 edition compiled by Aleksandr Afanas'ev, translated by Norbert Guterman, and illustrated by Alexander Alexeieff. The latest reissue of the standard anthology of Russian fairy tales, selected and translated from the 1936–40 three-volume edition of Afanas'ev's sizable collection. Dubbed "the Russian Grimm," the lawyer-cum-ethnographer Afanas'ev originally published his compilations from 1855 to 1863. Since then, his name both in Russia and abroad has become synonymous with the genre. This American edition contains two useful commentaries by one of Russia's leading linguists and literary critics, Roman Jakobson (1896–1982), who moved from Moscow to Prague (1920) and, after the Germans occupied Czechoslovakia, immigrated to the United States (1941). Publisher: Pantheon Books, 1945. Reissue, 1976.

then childbirth too carries an element of death—the death of the single human being and simultaneous birth of both child and mother.

In the stories where Baba Yaga kidnaps a child or has her minions do so, the heroine passes through a series of ritual rebirths once she has taken back the child. In Khudiakov's version of "The Brother," Baba Yaga's eagle notices that the stove that protects the maiden has gotten wider, and asks the apple tree, "Why have you, apple tree, gotten so curly, lowered your branches right down to the ground?" The tree answers: "The time has come [. . .] I'm standing here all fluffy." The wording, as well as the position of the girl and baby concealed beneath the lowered branches, suggests that the tree is pregnant, that its "time has come." Much as the testing tales lead into adulthood or marriage, the tales of girls who rescue babies stolen by Baba Yaga (or her avian psychopomps) could serve to socialize young mothers in caring for new babies, and girls to take care of their own new younger siblings. In some of these tales the girl might be seen as representing the new generation of parents, while the mother of the stolen child in the tale is *her* mother, an older woman who is nevertheless still young enough to have more children of her own, who knows how to keep a child alive in a dangerous world and now sends her daughter out to gain this knowledge. The various "pregnant" pauses in the narrative where girl and baby hide from pursuit show the girl emerging each time reborn as someone better fit to care for a child. The fact that the stolen child seems happy and safe with Baba Yaga—playing with golden apples or listening to a cat tell a story—suggests that infant mortality causes little pain for the infant, though more for the mother and other relatives who survive.[19]

In tales where Baba Yaga steals an older child, the child (usually a boy) must rescue himself. The gleeful description of how he tricks Yaga into eating her own daughter or daughters might work magic to make sure it is *her* child who will die, rather than the child of the tale-teller or listener. This gullible, stupid Baba Yaga is no longer so frightening, and making her devour her own child or children throws the fear and risk of death back onto her. We are more clever, we can use the magic of our tales to outwit the witch and survive into adulthood—where death is what we expect, rather than a premature tragedy that impacts the community's future. Telling a child a story about Baba Yaga may scare the child (pleasantly, like any frightening story, or as a way of compelling better behavior), while at the same time it has a prophylactic effect: after all, the very child who listens could soon be threatened with death. The story offers a mother or child a measure of power over Baba Yaga. In return, it prolongs Baba Yaga's life and vividness in folklore.

Baba Yaga's birds—geese, swans, eagles—are not just hunting birds. They are psychopomps who bear a dead person on a soul journey or a living person to the other world. Propp argues that no matter where Baba Yaga's house is located (forest; open field; sea shore), it is always at the border of the other realm, the realm of death and the afterlife, over thrice-nine lands and near the thrice-tenth. The forest lies at the heart of Russian civilization, as it held riches (the honey, wax, and furs that early Slavs traded along routes reaching from the Black Sea to Scandinavia) along with terrors.[20] The open field appears in traditional Russian spells (more properly called charms, according to specialists in magic; in Russian, *zagovory*, or incantations, *zaklinaniia*). The spells frequently begin with the words "I rise up, saying a blessing. I go out, crossing myself, and I go to an open field." An empty place where no one can see or hear what one says is the proper locus for working magic. Russia's traditional territory has a seacoast only in the far north, on the White Sea—but many cultures have imagined the afterlife as located beyond the sea, in the land where the sun sets (see, for example, the etymology of Brazil).[21]

In several of the tales included here, Baba Yaga herself is killed, baked in an oven (though sometimes she scratches her way out), or burned up after falling into a fiery river. She is strongly associated with fire. Vasilisa comes to her house asking for a light, and Yaga sends her back home with a fire-eyed skull that incinerates the offending stepmother and stepsisters. As Propp points out in his book *The Russian Folktale*, Baba Yaga is a recurring folk figure: if she burns up once, it only means that she no longer threatens the characters of *that* story. She'll be back in the next one.

The tale "Vasilisa the Beautiful" is unusual and possibly more archaic than most of the tales in Afanas'ev's collection. His publication was based on an earlier, eighteenth-century edition. The spooky details listed in the tale show Baba Yaga as the mistress of time: dawn, sun, and night are her servants, and they are physically present in her forest as horsemen, not only under her command as abstractions. Other tales mention twelve stakes with skulls around her hut; the number suggests twelve months. Her spinning hut models the turning of the heavens that causes and measures time itself.

BABA YAGA IN POPULAR CULTURE, EAST AND WEST

No doubt intrigued by Baba Yaga's potent dualities (death/life, senility/fertility, destruction/renewal, villainy/benevolence, masculine/feminine), young readers today seem as responsive to her magic as previous generations. Cultural creators and marketplaces testify to her enduring power in the forms of Russian "Palekh" lacquer boxes, dolls and figurines, carvings, holiday tree ornaments, children's storybooks, movies, Web sites, games, and music, from the classic *Pictures at an Exhibition* (part 15, "The Hut on Chicken Legs—Baba Yaga") by Modest Mussorgsky to compositions by Norwegian composer and musician Annbjørg Lien and punk-rock groups in England and Poland. Baba Yaga is a character in the Runequest/Gloriantha game, and the accompanying materials provide a sophisticated psychological and biographical background to explain why her house is on chicken legs and why she is so antisocial despite her many powers.[22] All

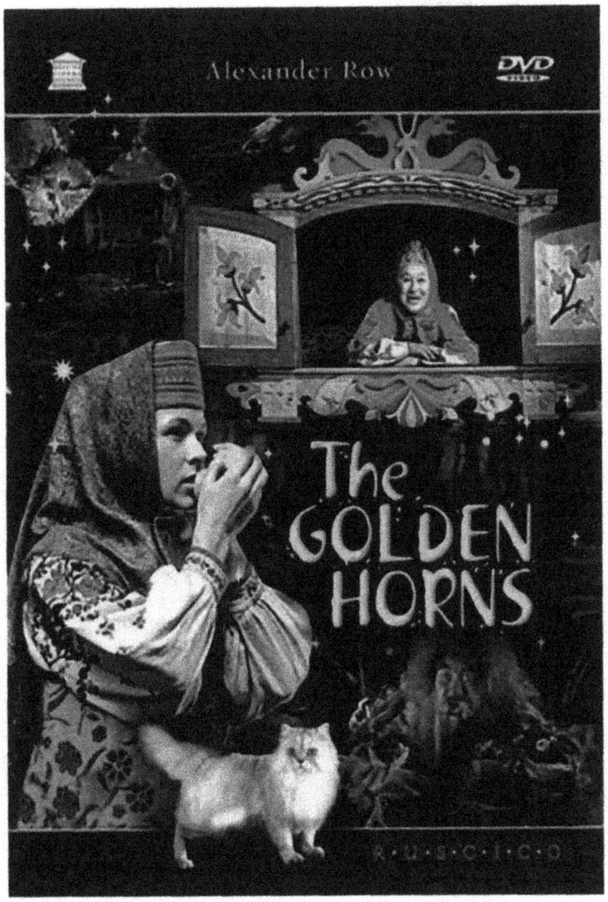

The Golden Horns, by Aleksandr Rou. For the genre-affirming third time, Georgii Milliar appears as Baba Yaga in Aleksandr Rou's *The Golden Horns* (Zolotye roga, 1972; DVD 2003) aka Baba Yaga, based on fairy-tale motifs that include a magical goat, deer, or stag. The film narrates a peasant widow's search for her twin daughters, whom Baba Yaga has kidnapped and magically changed into beguiling does. The Moon, Sun, Wind, and do-gooder deer with golden antlers in the forest aid the mother's quest, which culminates in a rescue by her son and the family cat—a counterpart to Baba Yaga's feline helper. This pseudo-animistic world is replete with a menacing forest, mushrooms, and somewhat cutesy effects clearly targeting a very young audience.

these prove the continuing attraction and vigorous legacy of the complex figure of Baba Yaga.

Baba Yaga is a popular figure in Russian films, especially but not only animated cartoons. She adds spice to a story, and the stories that include her are among the most central of the Russian wonder tale canon. Documentary filmmaker Jessica Oreck is now at work with her colleagues on a film that will examine the role of the forest in East European cultures, especially the mushroom (that ultimate forest treat, and one that until fairly recently could not be cultivated); the movie has the working title "The Vanquishing of Baba Yaga." Like the mushroom, sometimes nourishing and delicious but also sometimes poisonous, Baba Yaga is an ambiguous presence in the Russian forest.

Baba Yaga Vasilisa Dyad Cloth Doll by Melinda Small Patterson. Move over, Barbie! Perhaps more terrifying than Baba Yaga herself is the West's adoptive domestication of her role in Vasilisa the Beautiful, materialized in this fussy doll, which won first place in "Needle Sculpting" at the Santa Fe Doll Art Festival in 2000. The Baba Yaga doll (with pearl beads for teeth, no less) is but half of a "dyad doll pattern" by Patterson that includes Vasalisa (*sic*), who is supposed to hide under Baba Yaga's skirt—a union of doll and Vasilisa that is part of the West's enchantment with the "wild Baba Yaga" and the "intuition doll." http://www.smallwork.com/babayaga.html.

WHAT OTHER BOOKS SAY ABOUT BABA YAGA

Given her central place in many of the best-loved Russian wonder tales and her puzzlingly ambivalent character, it is no wonder that many scholars have written about Baba Yaga. I conclude this introduction by summarizing these works and what they offer for further reading. The short bibliography at the end of this introduction gives more complete bibliographic information about the works that are available in English and a filmography of movies and cartoons that involve Baba Yaga.

One might say that Andreas Johns "wrote the book" on Baba Yaga—*Baba Yaga: The Ambiguous Mother and Witch of the Russian Folktale.* (See the bibliography below for details of publication.) Summarizing and synthesizing hundreds of tales, he analyzes them as a professional folklorist and provides a range of information about the image of Baba Yaga and the many variant tales about her. Johns gives clear, well-founded readings of the tales without limiting his approach to a single theoretical perspective.

Baba Yaga by Boris Zvorykin, early twentieth century. Engaged in a surreptitious and enigmatic activity, the ornamentally inclined émigré artist's red-nosed Baba Yaga crouches in the forest that is her unchallenged realm. Though her physical appearance is domesticated, Zvorykin may intend to convey her symbolic status in the cosmic hierarchy by situating her at the base of the tree of life, with its roots underground as part of the chthonic world. Illustration by Boris Zvorykin (1872–1935/1942?).

The prominent Soviet folklorist Vladimir Propp (1895–1970) mentions Baba Yaga in several of his works. In his famous *Morphology of the Folktale* (1928), we see Baba Yaga fulfilling the functions of donor, tester, and villain, and he discusses her as a picturesque figure in his *Russian Folktale*. Most interestingly, she appears at length in *The Historical Roots of the Wonder Tale*, of which only fragments have been translated into English. Propp's project in *Historical Roots* is to trace each move of the wonder tale (or the "magical tale," *volshebnaia skazka*) back to its origins in rituals of initiation in primitive East Slavic society. He sees Baba Yaga as guardian of the boundary between the world of the living and the world of the dead: she gives the questing hero food that allows him or her to enter the world of the dead, and often she chases the hero back across the boundary as he returns to Rus', as if to make sure that he will not remain prematurely in the realm of death. Propp considers her connections with and power over birds and animals a trace of the primitive totemistic religion of a hunter/gatherer culture. Baba Yaga also reveals, according to Propp, a link to the period in human society when the male role in reproduction was not understood—hence her daughters, or her many vermin-children, conceived with no man in sight.

The Soviet reference book *Mify narodov mira* (*Myths of the Peoples of the World*) points out Baba Yaga's connections to analogous West Slavic figures (Czech, Polish, Slovak) and her importance in Ukrainian and Belarusian folklore.[23] The article on Baba Yaga in *Mify narodov mira* is written by Vyacheslav V. Ivanov and Vladimir N. Toporov, prominent Soviet semiotic

Baba Yaga Laid an Egg by Dubravka Ugrešić. This highly inventive, genre-defying book by one of Croatia's most gifted expatriate writers offers an irreverent gynocentric perspective on sickness, aging, death, and myths in Central Europe. Mixing autobiography, fiction, and critical commentary, Ugrešić reinterprets the Baba Yaga myth as a matrix paradigm for old women and their potential powers. Publisher: Grove Press, 2011.

scholars. They identify Baba Yaga as a relic of a priestess from initiation rituals, on the one hand, and note her status as an emblematic forest dweller on the other.

Robert Bly and Marion Woodman's book *The Maiden Tsar: The Reunion of Masculine and Feminine* gives an extended discussion of one of the tales we include here, "The Tsar Maiden" (in their translation, "The Maiden Tsar"). Because it includes Baba Yaga, they devote a chapter to her in particular. Their discussion places every element of the tale in a rich context of literary references (not Russian so much as European and Anglo-American) and popular culture (perhaps this is the first time Baba Yaga has met Bob Dylan?), bringing out the tale's implications for interpreting the universal vagaries of human experience. Bly's poetic sensibility sometimes leads him far afield from the character herself, and his musings on gender relations tend to presume that our own society is normative in every way. However, the poet and the Jungian therapist progress through the ideas that Baba Yaga suggests to them in ways that may provide insight for readers.

Clarissa Pinkola Estés is a Jungian therapist who writes about a number of narratives, including one about Baba Yaga. Her book *Women Who Run with the Wolves: Myths and Stories of the Wild Woman Archetype* treats the tale of Vasilisa the Beautiful, exploring Baba Yaga's role as an underground

Baba Yaga and Vasilisa the Brave, Marianna Mayer, illustrations by Kinuko Y. Craft. The partnership of Mayer and the Japanese-born American Craft has yielded some unusually beautiful fairy-tale picture books for children. Craft's impressive illustrations accompanying Mayer's retelling of "Vasilisa the Beautiful" are meticulously detailed, vividly ornamented, and, in the case of Baba Yaga, appropriately frightening. Publisher: HarperCollins, 1994.

character, tester, and source of wisdom. Pinkola Estés's discussion stresses the section of the tale involving Baba Yaga rather than the remainder, where Vasilisa spins wondrously fine linen cloth and wins the love of the tsar.[24]

Anthropologist Joanna Hubbs, in her book *Mother Russia: The Feminine Myth in Russian Culture*, draws on work by a variety of scholars. As a strong and mysterious female figure, Baba Yaga receives a chapter to herself as well as frequent mentions in other chapters. Hubbs's synthetic view of Baba Yaga connects her to other narratives or images of female divinity in Russian verbal and material culture, including the *rusalki*, the goddess Mokosh, Moist Mother Earth, and the later female Christian figures, Mary the Mother of God and Saint Paraskeva. To Hubbs, Yaga is a figure of occulted female power connected to goddess worship in which every mother was a priestess in her own house. Hubbs's work recalls and cites the works of archeologist Marija Gimbutas or the feminist scholar of comparative religion Barbara G. Walker.[25] Cherry Gilchrist's recent book *Russian Magic: Living Folk Traditions of an Enchanted Landscape* (2009) gives a detailed and accessible introduction to the place of magic in Russia today. Readers interested in Baba Yaga because of her resonance with these approaches will find all these authors rewarding.

Russian scholar Anna Natal'ia Malakhovskaia's 2007 book *Nasledie baby-iagi* (*The Heritage of Baba Yaga*) treats a similar range of topics, for readers who know Russian, though only part of her book is devoted to Baba Yaga. Like Hubbs, Malakhovskaia concludes her study in the realm of Russian literature. Discussing the ancient concepts that underlie the Russian wonder tale, she addresses matriarchy and initiation rituals. The larger part of the

A contemporary use of Bilibin's Baba Yaga, individualizing keds for kids. Bilibin's Baba Yaga from Vasilisa the Beautiful is one of many fairy-tale images imprinted on children's shoes, T-shirts, mugs, and numerous accessories in the SurLaLune (French for "On the Moon") line. Formerly available from SurLaLune Ked Shoes (ked is Russian for sneaker). SurLaLune also had produced shoes with familiar visuals by such famous Western fairy-tale illustrators as Gustave Doré, Arthur Rackham, and Walter Crane.

study finds traces of Russian folktales in nineteenth- and twentieth-century literature, concentrating in particular on the folk religious elements to be found in authors such as Dostoevsky, Platonov, and Valentin Rasputin. This book is in fact Malakhovskaia's second book on Baba Yaga: her first, a novel, is entitled *Vozvrashchenie k babe-iage* (*The Return to Baba-Yaga*). This novel treats the dilemmas of emigration and the differences between home and the West for individual émigrés, set in a kind of magical geography marked by traits of Russian folklore.

There are many treatments of Baba Yaga tales for children (some listed in the bibliography below). We can recommend not only Russian and North American books on Baba Yaga for adult readers, but also Dubravka Ugrešić's 2008 book *Baba Jaga je snijela jaje* (*Baba Yaga Laid an Egg*)[26] is great fun and quite intellectually rewarding. Ugrešić is one of the best-known writers today from former Yugoslavia, but before achieving her current international success she became a prominent specialist in Russian literature and culture. *Baba Yaga Laid an Egg* touches on a number of Yagian issues: the relationships between daughters and their aging mothers, the relationship between writers and their admirers, and the relationship between biographical experience and artistic invention. In the book's final section, Baba Yaga anagrams into a Bulgarian folklorist, and then . . . Well! We recommend that you read it.

BEYOND WORDS: BABA YAGA IN ILLUSTRATIONS, FILMS, GRAPHIC NOVELS, GAMES, AND OTHER MERCHANDISE

The illustrations that accompany these stories are crucial components of the image of Baba Yaga. Lush images from the late nineteenth and early twentieth centuries stylize the aesthetic values of old Russia. They have become inseparable from the narratives in the Baba Yaga canon, functioning not only as graphics, but also as vehicles for promoting products and, in the case of the luxurious Palekh lacquer boxes, as products themselves. More recently, Baba Yaga has fascinated artists and other creators with the same ambiguity that makes her a compelling figure in the tales. Her appearance in movies and cartoons, and in graphic novels and computer games, shows how much the idea of ancient wisdom—wise enough to change a hero's life, while powerful enough to inspire fear—continues to move our imagination today. As I write this, the online footwear vendor Zazzle is offering "Ivan Bilibin's Baba Yaga Shoe," a sneaker beautifully printed with Bilibin's portrait of Baba Yaga riding in her pestle, hair flying and a grim expression, for only $60.00.

The images in this volume were chosen by Helena Goscilo and Martin Skoro, and the descriptive captions by Helena Goscilo will quickly introduce the reader to the context of this fascinating world.

Sibelan Forrester
Swarthmore, Pennsylvania
August 4, 2012

BRIEF BIBLIOGRAPHY FOR FURTHER READING

EDITIONS/TRANSLATIONS OF RUSSIAN FOLKTALES

Afanas'ev, Aleksandr, ed. *Russian Fairy Tales.* Trans. Norbert Guterman. New York: Pantheon Books, 1943, 1973. A selection of tales from Afanas'ev's three-volume edition.

Balina, Marina, Helena Goscilo, and Mark Lipovetsky, eds. and trans. *Politicizing Magic: An Anthology of Russian and Soviet Folktales.* Evanston, IL: Northwestern University Press, 2005. This volume includes some more recent folktale-related stories, and the introductory essays for each section are quite valuable.

Chandler, Robert, ed. *Russian Magic Tales from Pushkin to Platanov.* Trans. Robert Chandler and Elizabeth Chandler, with Sibelan Forrester, Anna Gunin, and Olga Meerson. London: Penguin Books, 2012.

Gilchrist, Cherry. *Russian Magic: Living Folk Traditions of an Enchanted Landscape.* Wheaton, IL: Quest Books, 2009.

Haney, Jack, trans. *The Complete Russian Folktale* in seven volumes. Armonk, NY: M. E. Sharpe, 1999–2006. The first complete translation of Afanas'ev's tales into English, organized by theme.

Simonov, Pyotr. *Essential Russian Mythology: Stories That Change the World.* London: Thorsons, 1997. This short volume includes versions of some legends and epic songs as well as folktales.

OTHER WORKS ON BABA YAGA; USEFUL BOOKS ON WITCHCRAFT

Ankarloo, Ben, and Gustav Henningsen, eds. *Early Modern European Witchcraft: Centres and Peripheries.* Oxford: Clarendon Press, 1990.

Bly, Robert, and Marion Woodman. *The Maiden King: The Reunion of Masculine and Feminine.* New York: Henry Holt and Company, 1998.

Hubbs, Joanna. *Mother Russia: The Feminine Myth in Russian Culture.* Bloomington, IN: Indiana University Press, 1988.

Ivanits, Linda. *Russian Folk Belief.* Armonk, NY: M. E. Sharpe, 1989.

Johns, Andreas. *Baba Yaga: The Ambiguous Mother and Witch of the Russian Folktale.* New York: Peter Lang, 2004.

Maxwell-Stuart, P. G. *Witchcraft in Europe and the New World, 1400–1800.* Houndmills, Basingstoke: Palgrave, 2001.

Pinkola Estés, Clarissa. *Women Who Run with the Wolves: Myths and Stories of the Wild Woman Archetype.* New York: Ballantine Books, 1992.

Propp, Vladimir. *Morphology of the Folktale*. Trans. Laurence Scott. Austin: University of Texas Press, 1968.

Propp, Vladimir. *The Russian Folktale*. Trans. Sibelan Forrester. Detroit, MI: Wayne State University Press, 2012.

Ralston, W. R. S. *The Songs of the Russian People: As Illustrative of Slavonic Mythology and Russian Social Life*. London: Ellis & Green, 1872.

Sokolov, Y. M. *Russian Folklore*. Trans. Catherine Ruth Smith. Hatboro, PA: Folklore Associates, 1966.

Ugrešić, Dubravka. *Baba Yaga Laid an Egg*, translated by Ellen Elias-Bursać, Celia Hawkesworth, and Mark Thompson. New York: Cannongate, 2009.

TALES FOR CHILDREN

Arnold, Katya. *Baba Yaga: A Russian Folktale*. New York: North-South Books, 1993.

Arnold, Katya. *Baba Yaga and the Little Girl: A Russian Folktale*. New York: Norh-South Books, 1994.

Kimmel, Eric A., and Megan Lloyd. *Baba Yaga: A Russian Folktale*. New York: Holiday House, 1991.

Lurie, Alison, and Jessica Souhami. *The Black Geese: A Baba Yaga Story from Russia*. New York: DK Publishers, 1999.

Marshall Carey, Bonnie. *Baba Yaga's Geese, and Other Russian Stories*. Bloomington: Indiana University Press, 1973.

Mayer, Marianna, and Kinuko Craft. *Baba Yaga and Vasilisa the Brave*. New York: Morrow Junior Books, 1994.

McCaughrean, Geraldine, and Moira Kemp. *Grandma Chickenlegs*. Minneapolis, MN: Carolrhoda Books, 2000.

Oram, Hiawyn, and Ruth Brown. *Baba Yaga and the Wise Doll: A Traditional Russian Folktale*. New York: Dutton Children's Books, 1998. 1997.

Polacco, Patricia. *Babushka Baba Yaga*. New York: Philomei, 1993. (for children)

Small, Ernest, and Blair Lent. *Baba Yaga*. Boston: Houghton Mifflin, 1966.

FILMOGRAPHY
(WITH THANKS TO JACK ZIPES)

Jack Frost (Morozko, 1964)
Director: Aleksandr Rou
Russian, live-action film (84 minutes)

The Golden Horns (Zolotye roga, 1972)
Director: Aleksandr Rou
Russian, live-action film (74 minutes)

Baba Yaga (1973)
Director: Corrado Farina
Italian, live-action film (91 minutes)

Baba Yaga Is Against! (Baba Yaga protiv!, 1979)
Director: Vladimir Pekar
Russian, animated film (26 minutes)
The Little Dragon and the Old Witch (Malkiyat smey i Baba Yaga, 1985)
Director: Slav Balakov
Bulgarian, animated film (6 minutes)
Babka Yozhka and Others (Babka Yozhka i drugie, 2006)
Director: Valery Ugarov
Russian, animated film (70 minutes)
Emily and the Baba Yaga (2005)
Director: Clive Tronge
UK, animated film (10 minutes)

Tales of Baba Yaga

by Rima Staines, the young British painter, clockmaker, illustrator, and storyteller, who here clearly models her style on those of such ssian illustrators as Vasnetsov and Bilibin. Her creative violation of proportions, however, transforms Baba Yaga into a figure physically g the landscape, and her hut into an enlarged chicken-legged mailbox. http://www.intothehermitage.blogspot.com/.

Dancing Baba Yaga by Ivan Bilibin (1908). The extraordinary Terpsichorean Baba Yaga flies and rides in the tales, but generally abjures dance, though an early *lubok* (popular woodcut print) also shows her capering to the accompaniment of a bagpipe (see image #52). Here the angle of her preternaturally long arms suggests the boniness that is one of her salient features, while the festive red of her nose substitutes for its inordinate size. The tales repeatedly emphasize how her proboscis, sometimes unhygienically dripping snot, extends to the ceiling. Illustration by Ivan Bilibin (1876–1942).

Baba Yaga I

Once upon a time there lived a husband and wife, and they had a daughter. The wife up and died. The man married another woman and had a daughter with her, too. That wife took a dislike to her stepdaughter; the poor thing had no kind of life at all.

The man thought and thought about it and took his daughter into the woods. As they were driving through the woods, he looked and saw a little house standing on chicken legs. Then the man said, "Little house, little house, stand with your back to the woods and your front to me." The house turned around.

The man went into the house, and there inside was Baba Yaga, head facing straight ahead, one leg in one corner, one leg in the other. "There's a smell of something Russian!" said Yaga.

The man bowed to her and said, "Baba Yaga, bony leg! I've brought my daughter to serve you."

"Well, all right! Serve me, serve me," said Yaga to the girl. "I'll reward you for it."

The father said good-bye to her and went home. And Baba Yaga ordered the girl to spin stuff from the basket, stoke the stove, and prepare some of everything to eat, while she herself went out.

The girl started to work at the stove, but she was crying bitterly. Little mice ran out and said to her, "Maiden, fair maiden, what are you crying for? Give us some porridge, and we'll tell you something good." She gave them some porridge. "Here's what you need to do," they said. "You spin one thread on each spindle."

Baba Yaga came home: "So then," she said, "have you prepared some of everything?"

But the girl had everything ready. "Well then, come on—give me a wash in the bathhouse." Yaga praised the girl and gave her all kinds of fancy clothes.

Yaga went out again and assigned her even more difficult tasks. The girl began to cry again. The little mice ran out and said, "What are you crying for, lovely maiden? Give us some porridge, and we'll give you some good advice." She gave them some porridge, and once again they told her what to do and how.

Baba Yaga came back again, praised her and gave her even more nice clothes . . . After a while, the stepmother sent the man to see whether his daughter was alive.

Off the man went. He drove up to the house and saw that his daughter had become very rich. The Yaga was not at home, so he took his daughter home with him.

They drove toward their village, and the little dog at home couldn't keep quiet. "Woof, woof, woof! A lady is coming, a lady is coming!"

The stepmother ran out and let the doggie have it with a rolling pin. "You're lying," she shouted. "Say that bones are rattling in the basket!"

But the dog kept on saying what it wanted. They came to the house. The stepmother started to pester her husband to take her own daughter there, too. So the man took her off into the woods.

Baba Yaga assigned her some work and went out. The girl was beside herself with disappointment and started to cry. The little mice ran out and said, "Maiden, maiden! What are you crying for?"

But she didn't even let them finish speaking. She went after one and then another with the rolling pin. She kept on chasing them, and she didn't do the work she was supposed to. Yaga came home and got angry. The same thing happened a second time, so Yaga broke her up into pieces and put her bones in a box.

The mother sent her husband to go pick up her daughter. When the father got there, he found only bones to take away.

As he drove toward the village, the little dog started barking again on the porch: "Woof, woof, woof! They're bringing bones in a box!"

The stepmother ran out with the rolling pin. "You're lying," she shouted. "Say a lady is coming!"

But the doggie kept on repeating: "Woof, woof, woof! The bones are rattling in the box!"

The husband got home, and then the wife really started howling! For you there's a tale, and for me a cup of ale.

(Afanas'ev, no. 102)

Baba Yaga II

Once there lived an old man and his wife. The old man's wife died and he took another wife, but he had a little girl from his first wife. The evil stepmother did not like her. She beat her and thought about how to get rid of her once and for all.

Once the father went away somewhere, and the stepmother said to the girl, "Go see your aunt, my sister, and ask her for a needle and thread to sew a shirt for you." But this aunt was a Baba Yaga, bony-leg.

The girl wasn't stupid, so she stopped by to see her own aunt first. "Hello, Auntie!"

"Hello, my dear! Why are you here?"

"Mother's sent me to her sister to ask for a needle and thread to sew a shirt for me."

The aunt told her what to do. "My dear niece, a birch tree there will whip you in the eyes—you tie it back with a ribbon. The gate there will squeak and slam—you pour some oil under its hinges. The dogs there will tear at you—you toss them some bread. The tomcat there will scratch at your eyes—you give him some ham."

The girl set off. She walked and walked, and she got there.

A hut was standing there, and Baba Yaga, bony-leg, was sitting inside and waiting.

"Hello, Auntie!"

"Hello, my dear!"

"Mother sent me to ask you for a needle and thread to sew me a shirt."

"Good; sit down for a moment and weave."

The girl sat down there at the loom. But Baba Yaga went out and said to her maidservant, "Go, heat up the bathhouse and wash my niece, and be sure to do a good job. I want to have her for breakfast."

The girl sat there neither dead nor alive, all terrified. She begged the maidservant, "My dear girl! Don't light the wood as much as you pour on the water, and carry the water in a sieve," and she gave her a handkerchief.

Baba Yaga was waiting. She walked over to the window and asked, "Are you weaving, little niece, are you weaving, my dear?"

"I'm weaving, Auntie! I'm weaving, dear!"

Baba Yaga moved away again, and the girl gave the tomcat some ham and asked him, "Is there any way to get out of here?"

"Here are a comb and a towel for you," said the cat. "Take them and run away. Baba Yaga will chase after you. You put your ear to the ground, and when you hear that she's close, throw down the towel first—it will turn into a wide, wide river. If Baba Yaga crosses the river and starts to catch up with you, you put your ear to the ground again, and when you hear that she's close, throw the comb—it will turn into a thick, thick forest. She won't be able to get through it!"

The girl took the towel and the comb and ran out. The dogs wanted to tear at her; she threw them some bread, and they let her pass. The gate wanted to slam on her; she poured some oil under the hinges, and it let her pass. The birch tree wanted to lash her eyes out; she tied it back with a ribbon, and it let her pass. And the cat sat down at the loom and started to weave. He didn't weave as much as he tangled things. Baba Yaga came over to the window and asked, "Are you weaving, my little niece, are you weaving, my dear?"

"I'm weaving, Auntie! I'm weaving, dear!" the tomcat answered in a hoarse voice.

Baba Yaga raced into the hut, saw that the girl had run away, and started beating and scolding the tomcat. Why hadn't he scratched the girl's eyes out?

"I've been serving you for so long," said the tomcat. "You've never even given me a bone, but she gave me some ham."

Baba Yaga threw herself at the dogs, on the gates, on the birch tree, and on the maidservant. She started scolding each one and pounding them.

The dogs told her, "We've been serving you so long, and you've never thrown us a burned crust, but she gave us some bread."

The gate said, "I've been serving you for so long, and you've never even poured water under my hinges, but she poured some oil."

The birch tree said, "I've been serving you so long, and you've never tied me up with a thread, but she tied me up with a ribbon."

The maidservant said, "I've been serving you for so long, and you've never given me a rag, but she gave me a handkerchief."

Steam Powered Baba Yaga of the Future, also described by its creator, the young Bulgarian artist Aleksandr Nanitchkov aka Inca/Artofinca, as Baba Yaga—steam punked. Like most contemporary concepts of Baba Yaga, this one strives for originality and humor through temporal and physical recontextualization. Illustration by Aleksandr Nanitchkov. http://tsabo6.deviantart.com/www.artofinca.com.

Baba Yaga, the bony-leg, sat right down in her mortar, pushed along with a pestle, swept the tracks away with a broom, and set off to chase the girl. The girl put her ear to the ground and heard Baba Yaga chasing her and already getting close. She up and threw the towel. It turned into a river so wide, so wide!

Baba Yaga came to the river and her teeth squeaked with malice. She went back home, got her bulls, and drove them to the river. The bulls drank the whole river dry.

Baba Yaga set off again in pursuit. The girl put her ear to the ground and heard that Baba Yaga was close. She threw the comb, and it turned into a forest so thick and terrible! Baba Yaga started to chew it, but no matter how she tried she couldn't chew through it, so she went back home.

But the old man had already come back, and he asked, "Where on earth is my daughter?"

"She went to her aunt's," the stepmother answered.

A little later the girl herself ran up to the house. "Where were you?" asked her father.

"Oh, Dad!" she said. "It was like this. Mother sent me to my aunt's to ask for a needle and thread to sew me a shirt, but my aunt is a Baba Yaga, and she wanted to eat me."

"How did you get away, daughter?"

"Like this," and the girl told him the story.

When the old man found out all about it, he got angry at his wife and shot her. But he and his daughter went on living and living well and earning riches. And I was there, I drank mead and beer: it flowed down my mustache, but didn't go in my mouth.

(Afanas'ev, no. 103)

Baba Yaga and the Kid

Once there lived a tomcat, a sparrow, and a young man made three. The tomcat and the sparrow went to cut wood, and they said to the kid,[1] "You look after the house, but watch out. If Baba Yaga comes and starts counting the spoons, don't say anything—be quiet!"

"All right," said the kid.

The tomcat and the sparrow left, and the kid climbed up on the stove and sat behind the stovepipe. Suddenly a Baba Yaga appeared, picked up the spoons, and started counting: "This is the tomcat's spoon, this is the sparrow's spoon, and the third one is the kid's."

The kid couldn't bear it, and he shouted, "Baba-yaga, don't you touch my spoon!"

Baba Yaga grabbed the kid, got into her mortar, and rode off. She rode in the mortar, pushed along[2] with the pestle, and swept away her tracks with a broom.

The kid started to yell, "Run, cat! Fly, sparrow!"

They heard him, and they came running. The cat scratched Baba Yaga while the sparrow pecked her, and they took the kid away from her.

The next day they were getting ready to go into the forest again to cut wood, and they told the kid, "Watch out! If Baba Yaga comes, don't say anything. This time we're going far away."

No sooner had the kid settled down behind the stovepipe than the Baba Yaga appeared again and started to count the spoons. "This is the cat's spoon, this is the sparrow's spoon, and this one is the kid's."

The kid couldn't bear it, and he shouted, "Don't you touch my spoon, Baba Yaga!"

The Yaga-baba grabbed the kid and dragged him outside, but the kid shouted, "Cat, sparrow, help!"

Baba Yaga and Her Hut by Aleksandr Alexeieff. Illustration from *Russian Fairy Tales* by Aleksandr Afanas'ev and illustrated by Alexander Alexeieff, translated by Norbert Guterman, copyright 1945 by Pantheon Books and renewed 1973 by Random House, Inc.

They heard him and came running; the tomcat scratched, the sparrow pecked at the Yaga-baba! They got the kid away from her and went back home.

On the third day they got ready to go into the forest to cut wood, and they said to the kid, "Watch out! If the Yaga-baba comes, keep quiet. We're going far away now."

The tomcat and the sparrow left, and the third one, the kid, took a seat on the stove behind the pipe. Suddenly the Yaga-baba took the spoons again and started counting: "This is the cat's spoon, this is the sparrow's spoon, and the third one's the kid's."

The kid kept quiet.

The Yaga-baba started to count a second time: "This is the cat's spoon, this is the sparrow's spoon, and the third one's the kid's."

The kid kept quiet.

The Yaga-baba counted a third time: "This is the cat's spoon, this is the sparrow's spoon, the third one's the kid's."

The kid couldn't bear it. He started to bellow,[3] "Don't you touch my spoon, you slut!"

Yaga-baba grabbed the kid and dragged him away.

The kid shouted, "Run, cat! Fly, sparrow!" But his brothers didn't hear him.

Yaga-baba dragged the kid home, put him in the stove-box,[4] stoked the stove herself, and said to her eldest daughter, "So, girl! I'm going to Rus'. You roast up this kid for my lunch."

"All right!" her daughter answered.

The stove got nice and hot. The girl ordered the kid to come out. The kid came out, and the girl said, "Lie down in the pan!"[5]

The kid lay down, stuck one leg up toward the ceiling and the other down toward the floor.[6]

The girl said, "Not that way, not that way!"

The kid said, "Then how? You go ahead and show me."

The girl lay down on the pan.

The kid didn't lose his nerve. He grabbed the oven-fork and shoved the pan with Yaga's daughter right into the stove. He went back into the stove-box and sat there waiting for the Yaga-baba.

All at once Yaga-baba came running and said, "I want to roll, I want to loll around on the kid's bones!"

But the kid answered her, "Roll around, loll around on your own daughter's bones!"

The Brave Youth by Aleksandr Alexeieff. Illustration from RUSSIAN FAIRY TALES by Aleksandr Afanas'ev and illustrated by Alexander Alexeieff, translated by Norbert Guterman, copyright 1945 by Pantheon Books and renewed 1973 by Random House, Inc. Used by permission of Pantheon Books, a division of Random House, Inc.

Yaga-baba gasped and took a peek: it was her daughter who'd been roasted. She shouted, "Oh! You scoundrel, just you wait! You won't get out of this one!" She ordered her middle daughter to roast the kid, and she left.

The middle daughter stoked the stove and told the kid to come out. The kid came out, lay down in the pan, stuck one foot up toward the ceiling and the other down toward the floor. The girl said, "Not like that! Not like that!"

"Then show me how."

The girl lay down in the roasting pan. The kid up and shoved her into the stove, went back into the stove-box, and there he sat.

All at once Yaga-baba ran in: "I want to roll, I want to loll around on the kid's bones!"

He answered, "Roll around, loll around on your daughter's bones!"

Yagishna was furious: "Eh, just wait," she said, "you won't get away from me!" She ordered her youngest daughter to roast him. But nothing doing—the kid cooked that one, too!

Yaga-baba got even angrier. "Just wait," she said, "you won't get away from me!" She stoked the stove and shouted, "Come out, kid! Lie down there on the roasting pan."

The kid lay down, stuck one leg up toward the ceiling, the other toward the floor, and wouldn't fit into the oven.[7]

Yaga-baba said, "Not like that! Not like that!"

But the kid acted as if he didn't know: "I don't know how to do it," he said. "You show me!"

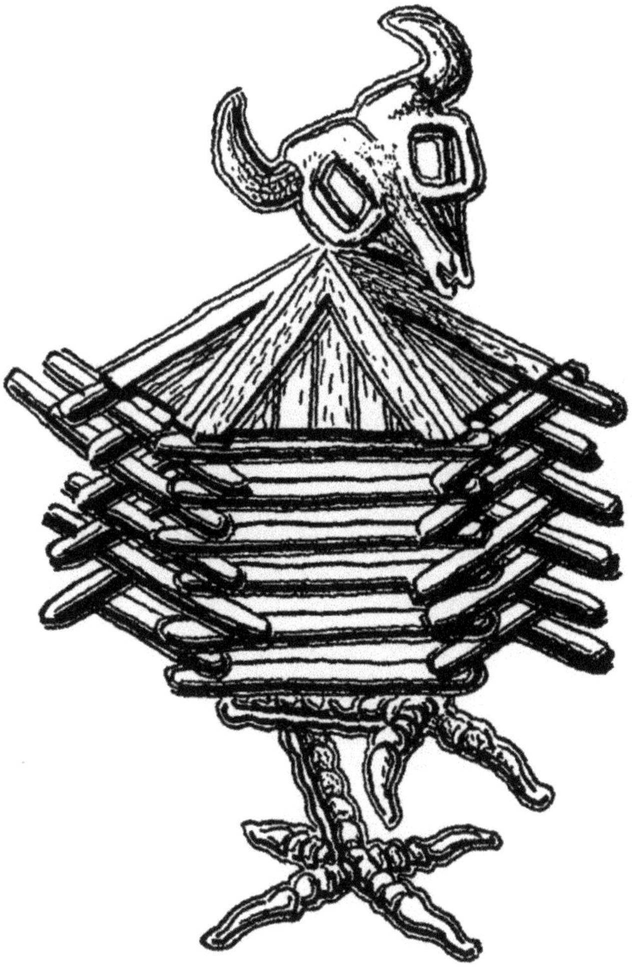

Baba Yaga's Hut by Aleksandr Alexeieff. Illustration from RUSSIAN FAIRY TALES by Aleksandr Afanas'ev and illustrated by Alexander Alexeieff, translated by Norbert Guterman, copyright 1945 by Pantheon Books and renewed 1973 by Random House, Inc. Used by permission of Pantheon Books, a division of Random House, Inc.

Yaga-baba lay right down and curled up on the pan.

The kid never hesitated. He went and shoved her into the stove. He ran home, went in, and told his brothers, "Let me tell you what I did to the Yaga-baba."

(Afanas'ev, no. 106)

Baba-Yaga and the Runt

There lived a man and a woman who had no children. No matter what they did, no matter how they prayed to God, the old woman still didn't bear any children. One day the man went into the woods to get mushrooms. On the road he ran into a very old man. "I know what's in your thoughts," he said. "You keep thinking about children. Go through the village, collect one egg from every household, and put a brood hen to sit on those eggs. You'll see for yourself what happens!"

The old man went back to the village. There were forty-one households in their village, so he went around all of them, took an egg from each, and put a brood hen on the forty-one eggs.

Two weeks passed. The old man took a look, the old woman took a look, too, and they saw that the eggs had hatched out a lot of boys. There were forty strong, healthy ones, but one hadn't turned out so well—he was puny and weak! The old man started to give names to the boys. He gave names to all of them, but there were no names left for the last one. "Well," he said, "you can be called Runt!"[8]

The old man and old woman's children grew. They grew not by the day but by the hour. They grew up and started to work, to help their father and mother. The forty fine lads were busy in the field, while Runt looked after things at home. It got to be time for haymaking, and the brothers mowed the grass, put up haystacks, worked for a week, and then came back to the village. They ate whatever God had sent and lay down to sleep. The old man looked and said, "Young and green! They eat a lot, and they sleep soundly, but they haven't done any work!"

"First, you go out and take a look, Dad!" Runt answered him.

The old man put on his jacket and went out to the meadows. He looked, and there were forty haystacks raked together. "Aye, the boys are good lads! They mowed so much in one week and raked it all into stacks."

The next day the father got ready to go to the meadows again, since he

Mike Mignola, *Hellboy, Vol. 3: The Chained Coffin and Others* (2004). Dark Horse; 2nd edition 2004, page 37. Hellboy: The Chained Coffin and Others™ © 2011 Mike Mignola.

wanted to admire his goods. He got there, and it seemed that one of the stacks was missing! He went back home and said, "Ah, children! Did you know that one stack has disappeared?"

"Don't worry, Dad!" answered Runt. "We'll catch the thief. Give me a hundred rubles, and I'll do it." He took a hundred rubles from his father and went to the blacksmith. "Can you forge me a chain long enough to wrap a person from head to foot?"

"Why wouldn't I be able to forge it?"

"Be careful, make it plenty strong. If the chain holds I'll pay you a hundred rubles, but if it snaps you've wasted your labor!"

The blacksmith forged an iron chain; Runt wrapped it around himself, stretched, and the chain snapped. The blacksmith made another twice as strong, and that one was good. Runt took this chain, paid the hundred rubles, and went to guard the hay. He sat down under one of the haystacks and waited.

At the stroke of midnight the weather changed, the sea grew rough, and a marvelous mare came out of the depths of the sea. She ran up to the first haystack and started to devour the hay. Runt jumped out, bridled her with the iron chain, and jumped up on her back. The mare started bucking, carrying him over hill and dale, but no, she wasn't strong enough to shake off the rider! She stopped and said to him, "Well, good lad! Since you've managed to keep your seat on me, then you must take my foals and break them."

Mike Mignola, *Hellboy, Vol. 3: The Chained Coffin and Others* (2004). Dark Horse; 2nd edition, page 40. Hellboy: The Chained Coffin and Others™ © 2011 Mike Mignola.

The mare ran up to the blue sea and neighed loudly. Then the blue sea grew rough and forty-one stallions came out on the shore, each more handsome than the last! You could go through the whole world and never find the likes of them anywhere! In the morning the old man heard neighing and stamping in the yard. What could it be? But it was his son Runt, who had driven the whole herd home. "Hi there, brothers!" he said. "Now there's a horse for each of us. Let's ride together to find brides for ourselves!"

"Let's go!" Their father and mother gave them their blessing, and the brothers set out on the long road.

They rode for a long time through the white world, but where could they find so many brides? They didn't want to get married separately, so that no one's feelings would be hurt, but what mother can brag that she had forty-one daughters at a time? The fine lads rode over thrice-nine lands and came upon a palace of white stone on a steep mountain, surrounded with a high wall, with iron columns placed at the gates. They counted, and there were forty-one pillars. So they fastened their forty-one *bogatyr* horses to those pillars and went into the courtyard. A Baba Yaga met them there.

Mike Mignola, *Hellboy, Vol. 3: The Chained Coffin and Others* (2004), page 38. A comics panel by the American artist/writer Mignola in his highly successful horror-cum-fantasy series titled Hellboy. The old witch in a mortar with pestle, blatantly modeled on Baba Yaga, follows her Russian predecessor's example by pressing an animated skeleton into service. Hellboy: The Chained Coffin and Others™ © 2011 Mike Mignola.

"Ah, you, uncalled and uninvited! How dare you hitch your horses without permission?"

"Well, old woman! What are you shouting for? First give us something to eat and drink, take us to the bathhouse, then afterward ask us for news."

Baba Yaga fed them, gave them something to drink, took them to the bathhouse, and then started to ask them: "What is it, good lads? Are you doing a deed or fleeing a deed?"

"We're doing a deed, grandmother!"

"What is it you need?"

"Why, we're looking for brides."

"I have daughters," said Baba Yaga. She ran into the high chambers and brought out forty-one maidens.

They got engaged right away and began to drink, to celebrate and hold the wedding. In the evening Runt went to look in on his horse. His good horse saw him and spoke up in a human voice, "Look out, master! When you lie down to sleep with your young wives, dress them in your clothes, and put on your wives' clothes yourselves. Otherwise we'll all be lost!" Runt told

Mike Mignola, *Hellboy, Vol. 3: The Chained Coffin and Others* (2004). Dark Horse; 2nd edition, page 38. Hellboy: The Chained Coffin and Others™ © 2011 Mike Mignola.

this to his brothers, and so they decked the young wives out in their clothes, put on the wives' clothes themselves, and then lay down to sleep. They all fell asleep, but Runt didn't close an eye. At the stroke of midnight Baba Yaga shouted loudly, "Hey, you, my faithful servants, cut the wild heads off these uninvited guests!" Her faithful servants came running and cut off the wild heads of Baba Yaga's own daughters. Runt woke up his brothers and told them everything that had happened. They took the heads and stuck them on the iron spikes around the wall, then saddled their horses and rode off in haste.

In the morning Baba Yaga got up, looked out the window—and all around the wall her daughters' heads were stuck on the spikes. She was horribly angry, ordered her fiery shield, rode off in pursuit, and started shooting fire from the shield in all four directions. Where could the fine lads hide themselves? Ahead of them was the blue sea, behind them was Baba Yaga, burning and shooting. They could all have died, but Runt had a good idea. He had thought to take a handkerchief from Baba Yaga, and he waved that kerchief in front of him. Suddenly a bridge appeared that stretched across the whole blue sea. The fine lads rode across it to the other side. Runt waved the handkerchief in the other direction and the bridge disappeared. Baba Yaga went back, and the brothers rode off for home.[9]

(Afanas'ev, no. 105)

Finist the Bright Falcon II

Once there lived an old man and an old woman. They had three daughters; the youngest was such a beauty that it can't be told in a tale or written down by a pen.

Once the old man was getting ready to go to the city for the market and he said, "My gracious daughters! Whatever you wish, give me your orders—I'll buy everything at the market."

The eldest asked, "Buy me a new dress, Father."

The middle one said, "Buy me a shawl kerchief, Father."

But the youngest said, "Buy me a little scarlet flower."[10]

The father laughed at the youngest daughter. "And what, silly little thing, do you need a little scarlet flower for? A great lot of good it would do you. I'd do better to buy you fancy clothes."

Only, no matter what he said, he couldn't persuade her at all. "Buy a little scarlet flower"—and that was all she wanted.

The old man set off for the market. He bought his eldest daughter a dress and the middle one a shawl kerchief, but he couldn't find a little scarlet flower in the whole city. He was already at the very gate of the city when he happened to meet an old man he didn't know, who was carrying a little scarlet flower in his hands. "Sell me your flower, old man!"

"It's not for sale; it's special.[11] If your youngest daughter will marry my son, Finist the bright falcon, then I'll give you the flower for nothing." The father sank into thought: not taking the flower would cause his daughter grief, but taking it would mean having to marry her off, and God knows to whom. He thought and thought, and finally he took the little scarlet flower, after all. "It's not a misfortune," he thought. "He'll come courting later on, and if he's no good then we can turn him down!"

The old man came home and gave his eldest daughter the dress and his middle daughter the shawl kerchief, but he gave the youngest one the little flower and said, "Your flower doesn't please me, my dear daughter, doesn't please me at all!" And he whispered in her ear, "You know, the flower was special, not for sale. I got it from an old stranger on the condition that I marry you to his son, Finist the bright falcon."

"Don't grieve, Father," answered the daughter. "He's so good and affectionate. He flies as a bright falcon through the sky, but as soon as he strikes the damp earth—then he turns into a fine young man!"

"Can it be that you know him?"

"I know him, I know him, Father! Last Sunday he was at church, he kept looking at me, and I spoke with him . . . you know, he loves me, Father!"

The old man shook his head, looked closely at his daughter, made the sign of the cross over her, and said, "Go to your room, my dear daughter! It's already bedtime. Morning's wiser than the evening. We'll make sense of it all later."

But the daughter locked herself in her room, put the little scarlet flower into water, opened the window, and looked out into the blue distance.

Out of nowhere, there before her appeared Finist the bright falcon, with jeweled feathers. He swooped in through the window, struck the floor, and turned into a fine lad. At first the girl was frightened, but then, once he began to talk with her, she felt ever so merry and good. They conversed until dawn, I don't know what about.

I only know that when it began to get light Finist the bright falcon with the jeweled feathers kissed her and said, "Every night, as soon as you put the little scarlet flower on the windowsill, I'll come to you, my dear! And here's a feather for you from my wing. If you need any kind of fine clothes, go out on the porch and just wave the feather to the right. In an instant everything your soul might desire will appear right in front of you!" He kissed her once more, turned into a bright falcon, and flew away over the dark forest.

The girl watched her intended leave, closed the window, and lay down to rest. From then on every night, as soon as she put the little scarlet flower in the open window, the fine lad Finist the bright falcon would come flying to her.

Sunday came, and the older sisters began to dress up for church. "And what will you put on? You have nothing new!" they said to the youngest one.

She said, "That's all right, I can pray at home, too!"

The older sisters went off to mass, but the little one sat by the window, all smudged, and looked at the Orthodox people going to God's church. She waited long enough for them to pass, went out on the porch, waved the jeweled feather to the right, and from out of nowhere a crystal carriage appeared before her, with a team of matching horses, and a servant in gold, dresses and all kinds of ornaments made of brightly colored jewels.

The fair maiden got herself dressed in a minute, got into the carriage, and hurried off to church. The people looked and marveled at her beauty. "You can see that some kind of princess has come!" the people said among themselves. When she heard the service drawing to an end,[12] she left the church right away, got in the carriage, and rode off home. The Orthodox people came outside, hoping to get a look and see where she was going, but there was no sign of her! Her tracks had cooled long ago. No sooner had our beauty driven up to the porch of her house than she waved the jeweled feather to the left. In no time the servant helped her take off the splendid dress, and the carriage disappeared. She was sitting there just as before, as if nothing at all had happened, looking out the window at the Orthodox people scattering to their homes.

Her sisters came home, too. "Well, sister!" they said. "What a beauty there was at mass in the church! A real pleasure to see, no tale could tell it and no pen could write it down! It must have been a queen from foreign lands who came visiting. She was just magnificent, all dressed up!"

A second Sunday came, and a third. The fair maiden kept teasing the Orthodox people, her own sisters, and her father and mother. Then once, when she was taking off her fine clothes, she forgot to take a diamond pin out of her hair. Her older sisters came from the church and were telling her about the beautiful princess, when they took a look at their little sister, and the diamond was just blazing in her plaits. "Ah, sister! What do you have there?" cried the girls. "Why, the princess today had exactly that kind of pin in her hair. Where did you get it?"

The fair maiden gasped and ran off to her bedroom. There was no end to the questions, guesses, and whispering back and forth. But the youngest sister kept quiet and laughed to herself.

Then the older sisters started paying close attention to her, listening at night outside her bedroom, and once they heard her conversation with Finist the bright falcon. At dawn they saw him with their own eyes as he shot out of the window and flew off over the dark forest. They were evil girls, it seems, the two big sisters. They decided to hide knives on the window of their sister's chamber in the evening so that Finist the bright falcon would cut his jeweled wings.

Once they got the idea, they did it, while the younger sister didn't suspect anything. She put her little scarlet flower on the windowsill, lay back on

Baba Yaga's hut. That Baba Yaga's hut in the forest represents a paradoxical locus of life and death is clear from its mélange of traits. Some connote reproduction and nurture (shelter from the elements; the organic support of chicken legs [chicken eggs = birth of chicks]; the oven that provides warmth and cooks food), while others evoke death (the skulls encircling the hut; the charm needed to access the entrance; the oven that transforms humans into food; the cannibalistic inhabitant). Hands function as locks and animals fulfill dread tasks, while Baba Yaga's body fills the hut—not unlike a corpse resting in a coffin. Yet the hut revolves, like the earth around the sun. The dark, windowless wooden hut here, coupled with the figure of Baba Yaga as totem, resembles structures reportedly housing figurines of ancient Siberian pagan gods.

her bed, and fell sound asleep. Finist the bright falcon came flying, but when he swooped into the window he cut his left leg. But the fair maiden knew nothing about it, she was sleeping so sweetly, so peacefully. The bright falcon soared up angrily into the open sky and flew away over the dark forest.

In the morning the beauty woke up and looked in every direction. It was already light, but there was no sign of the handsome young man! As soon as she glanced out the window, she saw sharp knives sticking out this way and that outside the window, and scarlet blood was dripping from them onto the little flower. For a long time the maiden drowned in bitter tears; she spent many sleepless nights by the window of her chamber, tried waving the jeweled feather—but all in vain! Finist the bright falcon didn't come flying to her, and he didn't send his servants, either!

Finally she went to her father with tears in her eyes and asked for his blessing. "I'm going, I don't know where," she said.

She ordered three pairs of iron shoes forged for her and three iron crutches, three iron caps, and three iron loaves. She put a pair of the shoes on her feet, a cap on her head, a crutch in her hands, and she set off in the same direction Finist the bright falcon had always come flying from to see her.

She walked along through a deep, dark forest, walked over stumps and stiles; the iron shoes were already getting worn, the iron cap was wearing out, the crutch was breaking, the loaf was gnawed away, but the fair maiden kept walking and walking, while the forest grew blacker and blacker, thicker and thicker. Suddenly she saw, standing in front of her, a cast-iron hut on chicken legs that constantly turned around.

The maiden said, "Little house, little house! Stand with your back to the woods, your front to me." The house turned its front toward her. She went into the house, and a Baba Yaga was lying inside from corner to corner, lips on the railing, nose stuck in the ceiling.[13] "Fie-fie-fie! Before the Russian smell[14] couldn't be seen with the sight, couldn't be heard with the hearing, but now the Russian spirit walks over the free world and appears before my very eyes,[15] throws itself into my nose! Where does your road lead, fair maiden? Are you doing a deed or fleeing a deed?"

"Granny, I had Finist the bright falcon, jeweled feathers, but my sisters harmed him. Now I'm searching for Finist the bright falcon."

"You'll have to go a long way, little one! You must pass through thrice-nine more lands. Finist the bright falcon, jeweled feathers, lives in the fiftieth kingdom, in the eightieth state, and he's already betrothed to a princess."

Baba Yaga fed the maiden whatever God had provided, gave her something to drink, and put her to bed. In the morning, as soon as the light began to spread, she woke her up and gave her a precious gift, a little gold mallet and ten diamond nails. And she instructed her: "When you come to the blue sea, Finist the bright falcon's bride will come out on the shore for a stroll. But you take this golden mallet in your hand and hammer in the diamond nails. She'll ask to buy them from you. Don't you take anything, fair maiden, only ask to see Finist the bright falcon. There now—go with God to see my middle sister!"

Again the fair maiden walked along through the dark forest—farther and farther, and the forest kept getting blacker and denser, its treetops curling up to the sky. The second pair of shoes was already down at heel, the second cap was already worn out, the iron crutch was breaking, and the second loaf was gnawed through—when there standing before her was a cast-iron house on chicken's legs, and it turned around without ever ceasing.

"Little house, little house! Stand with your back to the woods and your front to me. I must climb inside, to eat some bread."

The little house turned with its back to the woods, its front toward the maiden. She went inside, but a Baba Yaga was lying inside the little house from corner to corner, lips on the railing, nose stuck in the ceiling. "Fie-fie-fie! Before, the Russian smell couldn't be seen with the sight or heard with the hearing, but now the Russian smell has started walking all over the wide world! Where does your road lead, fair maiden?"

"Granny, I'm searching for Finist the bright falcon."

"He's about to get married. They're already holding the party for the bridesmaids," said the Baba Yaga. She gave the maiden food and drink and put her to sleep. In the morning, as soon as it got light, she woke her up, gave her a golden saucer with a diamond ball, and ordered her firmly-firmly, "When you come to the shore of the blue sea, start rolling the diamond ball on the golden saucer. Finist the bright falcon's bride will come out to you and start trying to buy the saucer with the ball. But don't you take anything for it, just ask to see Finist the bright falcon, jeweled feathers. Now go with God to see my older sister!"

Again the fair maiden walked through the dark forest—farther and farther, and the forest ever blacker and thicker. The third pair of shoes was already down at heel, the third cap was already worn out, the last crutch was breaking, and the last loaf was gnawed away. Before her a cast-iron house was standing on chicken's legs. It kept turning and turning around.

"Little house, little house! Turn your back to the woods, your front to me; I must go inside, to eat some bread." The house turned.

Once again there was a Baba Yaga in the house. She lay there from corner to corner, lips on the railing, nose stuck in the ceiling. "Fie-fie-fie! Before the Russian smell was not to be seen with the sight, not to be heard with the hearing, but now the Russian smell walks all over the wide world! Where does your path lead, fair maiden?"

"I'm looking for Finist the bright falcon, Granny."

"Ah, fair maiden, he's already married! Here's my swift horse, mount it and ride with God!" The maiden mounted the horse and raced onward, while the forest got thinner and thinner.

And there was the blue sea—wide and free—spreading out before her, and there in the distance, like fire, golden roofs burned on high towers of white stone. "That must be the kingdom of Finist the bright falcon!" thought

Illustration by Victor Bibikov.

the maiden. She sat down on the shifting sand and began to hammer in the diamond nails with the golden hammer. Suddenly a princess came walking down the beach with her nurses, with her nannies, and with her faithful servants. She stopped and started to bargain for the diamond nails and the golden mallet.

"Princess, just let me have a look at Finist the bright falcon, and I'll let you have them for nothing," the girl answered.

"But Finist the bright falcon is sleeping now; he ordered that no one be let in to him. Well, so be it, give me your wonderful nails and mallet—and I'll show him to you."

She took the mallet and the little nails, ran to the palace, and stuck a magic pin into Finist the bright falcon's clothes so he would sleep more soundly and wouldn't wake up from his sleep. Then she ordered the nurses to lead the fair maiden into the palace to her husband, the bright falcon, and she herself went for a walk. For a long time the girl wrung her hands, for a long time she cried over her darling, but there was no way she could wake him . . . Once she had strolled all she wanted, the princess came home, chased the fair maiden away, and pulled out the pin.

Finist the bright falcon woke up. "Ugh, how long I've been sleeping!" he said. "Someone was here and kept weeping and lamenting over me. Only there was no way I could open my eyes—it was so hard for me!"

"You were dreaming," answered the princess. "There was nobody here."

Illustration by Victor Bibikov. The artist Victor Bibikov uniquely catches Baba Yaga on the red-eye flight via mortar and broom—one of illustrators' favorite subjects, though in fairy tales mortals typically witness her flying by day.

The next day the fair maiden again sat on the shore of the dark-blue sea, and she rolled the diamond ball on the golden saucer. The princess came out to stroll. She saw it and asked, "Sell it to me!"

"Let me just take a look at Finist the bright falcon, and I'll let you have it for nothing!"

The princess agreed and again stuck a pin in Finist the bright falcon's clothes. Again the fair maiden wept bitterly over her darling and couldn't wake him. On the third day she sat on the shore of the dark-blue sea, so sorrowful and sad, feeding her horse glowing coals. The princess saw the horse being fed with fire, and she started asking to buy him.

"Let me just take a look at Finist the bright falcon, and I'll give him to you for nothing!"

The princess agreed, ran into the palace, and said, "Finist, bright falcon! Let me look in your hair for lice."

She sat down to search his head and stuck a pin in his hair. He immediately fell sound asleep. Then she sent her nurses to bring the fair maiden.

She came in, tried to wake her darling, embraced him, kissed him, and she herself cried bitterly-bitterly. No, he wouldn't wake up! She began to search in his hair and happened to pull out the magic pin. Finist the bright falcon, jeweled feathers, woke up right away, saw the fair maiden, and how he rejoiced!

She told him everything that had happened: how her evil sisters had begun to envy her, how she went wandering, and how she had bargained with the princess. He fell in love with her even more than before, kissed her sugared lips, and ordered without delay a gathering of boyars and princes and all kinds of people of rank.

He asked them, "What is your judgment, with which wife should I spend all my days—with that one, who sold me, or with this one, who bought me?"

All the boyars and princes and people of various ranks decided with one voice that he should take the one who had bought him, and that the one who had sold him should be hanged on the gates and shot. And that is what was done by Finist the bright falcon, jeweled feathers![16]

(Afanas'ev, no. 235)

Go I Don't Know Where, Bring I Don't Know What

In a certain state there lived a king who was an unmarried bachelor, and he had a whole company of musketeers. The musketeers would go out hunting, shoot migratory birds, and provide the ruler's table with game. A fine young musketeer by the name of Fedot served in that company. He had a sharp eye for shooting game: it was almost as if he never missed, and for that the king loved him more than all of his comrades.

One time it happened that he went out to hunt early-early in the morning, at the crack of dawn. He walked into a dark thick forest and saw a mourning dove sitting on a tree.[17] Fedot brought up his weapon, aimed, fired, and broke the bird's wing. The bird fell from the branch to the damp earth. The musketeer picked up the bird, was about to tear off its head and put it into his sack.

The mourning dove spoke to him. "Ah, you fine young musketeer, don't tear off my wild head, don't make me part from the white world. Better take me alive, bring me into your home, put me on the windowsill and watch. The moment I start to fall asleep, at that very time swing your right hand and strike me—and you'll win yourself great happiness!"

The musketeer was mightily surprised. "What is this?" he thought. "It looks just like a bird, but it speaks with a human voice! I've never seen anything like this before . . ."

He took the bird home, put it down on the windowsill, and stood there waiting. A little while passed, the mourning dove put its head under its wing and dozed off. The musketeer lifted his right hand, swung it, and hit the bird lightly. The mourning dove fell to the ground and turned into a beautiful girl, such a beautiful one that you couldn't imagine her, or guess, but only tell it in a fairy tale! There was no other beauty in the world to equal her!

She said to the fine young man, the king's musketeer, "You were able to catch me, so now figure out how to live with me. You'll be my betrothed husband, and I your God-given wife!"[18] And they agreed on that. Fedot got married and lived well. He amused himself with his young wife, but he didn't forget his duties. Every morning, before the sun rose, he would take his weapon, go into the forest, shoot all kinds of game, and take it over to the king's kitchen.

His wife saw he was exhausted from hunting, and she said to him, "Listen, my friend, I'm sorry for you. Every livelong day you're put to trouble, you wander through the forest and the swamps, you always come home soaking wet, but we have no gain from it. What kind of a trade is that! I know something here that will not leave you without profit. Get hold of a hundred or two hundred rubles, and we'll arrange the whole business."

Fedot ran to his comrades. He borrowed a ruble from one, two rubles from another, and got together exactly two hundred rubles. He brought them to his wife. "Well," she said, "now buy all kinds of silk with those two hundred rubles." The musketeer bought two hundred rubles' worth of silk. She took it and said, "Don't fret, say a prayer and go to bed. Morning's wiser than the evening!"

The husband fell asleep, and the wife went out onto the porch. She opened her magic book, and all at once two unknown young men[19] appeared before her. Tell them whatever you want! "Take this silk here and in a single hour make me a carpet, and such a wonderful one that its like has never been seen in the whole world. Let the whole kingdom be embroidered on the carpet, with cities, and with villages, and with rivers, and with lakes." They set to work and not only within an hour, but in ten minutes they had finished a carpet to make everyone marvel. They handed it over to the musketeer's wife and disappeared in a wink, as if they had never been there!

In the morning she handed the carpet over to her husband. "Here," she said. "Take this to the bazaar and sell it to the merchants, but listen: don't set your own price, but take what they offer."

Fedot took the carpet, unrolled it, hung it over his arm, and went to the tradesmen's rows. A merchant saw it, came running over, and asked, "Listen, honored sir! Are you selling this?"

"I'm selling it."

"And what does it cost?"

"You're a tradesman, you set the price."

The merchant thought and thought, but he couldn't set a price on the carpet—not at all! Another merchant jumped up, a third one after him, a fourth . . . and a huge crowd of them gathered, looking at the carpet, marveling, but they couldn't set a price on it. Meanwhile, the court commander was riding past the tradesmen's row when he caught sight of the crowd and wondered what the merchants were talking about. He got out of his carriage, walked over, and said, "Hello, merchants and tradesmen, guests from overseas! What are you speaking about?"

"It's like this, we can't set a price on the carpet."

The commander looked at the carpet and he himself began to marvel. "Listen, musketeer," he said. "Tell me the honest truth, where did you get such a marvelous carpet?"

"My wife embroidered it."

"What are you asking for it?"

"I myself don't know the price. My wife ordered me not to haggle, but whatever I'm offered, we'll take it!"

"Well, here are ten thousand for you!"

The musketeer took the money and handed over the carpet. But that commander was always near the king—he drank and ate at his table. So he rode off to the king's to dine and took along the carpet. "Would your majesty care to see what a wonderful carpet I bought today?"

The king took a look: he saw his whole kingdom, as if on the palm of his hand, and he gasped! "Now *that* is a carpet! I've never seen anything so cunning in my life. Well, commander, ask whatever you want, but I won't give the carpet back to you." Here the king took out twenty-five thousand and gave it to him, from hand to hand, but he hung the carpet up in his palace.

"That's all right," thought the commander. "I'll order another one for myself, an even better one."

He rode right to the musketeer's, searched out his house, walked into the main room, and the moment he saw the musketeer's wife, at that moment he forgot both himself and his business. He himself didn't know why he had come. There before him stood such a beauty that he could have stared at her for a hundred years without ever looking away! He looked at the other man's wife, and in his head thought after thought, "Who has ever seen, who has ever heard of a simple soldier having possession of such a treasure? Even though I serve the king himself, and I hold the rank of general, I've still never seen such a beauty!"

The general could barely force himself to come to his senses, and he went back home against his will. From that time, from that hour he was beside himself. Asleep or awake, he could only think of the musketeer's splendid wife. When he ate he could not be sated, and when he drank he could not drink his fill, her image kept appearing to him!

The king noticed this and asked him, "What's happened to you? Is it some kind of grief?"

Vasilisa the Beautiful, Artist: Figurin Alexey, From the village of Palekh. http://tinyurl.com/cpfq54q

"Ah, your highness! I saw the musketeer's wife. There's no other such beauty in the world. I keep thinking about her: I can't be satisfied by food and drink, I can't be delighted by any kind of nourishment!"

The king felt the wish to admire her himself. He ordered his carriage prepared and rode to the musketeer's part of town. He came into the main room and saw an indescribable beauty! No matter who looked at her, an old man or a young man, everyone fell madly in love. He was crushed by the fever in his heart. "What?" he thought to himself. "Why am I walking around an unmarried bachelor? I would like to marry this beauty; why should she be a musketeer's wife? She was destined from birth to be a queen."

The king returned to his palace and said to the commander, "Listen! You knew how to show me the musketeer's wife, an unimaginable beauty. Now figure how to get rid of her husband. I want to marry her myself . . . And if you don't get rid of him, you'll have yourself to blame. Even though you're my faithful servant, you'll swing on the gallows!"

The commander went out, even more sorrowful than before. He couldn't figure out how to get rid of the musketeer.

He walked through empty lots, back alleys, and he met a Baba Yaga. "Stop, servant of the king! I know all your thoughts. Would you like me to help your inescapable grief?"

"Help me, grandmother! I'll pay you whatever you want."

"The king has told you his order, that you should get rid of Fedot the musketeer. That would be no great matter, he's simple himself, but his wife's awfully sly! Still, we'll set such a task that he won't be able to handle it quickly. Go back to the king and tell him this: over thrice-nine lands, in the thrice-tenth land there's an island. On that island walks a stag with golden horns.[20] Let the king gather fifty sailors—the most useless, hopeless drunks—and let him order an old, rotten ship that's been considered retired for thirty years prepared for the quest. Let him send Fedot the musketeer on that ship to get the stag Golden Horns. In order to get to the island, he'll have to sail neither much nor little—three years, and then three years back from the island—six years altogether. When the ship goes to sea, it will serve for a month, and then it will sink. The musketeer, the sailors—they'll all go to the bottom!"

The commander listened to these words, thanked the Baba Yaga for her advice, rewarded her with gold, and ran to the king.

"Your highness," he said, "it's like this, and like that—we can surely get rid of the musketeer."

The king agreed to the plan, and he gave the order to his navy at once: to prepare for the quest an old, rotten ship, load it up with six years' worth of provisions and find a crew of fifty sailors—the most debauched and bitter drunks. The heralds ran through all the taverns and got together such sailors that it was a treat to see: one had two black eyes, one had his nose punched sideways. As soon as they reported to the king that the ship was ready, at that moment he ordered the musketeer to come to him. "Well, Fedot, you're a fine young man, the best musketeer in the company. Do me this favor: sail over thrice-nine lands, and in the thrice-tenth kingdom there's an island. On that island walks the stag Golden Horns. Catch him alive and bring him here."

The musketeer thought about it. He didn't even know what to answer. "Think or don't think," said the king, "but if you don't do this deed, then my sword will take your head off your shoulders!"

Fedot turned around leftward and went out of the palace. That evening he came home sorely sorrowful, he didn't want to say even a word.

His wife asked, "What are you sad about, my dear? Has something bad happened?"

He told her everything in full.

"So you're grieving about that? No wonder! That's a great service, not a small one! Say a prayer and go to sleep. Morning's wiser than the evening: everything will be done."

A lacquer box depicting Baba Yaga's abode, here reduced to its bare essentials. Boxes, plates, jewelry, and various other items featuring fairy tales were created by the four major centers of lacquer miniature production specializing in folklore iconography: Palekh (a center of icon-painting in the sixteenth century and of lacquer box manufacture in the 1920s), Fedoskino (established in 1796), Mstera (founded in 1931), and Kholui (dating from 1934). Artist unknown. http://babayagawassilissa.blogspot.com/2007_09_01_archive.html.

The musketeer lay down and fell asleep, and his wife opened her magic book. Suddenly two unknown young men appeared before her. "What do you need, what do you wish?"

"Go over thrice-nine lands, to the thrice-tenth kingdom—to the island, catch the stag Golden Horns and bring him here."

"We obey! By sunrise it will all be done."

They flew off like a whirlwind to that island, caught the stag Golden Horns, and brought him straight to the musketeer's yard. An hour before dawn they had done the whole deed and vanished, as if they had never been there.

The musketeer's beautiful wife woke her husband extra early and told him, "Go and look, the stag Golden Horns is strolling in your yard. Take him on the ship with you, sail away for five days, and on the sixth day turn back." The musketeer put the stag in a thick, closed cage and put it on the ship. "What's this?" asked the sailors.

"All kinds of provisions and food. The way is long, we're likely to need all kinds of things!"

When the time came for the ship to leave the dock, many people came to see it off. The king himself came, said good-bye to Fedot, and made him the commander of all the sailors. For five days the ship sailed over the sea; they were already far from shore. Fedot the musketeer ordered a forty-bucket cask of wine rolled onto the deck and said to the sailors, "Drink, lads! Don't stint yourselves: the soul's your measure!" And they were glad of this: they rushed over to the cask and started drinking the wine, drinking so much that they toppled over and fell into a sound sleep right there beside the cask. The musketeer took hold of the wheel at the helm, turned the ship, and sailed back. To keep the sailors from noticing this, he kept them full of wine from morning to night. The moment they pried their eyelids open from one spree, a new cask would be ready—good reason to take a hair of the dog that bit them.

On exactly the eleventh day the ship hove to the dock, threw up its flag, and began to fire its cannons. The king heard the firing, got angry, and jumped on Fedot with all possible severity. "How dare you return before the time was up?"

"But where was I supposed to go, your highness? Perhaps some fools would sail around for ten years without doing anything sensible, but instead of ten years we took only ten days to make the voyage and do the deed. Wouldn't you like to have a look at the stag Golden Horns?"

They immediately brought the cage off the ship, let out the golden-horned stag. The king saw that the musketeer was right; you couldn't blame him for anything! He allowed him to go home, but he gave the sailors who had voyaged with him freedom for a whole six years. No one could dare ask them to come and serve, for the very reason that they had already served those years.

The next day the king summoned the commander and went for him with threats. "Why did you allow this?" he said. "Or are you playing a joke on me? Your own head's not dear to you, it seems! Do whatever you can, but find a way to send Fedot the musketeer to an evil death."

"Your royal majesty! Allow me to think. Perhaps this can be remedied."

The commander set off through empty lots and back alleys, and he saw the Baba Yaga coming to meet him. "Stop, servant of the king! I know your thoughts; would you like me to ease your grief?"

"Ease it, grandmother! For the musketeer has returned and brought the stag Golden Horns."

"Oh, I already heard! He himself is a simple man. It wouldn't be hard to get the better of him—just like sniffing a pinch of snuff! But his wife's a real crafty one. Well, we'll set her another task, one she won't be able to handle so quickly. Go to the king and tell him to send the musketeer I don't know where, to bring back I don't know what.[21] He won't be able to complete this task for all of eternity. Either he'll disappear without a trace or he'll come back empty-handed."

The commander rewarded the Baba Yaga with gold and ran to the king. The king heard him out and ordered the musketeer brought to him. "Well, Fedot! You're a fine lad, the first musketeer in the company. You've done me one service—you got the stag Golden Horns. Now do me another service: go I don't know where and bring back I don't know what. But remember, if you don't bring it then my sword will see your head off your shoulders!"

The musketeer turned around leftward and left the palace. He came home sorrowful and pensive. His wife asked him, "Why, my dear, are you grieving? Has there been another misfortune?"

"Eh," he said, "I shook one piece of bad luck off my neck, but another came falling on me. The king is sending me I don't know where, and he orders me to bring back I don't know what. Because of your loveliness I have to bear all kinds of misfortunes!"

"Yes, this service is no small one! In order to get there, you'll have to travel for nine years, and nine years back—altogether eighteen years. And God only knows whether you'll have any use from it!"

"What can I do, how should I act?"

"Say a prayer and go to sleep. Morning's wiser than the evening. Tomorrow you'll find out everything."

The musketeer lay down to sleep, and his wife waited until nightfall, opened her magic book, and at once the two lads appeared before her. "What do you wish, what do you need?"

"Do you happen to know how to go I don't know where, to bring back I don't know what?"

"No, we don't!"

She closed the book, and the lads disappeared before her eyes.

In the morning the musketeer's wife woke her husband. "Go to the king, and ask him for golden treasure for the road. After all, you'll have to wander for eighteen years. When you get the money, come say good-bye to me."

The musketeer visited the king, got a whole sack[22] of gold from the treasury, and came back to say good-bye to his wife. She gave him a piece of cloth and a ball. "When you leave the city, throw this ball ahead of you. Wherever it rolls, you walk that way. And here is some of my handiwork for you. Wherever you may be, whenever you go to wash, always dry your face with this cloth."

The musketeer said good-bye to his wife and to his comrades, bowed in all four directions, and set off to the edge of town. He threw the ball ahead of him. The ball rolled and rolled, and he followed after it.

About a month had passed, the king called the commander and said to him, "The musketeer has set out for eighteen years to drag around the white world, and all the signs are clear that he won't remain alive. After all, eighteen years isn't two weeks. All kinds of things can happen on the road! He's carrying a lot of money. Perhaps robbers will fall upon him, rob him, and subject him to an evil death. It seems that now I can get started on his wife. You take my carriage, drive to the musketeers' part of town, and bring her here to the palace."

The commander drove to the musketeers' part of town, came to the house of the musketeer's beautiful wife, walked into the house, and said, "Hello, clever woman. The king has ordered you to present yourself at the palace."

She came to the palace. The king welcomed her with joy, led her into gilded chambers, and said these words to her: "Would you like to be the queen? I'll marry you."

"Where is it seen, where is it heard of, to try to take the wife away from a living husband! No matter who he is, even just a simple musketeer, but to me he's my lawful husband."

"If you won't come of your own free will, I'll take you by force!"

The beauty smiled, struck the floor, turned into a mourning dove, and flew out the window.

The musketeer passed through many lands and kingdoms, but the ball kept on rolling. When they met a river, there the ball would cast itself across as a bridge. When the musketeer wanted to rest, there the ball would turn into a feather bed. For a long time, for a short time—quickly may a tale be spun, but not so soon a deed is done—the musketeer came to a great, beautiful palace. The ball rolled up to the gates and disappeared.

So the musketeer stood and thought, "Let me go straight ahead!" He went up the stair into the rooms, and there he met three maidens of indescribable beauty. "Where are you come from, young man, and why have you come to visit?"

"Ah, fair maidens, you didn't let me rest after the long journey, but you started to ask questions. If you gave me food and drink first, laid me down to rest, then you could ask me for news." They immediately set the table, sat him down, fed him and gave him drink, and put him to bed.

The musketeer slept his fill and rose from the soft bed. The fair maidens brought him water and an embroidered towel. He washed up with spring water, but he didn't take the towel. "I have my own cloth," he said, "I have something to wipe my face."

Baba Yaga by Waldemar von Kazak. Reminiscent of Snoopy's fantasized Red Baron, this military Baba Yaga, accompanied by her armed feline helper, could have starred in Stanley Kubrick's *Apocalypse Now*. Executed by Waldemar von Kazak from Tver', this is a fantastically modern and westernized Baba Yaga. Info@kazakdesign.com, kazakdesign.com.

He took out the cloth and began to wipe his face. The fair maidens asked him, "Good man! Tell us: where did you get that cloth?"

"My wife gave it to me."

"Then you must be married to our own dear sister!"

They called their old mother. As soon as she took one look at the cloth, she said right away, "That's my daughter's handiwork!" She began to ask their guest about everything. He told her how he had married her daughter and how the tsar[23] had sent him I don't know where, to bring I don't know what. "Ah, my dear son-in-law! But even I haven't heard of that wonder! Wait here, perhaps my servants know."

The old woman went out onto the porch, called in a loud voice, and suddenly—where did they come from?—all kinds of beasts ran up, and all kinds of birds came flying. "Greetings, forest beasts and birds of the air! You beasts search everywhere, you birds fly everywhere: have you heard how to get I don't know where and to bring back I don't know what?"

All the beasts and birds answered in one voice, "No, we've never heard of that!"

The old woman sent them back to their own places, in overgrown places, in forests, in groves. She returned to the main room, got out her magic book, opened it—and right away two giants appeared to her. "What do you wish, what do you need?"

"Here's what, my faithful servants! Take me along with my son-in-law to the wide ocean-sea and stand exactly in the middle—on the very surface of the waves."

They immediately picked up the musketeer and the old woman, carried them off as if they were restless whirlwinds to the wide ocean-sea, and stopped in the middle—on the very surface of the waves. They themselves stood like pillars, and they held the musketeer and the old woman in their arms.

The old woman called with a loud voice, and all the monsters and fish of the sea swam to her: they were just teeming! Their bodies hid the blue sea! "Hail, monsters and fish of the sea! You swim everywhere, you visit all the islands. Have you heard how to go to I don't know where, and to bring back I don't know what?"

All the monsters and fish answered in one voice, "No! We've never heard of that!"

Suddenly an old lame frog, who had been living in retirement for thirty years already, pushed her way forward, and she said, "Kva-kva! I know where to find such a marvel."

"Well, my dear, you are the one I need," said the old woman. She picked up the frog and ordered the giants to take her and her son-in-law back home.

In a moment they found themselves back in the palace. The old woman started to ask the frog questions. "How and by what road must my son-in-law go?"

The frog answered, "This place is on the edge of the world—far, far away! I would come along myself, but I'm already mighty old. I can barely move my legs, I couldn't hop there if I had fifty years." The old woman brought a large jar, filled it with fresh milk, put the frog in it, and gave it to her son-in- law. "Carry this jar," she said, "and let the frog show you the way."

The musketeer took the jar with the frog, said good-bye to the old woman and her daughters, and set off on his way. He walked along, and the frog told him which way to go.

Close or far, long or short, he came to a fiery river. Beyond that river stood a high mountain, and you could see a door to the inside of the mountain. "Kva-kva!" said the frog. "Let me out of the jar; we have to cross the river." The musketeer took her out of the jar and put her on the ground. "Well, fine young lad! Sit down on me, and don't feel pity. You won't be able to squash me!"

The musketeer sat down on the frog and squashed her into the earth. The frog started to puff up. She puffed and puffed until she was as big as a haystack. All the musketeer could think of was how to keep from falling off. "If I fall, I'll be smashed to death!"

The frog puffed up and made such a jump that she jumped all the way across the fiery river, and then she turned small again. "Now, good lad, go in that door, and I'll wait for you here. You'll go into a cave, and hide yourself well in there. After a while two old men will come in. Listen to what they say and do, and after they leave you do the same thing!"

The musketeer went up to the mountain, opened the door—and the cave was awfully dark, as if you'd poked your eyes out! He walked crouching over and started feeling with his hands. He felt an empty space, sat down in it, and hid himself. Then a little bit later two old men came and said, "Hey, Shmat-Razum![24] Give us something to eat."

That very moment—out of nowhere!—the chandeliers began to burn, plates and dishes rattled, and all kinds of wine and food appeared on the table. The old men ate and drank their fill and then ordered, "Hey, Shmat-Razum! Clear everything away." Suddenly everything disappeared—the table, the wines, the food—and the chandeliers went out.

The musketeer heard the two old men leave, got out of the cupboard, and shouted, "Hey, Shmat-Razum!"

"What do you wish?"

"Feed me!" Again the lit chandeliers appeared, and the laden table, and all kinds of drinks and foods.

The musketeer sat down at the table and said, "Hey, Shmat-Razum! Sit down with me, brother, let's eat and drink together, it's boring by myself."

An unseen voice answered, "Ah, good man! Where did God bring you from? I've been serving the two old men in faith and truth for nearly thirty years, and in all that time they've never asked me to sit with them."

The musketeer took a look and was surprised. He couldn't see anyone, but it was as if someone was sweeping food from the plates with a little broom, and the bottles of wine lifted themselves, poured themselves into the goblets, and look—they were already empty! The musketeer ate and drank

Baba-Yaga by Artus Scheiner for the Prague Otta Detergent Co. (circa 1900). Reproduced courtesy of the Cotsen Children's Library, Princeton University Library.

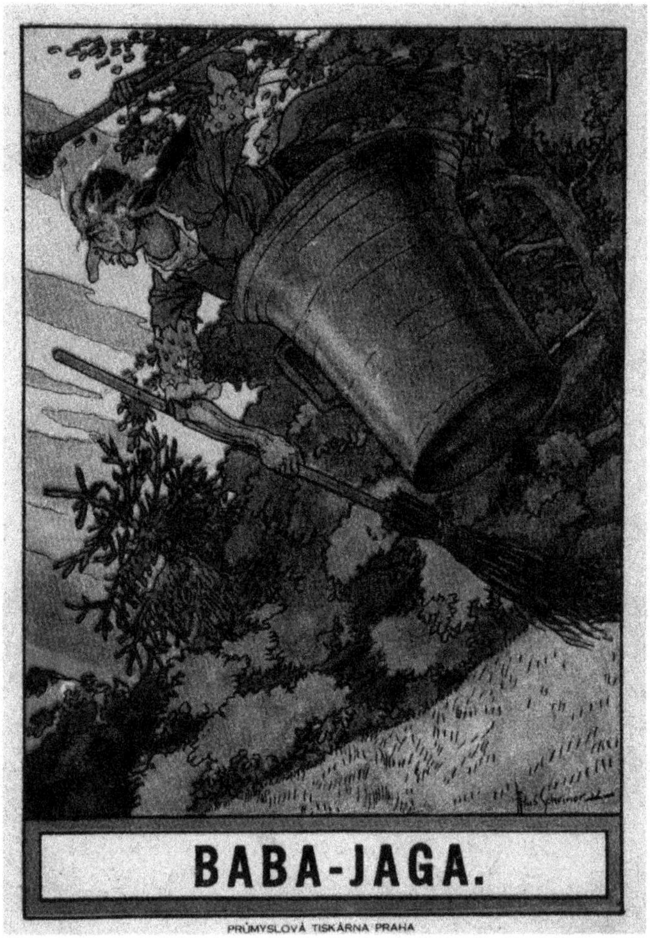

his fill and said, "Listen, Shmat-Razum! Would you like to serve me? I have a good life."

"Why wouldn't I want to! I've been bored here for a long time, and I can see that you're a good man."

"Well, gather up everything and come along with me!"

The musketeer came out of the cave, looked behind and there was nothing . . . "Shmat-Razum! Are you here?"

"Here! Don't fear, I won't fall behind you."

"All right!" said the musketeer and sat down on the frog. The frog puffed herself up and jumped across the fiery river. He put her back into the jar and set off on his journey back.[25]

He came back to his mother-in-law and made his new servant give a good treat to the old woman and her daughters. Shmat-Razum showed them such a time that the old woman almost started to dance with joy, and the frog, as a reward for her faithful service, was to be given three jars of milk every day.

The musketeer said good-bye to his mother-in-law and set off for home. He walked and walked and got very tired; his swift feet were weary, and his white arms drooped. "Eh," he said. "Shmat-Razum! If you knew how tired I am. My legs are just paralyzed."

"Why didn't you say so a long time ago? I'd have gotten you there in no time."

He immediately picked the musketeer up like a restless whirlwind and carried him through the air so fast that his hat fell off. "You reached for it too late, my lord! Now your hat's five thousand *vyorsts* behind us." Cities and villages, rivers and forests flickered before his eyes . . .

The musketeer was flying over a deep sea, and Shmat-Razum said to him, "Would you like me to build a golden pavilion on this sea? You could rest and have some good luck."

"All right, do it!" said the musketeer, and he began to sink toward the sea. Where the waves had been rising a minute before, a little island appeared, and a golden pavilion appeared on the island. Shmat-Razum said to the musketeer, "Sit down in the pavilion, rest, and watch the sea. Three merchant ships will sail by and come to anchor by the island. You invite the merchants in, treat them as guests, and trade me for the three wonders the merchants are carrying with them. I'll return to you in my own good time!"

The musketeer watched, and he saw three ships sailing from the west. The sailors saw the island and the golden pavilion. "What a wonder!" they said. "How many times have we sailed here, and there was nothing but water, but now just look here! A golden pavilion has appeared. Let's anchor by the shore, brothers, take a look and admire." At once they stopped the course of the ships and threw down their anchors. The three merchant masters got into a light boat and sailed to the island. "Hello, good man!"

"Hello, merchants from foreign lands! Welcome; please take a walk, enjoy yourselves, catch your breath. The pavilion is built expressly for passing guests."

The merchants came into the pavilion and sat down on a bench. "Hey, Shmat-Razum!" cried the musketeer, "give us something to eat and drink." A table appeared, on the table wines and dishes, as much as the soul could desire—all ready in a moment!

The merchants simply gasped. "Let's trade!" they said. "You give us your servant, and for that take any wonder that we have."

"But what kinds of wonders do you have?"

Illustration by Artus Scheiner for the Prague Otta Detergent Co. (circa 1900). Reproduced courtesy of the Cotsen Children's Library, Princeton University Library.

"Take a look, you'll see!"

One of the merchants pulled a tiny box out of his pocket, and the moment he opened it a wonderful garden immediately grew up, with flowers and with paths, but when he closed the little box the garden disappeared.

The second merchant pulled an axe from under the hem of his coat and began to chop. Chop and chop—he'd made a boat! Chop and chop—another boat! He chopped a hundred times and made a hundred boats, with sails, with cannon, and with sailors. The boats sailed around: they shot their cannons, and they asked the merchant for his orders . . . When he'd had enough of the amusement, he hid his axe—and the ships disappeared, as if they'd never been there!

The third merchant took a horn, blew into one end, and all at once an army appeared, infantry and cavalry, with rifles, with cannon, with banners. All the regiments sent couriers to the merchant, and he gave them orders. The regiments marched, music thundered, the banners unfurled . . . When the merchant had had enough fun, he took his trumpet, blew into the other end—and there was nothing; where had all the forces gone to?[26]

"Your wonders are just fine, but I don't need them!" said the musketeer. "Armies and ships are tsars' business, and I'm a simple soldier. If you want to trade with me, then give me all three wonders for my one invisible servant."

"Won't that be too much?"

"Well, as you prefer; otherwise, I won't trade!"

The merchants thought to themselves, "What good is that garden to us, these regiments and warships? Better to trade; at least we'll be fed and drunk without any effort at all." They gave the musketeer their wonders and said, "Hey, Shmat-Razum! We're taking you with us; will you serve us with faith and truth?"

"Why shouldn't I serve you? It's all the same to me who I live with."

The merchants returned to their ships and started to treat all the mariners to food and drink. "Well then, Shmat-Razum, stir your stumps!"

They all drank until they were drunk and fell fast asleep. But the musketeer sat in his golden pavilion, started thinking, and said, "Ah, it's too bad! Where's my faithful servant Shmat-Razum now?"

"I'm here, sir!"

The musketeer was delighted. "Isn't it time for us to get home?"

No sooner had he said it than he was picked up by a restless whirlwind and carried through the air.

The merchants woke up, and they wanted to drink some more. "Hey, Shmat-Razum, give us something for our hangovers!" No one answered: no one was serving them. No matter how much they shouted, no matter how they gave orders, it was no use. "Well, gentlemen! That swindler[27] cheated us. Now only the devil will find him! The island's disappeared, and the golden pavilion, too." The merchants grieved and grieved for a while, lifted their sails, and set off for where they were supposed to be going.

The musketeer quickly flew to his own land and came down beside the blue sea in a deserted place. "Hey, Shmat-Razum! Couldn't we build a palace here?"

"Why not? It will be ready right away."

In a wink there was such a delightful palace that it can't even be described, twice as good as the king's. The musketeer opened the little box, and around the palace a garden appeared with rare trees and flowers. The musketeer sat there at the open window and admired his garden. Suddenly a mourning dove flew in at the window, struck the floor, and turned into his young wife. They embraced, said their greetings, and began to ask each other questions, tell each other everything. The wife said to the musketeer, "Since the very moment when you left home, all that time I've been flying through the forests and groves as a lonely mourning dove."

The next morning the king came out on his balcony, looked toward the blue sea, and saw that a new palace was standing on the very shore of the sea, and around the palace a green garden. "What ignoramus got the idea of building on my land without permission?"

The couriers went running, found out everything, and reported that the palace had been built by the musketeer, and that he himself was living in it with his wife at his side. The king became even more enraged and ordered an army collected and sent to the shore, to raze the garden to its foundations, to break the palace up into little pieces, and to put the musketeer himself and his wife to a cruel death. The musketeer observed that the king's strong army was marching on him, and he quickly grabbed the axe. Chop and chop—out came a ship! He chopped a hundred times and made a hundred ships. Then he took out the horn, blew into it once—the infantry tumbled out of it; he blew twice and out tumbled the cavalry.

The commanders of the regiments came running to him, and the ships were waiting for his orders. The musketeer ordered them to enter the battle. At once music began to play, they beat the drums, and the regiments moved. The infantry smashed the king's soldiers; the cavalry chased them the rest of the way, took them captive, and the cannons from the ships rained fire on the capital city. The king saw that his army was running away; he wanted to rush and stop the army—but how could he? Before even a half-hour had passed, he himself was killed.

When the battle ended, the people gathered and asked the musketeer to take the whole kingdom into his hands. He agreed to that and became the king, and his wife became the queen.

(Afanas'ev, no. 212)

Ivanushka

There was a lady, and she had a son, Ivanushka. He got into a little boat and went sailing. He sailed and sailed. The lady came to the shore. "Ivanushka! Sail over to me, I've brought you something to eat and drink!" He sailed over. She gave him something to eat and drink, and she sent him off to sail some more.

Baba Yaga came. "Ivanushka! Sail over to me, I've brought you something to eat and drink!"

Ivanushka heard that it wasn't his mother's voice, and he didn't sail over to her. Then the Baba Yaga ran to the smithy. "Blacksmith, blacksmith! Forge me a voice like Ivanushka's mother's!" So he forged her a voice, and she ran down to the bank. "Ivanushka! Sail over to me, I've brought you something to eat and drink!" He heard his mother's voice and sailed over. Baba Yaga grabbed him and dragged him off.

The lady realized that Ivanushka was missing. She sent her maid to look for him. The maid walked and walked. She came to a palace, and there she saw a girl sitting on the meadow, spinning and playing with a little boy. The child had a golden saucer, and on that saucer was a golden egg. "Fair maiden! Do you happen to know where I could find my child? My lady will drive me away if I don't find him!"

She said, "You sit down, spin some of my flax for me, and I'll go and bring you a ball of thread. Wherever that ball of thread rolls, follow it."

She said to her, this girl, "Eh, how can I spare the time to work, my dear? I have to go, I have to find the child. You tell me, my dear, where can I find him?"

"Well," she said, "off you go. I don't know where your child is."

So she walked and walked and came to another palace, where she saw a girl sitting. She was winding the spun thread, playing with a little boy, and the child had a golden apple with a golden egg. "Fair maiden, do you happen to know where I can find my child?"

Baba Yaga dines, with iron teeth by Forest Rogers. Contemporary artist Forest Rogers's *Baba Yaga at Dinner,* inspired by Vasilisa the Beautiful. The visual captures Baba Yaga's gluttonous consumption of gigantic meals typically prepared by a young female visitor forced to stay in the chicken-legged hut as her servant. Such girls may court the risk of becoming the cannibalistic witch's feast, as foreshadowed here by the foreplay of Baba Yaga's grasp on her victim's braid. Yet that threat is never explicitly realized in the tales. Illustration by Forest Rogers, http://www.forestrogers.com/.

"You sit down," she said, "wind my thread, and I'll go and bring you a ball of thread. Wherever the ball rolls, you must follow after it."

The maiden said to her, "Eh, my dear, do I have the time to work? I have to go and look for the child. You tell me, my dear, where I'm to find him!"

"Well," she answered, "off you go. I don't know where your child is."

She went along farther, and she came into the forest. A little house stood there on chicken legs, on shuttle heels. She said to this house, "Little house, little house! Stand with your back to the woods, with your front to me!" The house turned around. She stepped up into it and said a prayer to God.

Baba Yaga turned over onto her other side. "Fie, fie, fie! It smells of a Russian smell!" she said. "Before there was neither sight nor smell of the Russian spirit, but now the Russian spirit rolls around before my eyes! What are you doing, fair maiden, flying from a deed or trying a deed?"

"No, granny," she said, "I was walking and walking, I dropped in here to warm up."

"Well, then, sit by my head and search my head for gunpowder."

The girl got some pitch in a little pottery shard, put it into the stove, got some pieces of cotton ready, and sat down to search Baba Yaga's head. She searched and kept repeating, "Fall asleep, little eye, fall asleep, second eye! If you don't sleep, I'll pour pitch into you, I'll stop you up with cotton!" She kept repeating it until Baba Yaga fell asleep. When she fell asleep, the girl poured pitch into her eyes and stopped them up with cotton balls. She took the child and ran off with him.

She ran up to the first girl and said, "Fair maiden, hide me, or else Baba Yaga will eat me!"

"No," she said. "You didn't want to wind my thread!"

She ran on further. But meanwhile the cat began to purr, and Baba Yaga woke up and realized the child was gone. She chased after her, ran up to the palace, and asked the maiden, "Tell me, did a fair maiden run past here with a little boy?"

"She left just this minute!"

Baba Yaga ran and chased down the girl. She took the little boy away from her and tore her up into pieces.

The lady waited a long time, but no one came home. She had to send out another girl. The same thing happened to the second girl. Baba Yaga tore that one to pieces, too.

Finally, the lady sent a third girl. She came to the palace, saw the girl and the little boy, and asked, "Fair maiden, do you happen to know where I can find my child?"

"Here," she says, "you spin this and watch the child, and I'll bring you a ball of thread. You must give it to my sister!"

The girl sat down to spin, and the other girl went to get the ball of thread and gave it to her. "Well," she said, "off you go!"

The girl came to the next palace. All she saw was the little boy again with the girl. "Here, fair maiden," she said. "Your sister sends her greetings and a ball of thread. But I'm looking for my child. Do you happen to know where I can find him?"

"I know, my girl! Now sit down, spin a bit for me, and I'll go get you a lump of butter."

She sat down to spin, while the maiden brought a lump of butter and gave it to her.

"Now go into the forest," said the maiden. "There's a little house standing in the forest, and your child is there."

The girl set off and went into the forest. There stood a little house on chicken legs, spinning around on shuttle heels.

She said, "Little house, little house! Turn your back to the forest, your front to me."

When the little house turned toward her, she stepped up into it, said a prayer to God, and saw the child.

Baba Yaga caught the smell of Russian breath and turned around. "Fie, fie, fie! Before there was neither smell nor sight of the Russian spirit, but now the Russian spirit appears before my eyes! What is it, fair maiden, are you doing a deed or fleeing a deed?"

"No, granny, I was walking and walking, and I came in here to warm up!"

"Well," she said, "sit down and look for things on my head."

This girl put a pottery shard with pitch into the stove, got some balls of cotton ready, and sat down to search Baba Yaga's head. She searched and kept repeating, "Fall asleep, one eye, fall asleep, second eye! If you don't sleep, I'll pour in pitch, I'll stop you up with cotton."

When Baba Yaga fell asleep, the girl poured pitch over her eyes and stopped them up with cotton. She gave the cat the piece of butter, grabbed the child, and ran off.

She ran to the palace and said, "Fair maiden, hide me, or else Baba Yaga will eat me up."

"Sit down, fair maiden, I'll hide you. After all, you yourself did some work for me."

No sooner had she hidden the girl in the basement, Baba Yaga flew up to her. "Fair maiden, did you happen to see—did a girl run by here with a little boy?

"No, Baba Yaga, I didn't see anyone."

Baba Yaga ran home and scratched the cat for not guarding the child.

While she was scratching him, that girl with the child ran on to the other palace. "Fair maiden, hide me."

"Sit down, fair maiden," she answered. "After all, you yourself did some work for me." She hid her in a trunk.

No sooner had she hidden the girl in the trunk than Baba Yaga flew up to her. "Fair maiden, did you happen to see—did a girl run by here with a little boy?"

"No, Baba Yaga, I didn't see anyone."

Baba Yaga flew off home again and started to pinch that cat for not guarding the child. She pinched him so hard that she pinched him to death. Meanwhile, the girl ran up to the house with the child.

The lady was so happy, she rewarded the girl for rescuing her child, and she herself went on living with the child, earning riches, and making it through the bad times.

(Khudiakov, no. 52)

Mar'ia Morevna

In a certain kingdom, in a certain state lived Prince Ivan. He had three sisters: one was Princess Mar'ia, the second was Princess Olga,[28] and the third was Princess Anna. Their father and mother had died, and as they were dying they ordered their son, "Marry each of your sisters to the first man who comes to court her. Don't keep them here for long!"

The prince buried his parents, and from grief he went out to stroll with his sisters in the green garden. Suddenly a black cloud came over them, and a horrible thunderstorm arose. "Let's go home, sisters!" said Prince Ivan.

The moment they went into the palace, it was as if thunder struck: the ceiling opened, and a bright falcon flew into their room. The falcon struck against the floor, turned into a handsome young man, and said, "Hello, Prince Ivan! I used to live here as a guest but now I've come as a suitor; I want to court your sister Princess Mar'ia."

"If you please my sister, I won't interfere with her. May God protect her!"

Princess Mar'ia agreed. The falcon married her and took her away to his kingdom.

One day passed after another, hours ran after hours, and a whole year passed as quickly as if it had never been. Prince Ivan went out to stroll in the green garden with his two sisters. Again a storm cloud arose with a whirlwind, with lightning. "Let's go home, sisters!"

The moment they came into the palace, it was as if thunder struck: the roof fell open, the ceiling split in two, and an eagle flew in. The eagle struck the floor and turned into a handsome young man. "Hello, Prince Ivan! Before I lived here as a guest, but now I've come as a suitor." And he asked to marry Princess Olga.

Prince Ivan answered, "If you please Princess Olga, then let her marry you. I won't interfere with her freedom." Princess Olga agreed and married the eagle. The eagle snatched her up and took her away to his kingdom.

Another year passed. Prince Ivan said to his youngest sister, "Let's go and stroll in the green garden!" They strolled a bit, and once again a storm arose with a whirlwind, with lightning. "Let's go back home, sister!"

They went back home, and they hadn't yet had a chance to sit down when thunder boomed, the ceiling split in two, and a raven flew in. The raven struck the floor and turned into a handsome young man. The first two were handsome, but this one was even more handsome. "Well, Prince Ivan! Before I came as a guest, but now I've come as a suitor. Let me marry Princess Anna."

"I won't limit my sister's freedom. If you please her, she may marry you."

Princess Anna married the raven, and he took her away to his kingdom.

Prince Ivan was left alone. For a whole year he lived without his sisters, and he started to feel bored. "I'll go find my sisters," he said. He got ready to travel, walked and walked, and saw a great army lying dead in the field. Prince Ivan asked, "If there's anyone here alive, answer me! Who destroyed this great army?"

A man who was still alive called back to him, "This whole army was killed by Mar'ia Morevna, the beautiful princess."

Prince Ivan went on farther. He saw some white tents, and the beautiful princess Mar'ia Morevna came out to meet him. "Welcome, Prince! Where is God taking you—by your will or by compulsion?"

Prince Ivan answered her, "Fine young men don't travel under compulsion!"

"Well, if there's no hurry, come and be a guest in my tents."

Prince Ivan was glad to do so. He spent two nights in the tents, won Mar'ia Morevna's love, and married her.

Mar'ia Morevna, the beautiful princess, took him with her to her realm. They lived together for a certain time, and then the princess decided to go to war. She left all the household affairs to Prince Ivan and told him, "You may go everywhere and keep an eye on everything, but don't let yourself look into that shed!"

He couldn't stand it, and the moment Mar'ia Morevna rode away he dashed straight to the shed, opened the door, and took a look. Koshchei the Deathless was hanging there, shackled with twelve chains. Koshchei begged Prince Ivan, "Take pity on me, give me a drink of water! I've been suffering here for ten years, I haven't had anything to eat or drink. My throat's all dried up!"

The prince gave him a whole bucket of water. Koshchei drank it up and asked for more.

"I can't quench my thirst with one bucket. Give me more!"

The prince gave him a second bucket.

Koshchei drank it up and asked for a third. As soon as he drank up the third bucket he regained his former strength, shook the chains, and broke all twelve at once.[29]

"Thank you, Prince Ivan!" said Koshchei the Deathless. "Now you'll never see Mar'ia Morevna again, no more than your own ears!" He flew out the window in a terrible whirlwind, caught up with Mar'ia Morevna on the road, snatched her up, and took her away to his palace.

But Prince Ivan cried very bitterly, armed himself, and set off on his way. "No matter what, I'll find Mar'ia Morevna!"

He walked for a day, he walked for another, and at dawn on the third day he saw a marvelous palace. An oak tree stood by the palace, and on the oak tree sat a bright falcon. The falcon flew down from the oak tree, struck the ground, turned into a handsome young man, and cried, "Ah, my gracious brother-in-law! How is the Lord favoring you?"

Princess Mar'ia ran out, greeted Prince Ivan joyfully, and began to ask about his health, to tell him about her daily life and being. The prince was their guest for three days, and then he said, "I can't stay with you long. I'm going to search for my wife, Mar'ia Morevna, the beautiful princess."

"It won't be easy for you to find her," answered the falcon. "Leave your silver spoon here just in case. We'll look at it and think of you." Prince Ivan left his silver spoon with the falcon and set off on his way.

He walked a day, he walked a second day, and at dawn on the third day he saw a palace even better than the first one. An oak tree stood beside the palace, and on the oak tree sat an eagle. The eagle flew down from the tree, struck the ground, turned into a handsome young man, and cried, "Get up, Princess Olga! Here comes our dear brother."

Princess Olga ran out at once to greet him. She began to kiss and hug him, ask after his health, and tell him about her own life. Prince Ivan spent three days as their guest, and then he said, "I can't stay any longer. I'm going to search for my wife, Mar'ia Morevna, the beautiful princess."

The eagle answered, "It won't be easy for you to find her. Leave us your silver fork, we'll look at it and think of you." He left the silver fork and set out on his way.

He walked a day, he walked for two, and at dawn on the third day he saw a palace even better than the first two. An oak tree stood beside the palace, and on the oak tree sat a raven. The raven flew down from the oak tree,

Baba Yaga by Viktor Korolkov from the *Entsiklopediia slavianskoi mifologii* by Bychkov, Aleksei Aleksandrovich. Moscow: AST, 2008, 2010. Ed. Elena Grushko and Iurii Medvedev.

struck the ground, turned into a handsome young man, and cried, "Princess Anna! Come out right now, here's our brother."

Princess Anna ran out. She greeted him joyfully, began to kiss and hug him, ask after his health, tell him about her own life. Prince Ivan spent three days as their guest, and then he said, "Farewell! I'm off to search for my wife—Mar'ia Morevna, the beautiful princess."

The raven answered, "It won't be easy for you to find her. Why don't you leave your silver snuffbox with us? We'll look at it and think of you."

The prince handed over his silver snuffbox, said good-bye, and set off on his way.[30]

He walked for one day, he walked for a second, and on the third day he reached Mar'ia Morevna. She saw her dear one, she threw herself onto his neck, dissolved in tears, and said, "Ah, Prince Ivan! Why didn't you listen to me? You looked in the shed and set Koshchei the Deathless free!"

"Forgive me, Mar'ia Morevna! Let's not mention things in the past. Better come along with me while Koshchei the Deathless is not in sight. Perhaps he won't be able to catch up to us!"

They got their things together and left. Koshchei was out hunting, but toward evening, as he was coming home, his good horse stumbled underneath him. "You insatiable nag, what are you tripping for? Or do you sense some misfortune?"

The horse answered, "Prince Ivan was here, he's taken Mar'ia Morevna away."

"But can we catch them?"

"We could sow wheat, wait for it to grow, reap it, thresh it, make it into flour, prepare five ovens full of bread,[31] eat that bread, and then start in pursuit—and even then we'd catch them!"

Koshchei galloped off and caught up with Prince Ivan. "Well," he said, "this first time I forgive you thanks to your kindness, because you gave me water to drink. I'll pardon you a second time, too, but the third time beware—I'll cut you up into pieces!" He took Mar'ia Morevna away from Ivan and rode away with her, but Prince Ivan sat down on a rock and started crying.

He cried and cried, and then he went back again to get Mar'ia Morevna. Koshchei the Deathless happened to be out of the house. "Let's ride away, Mar'ia Morevna!"

"Ah, Prince Ivan! He'll catch us!"

"Let him catch us. At least we'll spend an hour or two together." They got their things together and rode away.

Koshchei the Deathless was returning home, and his good horse stumbled underneath him. "What are you tripping for, you insatiable nag? Or do you sense some misfortune?"

"Prince Ivan was here, he's taken Mar'ia Morevna away with him."

"And can we catch up to them?"

"We could sow barley, wait for it to grow, reap and thresh it, brew beer, drink ourselves drunk, sleep it off, and then set off in pursuit—but we'd still make it!"

Koshchei galloped off and caught up with Prince Ivan. "I told you you'd never see Mar'ia Morevna, no more than your own ears!" He took her and rode back to his palace with her.

Prince Ivan was left alone. He cried and cried, and then he went back again for Mar'ia Morevna. At that time Koshchei the Deathless was not at home. "Let's go, Mar'ia Morevna!"

"Ah, Ivan Tsarevich! But he'll catch us, he'll cut you up into pieces."

"Let him cut me up! I can't live without you." They got their things together and set off.

As Koshchei the Deathless was returning home, the good horse stumbled underneath him. "What are you tripping for? Or do you sense some misfortune?"

"Ivan Tsarevich was here, he took Mar'ia Morevna with him."

Koshchei galloped off, caught up with Prince Ivan, cut him up into little pieces, and put the pieces in a barrel sealed with pitch. He took that barrel, reinforced it with iron hoops, and threw it into the blue sea. Then he took Mar'ia Morevna back home with him.

Just then the silver Prince Ivan had left with his brothers-in-law turned black. "Oh no," they said, "it seems something bad has happened!" The eagle rushed to the blue sea, grabbed the barrel, and dragged it out onto the shore; the falcon flew to get living water, and the raven flew for dead water. All three of them flew back to the same place, broke open the barrel, took out the pieces of Prince Ivan, washed them and put them in order, the way they're meant to be. The raven sprinkled him with dead water, and his body grew back together. The falcon sprinkled him with living water.

Prince Ivan jumped, stood up, and said, "Ah, I was asleep for such a long time!"

"You'd have slept even longer, if not for us!" his brothers-in-law answered. "Now come, stay with us as a guest."

"No, brothers! I'm off to search for Mar'ia Morevna."

He came to her and asked her, "Find out from Koshchei the Deathless where he got hold of such a good horse."

So Mar'ia Morevna chose a good moment and started to ask Koshchei questions. Koshchei said, "Over thrice-nine lands, in the thrice-tenth kingdom, past a fiery river lives Baba Yaga. She has a special mare; every day she flies around the world on her. She has many other wonderful mares. I spent three days as her herdsman, I didn't let a single mare out of my sight! And for that Baba Yaga gave me one little foal."

"How did you make it across the fiery river?"

"I have a special handkerchief. When I wave it to the right three times, it makes a high-high bridge, and the fire can't reach it!"

Mar'ia Morevna listened to this, told it all to Prince Ivan, took away the handkerchief, and gave it to him.[32]

Prince Ivan made his way across the fiery river and went to see Baba Yaga. He walked for a long time without drinking or eating. He came across an overseas bird with its little young. Prince Ivan said, "I'll eat one of your chicks."

"Don't eat it, Prince Ivan!" begged the overseas bird. "There'll be a time when I'll come in handy to you."

He went along farther, and he saw a beehive in the forest. "I'll take a bit of honey," he said.

The queen bee called out, "Don't touch my honey, Prince Ivan! There'll be a time when I'll come in handy to you."

He didn't touch it and went on. He came across a lioness with her cub. "I'll at least eat this lion cub. I'm so hungry I feel sick!"

"Don't touch it, Prince Ivan!" begged the lioness. "There'll be a time when I'll come in handy for you."

"Very well, I'll do what you say!"[33]

He wandered along hungry, walked and walked—and there stood the house of Baba Yaga. Twelve poles stood around the house. Eleven of the poles had human heads on top; only one of them was empty.

"Hello, granny!"

"Hello, Prince Ivan! How have you come—by your own good will, or in need?"

"I've come to serve you for a *bogatyr* horse."

"Go right ahead, Prince! You don't have to serve me for a year, but only for three days. If you manage to herd my mares, I'll give you a *bogatyr* horse, but if not, don't be wrathful—your head will be stuck on the last pole."

Prince Ivan agreed. Baba Yaga fed him, gave him something to drink, and ordered him to get to work.

No sooner had he driven the mares out to the field than the mares all lifted their tails and all ran off to different meadows. Before the prince even had time to take a look, they had all disappeared. Then he started to cry and grieve, sat down on a stone, and fell asleep. The sun was already setting when the overseas bird came flying to him and said, "Wake up, Prince Ivan! The mares are home now."

The prince got up and went back, but Baba Yaga was making a fuss and shouting at her mares. "Why did you come home?"

"How could we stay away? Birds came flying from all over the world, they almost pecked our eyes out."

"Well, tomorrow don't run over the meadows, but scatter in the deep forest."

Prince Ivan slept all night. In the morning Baba Yaga said to him, "Watch out, prince! If you don't herd the mares, if you lose even one of them, then your wild head will be on a pole!"

He drove the mares out into the field. They immediately lifted their tails and ran off into the deep forest. The prince sat down on a stone again, cried and cried, and fell asleep. When the sun was sinking behind the forest, the lioness came running up to him. "Get up, Prince Ivan! The mares are all together."

Prince Ivan stood up and went home. Baba Yaga was making even more noise than the first time and shouting at her mares, "Why did you come back home?"

"How could we stay away? Wild beasts came running from all over the world, they almost tore us to pieces."

"Well, then, tomorrow you run into the blue sea."

Prince Ivan slept through the night again. In the morning Baba Yaga sent him to herd the mares. "If you don't herd them, then your wild head will be on a pole."

He drove the mares out into the field. They immediately lifted their tails, disappeared, and ran into the blue sea. They stood there with water up to their necks. Prince Ivan sat down on a stone, started to cry, and fell asleep. When the sun was setting behind the forest, a little bee came flying and said, "Get up, prince! The mares are all together. When you go back, don't let Baba Yaga see you, but go into the stable and hide behind the crib. There's a mangy foal there, rolling in the muck. You steal him and leave the house at the stroke of midnight."

A lacquer box by the young Fedoskino miniaturist Vladislav Maslov captures Baba Yaga in her signature mode of transportation. Artist: Vladislav Maslov, from the village of Fedoskino, http://tinyurl.com/c8vayzy.

Prince Ivan got up, sneaked into the stable, and lay down behind the crib.

Baba Yaga made a lot of noise and shouted at her mares, "What did you come back for?"

"How could we help coming back? Bees came flying visibly and invisibly from all over the world, and they started to sting us from all sides until we were bleeding!"[34]

Baba Yaga fell asleep, and at the stroke of midnight Prince Ivan stole her mangy foal, saddled him, mounted him, and galloped to the fiery river. He came to the river, waved the handkerchief three times to the right, and suddenly, out of nowhere, a great high bridge stood over the river. The prince crossed over the bridge and waved the handkerchief to the left only twice—a thin, thin bridge was left hanging there over the river!

In the morning Baba Yaga woke up, and there was no sign of the mangy foal! She raced in pursuit; she galloped at full speed in her iron mortar, driving with the pestle, sweeping away her tracks with a broom. She galloped up to the fiery river, took a look, and said, "A good bridge!" She started to cross the bridge. She had only made her way to the middle when the bridge broke, and Baba Yaga went *flump*! into the river. There she met a cruel death!

Prince Ivan fed his foal in green meadows, and it turned into a marvelous horse.

The prince came riding to Mar'ia Morevna. She ran out and threw her arms around him. "How has God resurrected you?"[35]

"This is what happened, and that," he said. "Come away with me."

"I'm afraid, Prince Ivan! If Koshchei catches us, you'll be cut into pieces again."

"No, he won't catch us! I have a wonderful *bogatyr* horse now, he flies like a bird." They both climbed onto the horse and rode away.

When Koshchei the Deathless came home, his horse stumbled under him. "What are you tripping for, you insatiable nag? Or do you sense some misfortune?"

"Prince Ivan was here, he's taken Mar'ia Morevna away."

"And can we catch them?"

"God knows! Now Prince Ivan has a *bogatyr* horse better than I am."

"No, I can't bear it!" said Koshchei the Deathless. "I'm going to chase them."

For a long time, for a short time—he rode and caught up with Prince Ivan, jumped to the ground, and was about to stab him with his sharp sword. But just then Prince Ivan's horse kicked him with all his strength and knocked the brain out of his head, while the prince finished him off with a club.[36] After that, the prince piled up a mound of firewood, started a fire, burned Koshchei the Deathless on the bonfire, and scattered even his ashes to the wind.

Mar'ia Morevna mounted Koshchei's horse, while Prince Ivan rode his own. They went to visit first the raven, then the eagle, and then the falcon. Wherever they arrived, they were met everywhere with joy. "Ah, Prince Ivan! And we feared we'd never see you again. Well, you didn't go to all that trouble for nothing. You could search the whole world for such a beauty as Mar'ia Morevna, but you'd never find a second one!"

They stayed a while as guests, feasted a while, and then they set off for their own kingdom. They came home and started to live and live well, to earn wealth and to drink mead.

(Afanas'ev, no. 159)

Moon and Star

In a certain kingdom, in a certain state there lived a tsar, and he had no children. So he and his wife begged God to give them a child for consolation. After a certain time the tsar's wife grew heavy with child, and they rejoiced greatly. They had a daughter, and they gave her the name Moon. And how glad the tsar was! They hired all kinds of courtiers to teach her . . . After a certain time the tsar's wife grew heavy again, and everyone was glad that God had given her such a gift. They had another daughter, and they gave her the name Star.[37] And what beauties they both were, so beautiful that it's impossible to describe. It was more than the mind could grasp! And as those beautiful girls grew, people kept coming to visit to marvel at them . . .

When they were about twelve years old, one of the daughters had a birthday. The tsar arranged a magnificent ball. People came from every city and province to offer their congratulations, and everyone wanted to admire their beauty. At one point the girls went out into the garden to take a walk, and they left their papa and mama inside. Suddenly a Whirlwind came rushing up, snatched both sisters, and carried them off . . . All the guests shouted; there was a great commotion. But the Whirlwind carried them higher and higher. All the guests were shouting, so the tsar ran outside: "What is it, what is it?"

"Oh, father tsar! Your children are up there!"

When the tsar heard this, he fell right over in a faint . . . The senators immediately sent all the soldiers to search for the girls: perhaps they had fallen somewhere. They searched and searched, but they didn't find them anywhere. They looked for them; they looked into a special mirror: could they be seen anywhere? No, they couldn't be seen. They asked the sorcerers; the sorcerers searched for a day, and two, and three, for a week and more. A month passed, and no, there was no sign . . . They searched in the forest but didn't find them. "It must be," they said, "that they fell into the sea!"

A year passed, and another . . . Then after several years the tsaritsa grew heavy with child and gave birth to Prince Ivan. And he grew not by the day but by the hour, and so smart, so clever! But the tsaritsa kept on crying, she cried inconsolably for her daughters, for Moon and Star. Prince Ivan came in and asked, "Mama, dear one, why are you crying?"

"It's nothing," she said.

"Mama, dear one, tell me!"

"Oh, my dear friend Vanechka, I had two daughters before you . . ."[38]

"Where are they?"

She told him the story . . . "And there's been neither sight nor sound nor any word of them!"

"Mama," he said, "permit me to go search for my sisters."

"No," she said, "don't go! You won't find them . . . We lost our daughters," she said, "and we'll lose you too!" She begged him in every possible way.

His father found out about this, asked about it, and then summoned his ministers. "Gentlemen," he said, "my son cries day and night, he wants to go search for his sisters!"

The senators said, "Why not give him your blessing, if he has such a wish?"

"How can he do this," said the king, "at such a youthful age? How can he have such ideas?" Then he grew angry at his wife, "Why did you suggest it to him?"

They thought and thought about it, and then they gave him their blessing.

Prince Ivan said, "I could do without anything, but I would never go without your blessing!" He set off, saying, "Mama! Don't cry, don't grieve, I'll find my sisters!"

He walked for a week and for two through a forest, and suddenly he saw two forest spirits, ever so tall, who were fighting.

"Oh," they said, "Prince Ivan, please be a judge for us."

These forest spirits had three things: a self-setting tablecloth, a pair of seven-league boots, and an invisible hat.

Prince Ivan agreed and said, "Here's a milepost. Whoever reaches it first will get two of the things, and the one who comes after will get one of them."

They ran off, overtaking each other, reached the milepost and turned around, but Prince Ivan had put on the invisible hat and they couldn't see him.

"Oh, where's Prince Ivan? Where's Prince Ivan?"

They ran around him, but they couldn't see him. They searched for three hours, they cried, and they dashed off into the forest to search. But Prince Ivan took off the invisible hat and put on the seven-league boots. When he took a step, he'd go five *vyorsts*, if he took another step he'd go another five *vyorsts*.

Now Ivan felt like eating. "So," he said, "tablecloth, spread out!" Suddenly all kinds of dishes and drinks appeared. Some men were coming down the road. He called to them, "Men! Please come over here. Sit down please," he said. They sat down and ate and drank their fill. Prince Ivan thought, "Thank God, I have everything I could need!" Meanwhile, the men he had invited were marveling, too; they thanked him and went on their way.

He set off, too, and he came into a deep forest. He came upon a house that stood on chicken knees, turning this way and that. "Little house, little house! Stand with your back to the forest, your front to me!"

The house turned around and Ivan went inside. There was a Baba-Yaga, an old woman sorceress. "Now," she said, "the Russian spirit appears before my eyes! What, Prince Ivan, are you doing a deed or fleeing a deed?"

"I had two sisters who disappeared," he said. "Do you know about them? Have you heard anything?"

"I know your sisters. The spirits took them away, and you won't be able to get them. The Whirlwinds are so strong, magical. You can't even get close. Your sister Moon," she says, "is in the silver palace, and Star is in the golden palace. You won't find them: it's far, far away!"

"No," he said, "I'll go."

"Well, go then; my sister lives closer to there. Here's a ball of thread for you. Wherever the ball of thread rolls, follow it, and you'll come to my sister."

He thanked the Baba-Yaga, and when the ball of thread rolled off, he followed. He walked for about a week and came to her second sister. He went into her house. This one was even angrier, meaner. "I'm mean, crafty and wise," she said, "but our third sister is even meaner. Here's a kerchief for you," she said. "Give it to her as a present from me. Then she'll let you come in."

Then he set off again after the ball of thread. He came to the house of the third Baba-Yaga, and he gave her the kerchief from her sister as a present. "Well," she said, "what's your business?"

"I'm searching for my sisters," he said. "Do you happen to know where my sisters are?"

"Moon," she said, "is with the first Whirlwind; only there's a stone wall, and twelve men stand guard day and night. They won't let you through. And about the other Whirlwind there's nothing to say: he's very mean." So the prince said good-bye and went on his way.

Artist unknown.

He came to the first palace. The stone wall was exceedingly high: there was no way at all to climb it, and twelve men stood there day and night. He came up and asked them to let him in, but they wouldn't agree for anything. He put on the invisible hat and flew across. The sentries saw him walking in the courtyard. "Well," they said, "it's as if we'd let him in! It must have been a spirit testing us!"

But Prince Ivan went into the palace. He went into one room, but there was no one there. He went into a second room, a third, into the fifth, and there was his sister Moon resting on a couch, such a beauty . . . She was lying there, resting in sound sleep. "Dear sister! Wake up, wake up! Papa and mama send their respects."

"I don't have any brothers," she said.

Then he told her everything, and she rejoiced and was frightened. She cried and cried with joy. "Oh," she says, "you know, the Whirlwind will come flying home now, and he'll tear you into little pieces."

"I'm not afraid," he said, "of anyone in the world."

"Oh," she said, "he's a mean one!"

Prince Ivan showed her his invisible hat and calmed her down. Suddenly the Whirlwind came flying. Right away Prince Ivan put on his invisible hat, and he couldn't be seen.

"Oh," said the Whirlwind, "Moon, it smells of Russian spirit; it must be that your brother has come."

"I don't have any brothers."

So the Whirlwind raced to search for him. He looked everywhere, in the cupboards and in the trunks, but he couldn't find him anywhere. "It must be," he said, "that your brother's here!"

"Even if he is, what would you do?"

"Nothing," said the Whirlwind.

"Prince Ivan, show yourself!" she said.

He took off the invisible hat. The Whirlwind saw him and said, "I am crafty, but he's even more sly. How did you get here?"

"Yes," he said, "blood made me search, so I found her."

Then his sister ran to bring something to eat.

"Don't trouble yourself!" said Prince Ivan. "I'll feed you. Tablecloth, spread yourself!"

Then all sorts of food and drink appeared.

The Whirlwind ate and praised it all. "Oh, what food, what drinks there are in Rus'!"

Prince Ivan stayed there for a week and then two.

Then his sister said, "You had better go to see Star. The Tsar-Maiden lives just beyond her, and she has great power over these spirits."

Prince Ivan said good-bye to Moon, and he set out to see his other sister, Star.

He came to the palace; it had a very high wall. Twelve men were standing there, and they didn't let anyone into the palace. Star's husband was the Whirlwind above all Whirlwinds, the most smothering. Just as before, the sentries wouldn't let Prince Ivan pass. He put on his invisible hat and went through. They said, "There he is, walking around in the courtyard. It's a spirit who was curious about us."

Prince Ivan went up into the first room—there was no one; into the second, the third, and in the fifth room he found his sister Star, even more splendid, resting in a sound sleep.

"My dear sister! Wake up, wake up; your brother has come to see you, and he brings respects from your father and mother."

"No," she said, "I don't have any brothers."

Then he told her everything. She was so glad, so glad. But she said, "My Whirlwind is furious, though, and he'll tear you to pieces."

"Don't worry," he said, "he won't see me." He showed her the invisible hat.

The Whirlwind came flying in. "Oh," he said, "Star, it must be that your brother is here. It smells of the Russian spirit. He must be here, show him to me!"

"But you'll tear him apart!"

"I swear," he said, "I won't tear him apart."

So Prince Ivan took off the invisible hat and stayed as a guest with them as well. Then he said to Star, "I'll take you away!"

"No, the Whirlwind would catch up with us . . . But in this kingdom there's a Tsar-Maiden, and she has great power over these spirits . . . She wants to meet you."

So Prince Ivan stayed as a guest of his sister for a week and for two, said good-bye, and set off . . . He came to the Tsar-Maiden, and she was so glad. The Tsar-Maiden was a true beauty.

"Oh, Prince Ivan, how did God bring you here?"

"Blood led me here," he said. "Can you fulfill my request and help me rescue my sisters? I'll take you as my spouse."

"All right," she said. "I have a twelve-headed dragon. He's been shackled in chains for twelve years, but I'll let him free, and he'll defeat the Whirlwinds."

Then they spoke for a while.

"Well," she said, "Prince Ivan, let's go get the dragon!"

They went there, and she asked her dragon, "Could you defeat those two spirits—the Whirlwinds?"

"I can," he said, "only give me time for a month to eat as much beef and drink as much beer as I want."

They set the dragon free, and every day they gave him a whole bull to eat and a vat of beer. The dragon began to gain weight. A month passed; the dragon took his weapons, and he flew off. "Wait here," he said.

He flew to those spirits. The spirits flew toward him; they fought, and they fought, they knocked off ten heads, but he got them with fire, with his claws . . . He killed them, threw their bodies into the sea, and brought their heads to the Tsar-Maiden.

Prince Ivan and the Tsar-Maiden came riding to the field and met the dragon with joy. Then they went to Star.

"My dear sister!" said Prince Ivan. "Here's what the Tsar-Maiden has done for you!"

They rejoiced and celebrated. And they gave the dragon his own dear freedom, and he could eat and drink all he wanted. The dragon was so glad, so glad to be free. And once again he grew twelve heads: for the dragon is a spirit . . .

They feasted with Star for a week. Then she said, "What's Moon thinking now? She doesn't see her spirit!"

Prince Ivan said, "Well, dear sister, pack your things and let's go!"

"What should I pack?"

They went out onto the porch. She said a word[39] and rolled an egg on a golden saucer: "Roll my house into the golden egg! Flying carpet! Fly in to me!"

A flying carpet appeared, and all three of them flew to see Moon.

When they came to his sister, he said, "Well, my dear sister, we have to get our things together!" She came out on the porch, said a word, rolled an egg on a silver saucer, and the house rolled up into the silver egg. They sat down on the flying carpet and flew away like birds to their own country. They came to the garden and unrolled the egg—and a palace appeared. They unrolled the other egg—another palace . . .

Just then an ambassador was out riding, and he reported to the tsar, "Two palaces have appeared in your garden!" The tsar came out and found out about everything. What joy it was . . . The tsar arranged a ball, Prince Ivan got married, and the tsar gave him his kingdom. Then they began to live and live, and to store up riches.[40]

(Khudiakov, no. 108)

Prince Danila-Govorila

Once there lived an old princess. She had a son and daughter who were still growing, both so noble and good.[41]

An evil witch took a dislike to them and wondered how she could ruin them. She mulled it over and came up with an idea. She turned herself into a fox, went to their mother, and said, "My dear gossip! Here's a little ring for you. Put it on your son's finger. It'll make him rich and quick on the uptake, if only he never takes it off and if he marries a girl whose finger fits the ring!"

The old woman believed her and was happy. As she was dying, she ordered her son to marry a girl whose finger fit the ring.

Time passed, and her son was growing up. He came of age and started to look for a bride. One pleased him, another caught his eye, but when they tried on the ring it was either too small or too big. It didn't fit one or the other. He traveled and traveled through towns and cities, tried all the lovely maidens, but didn't find anyone to be his intended.

He came home and got pensive. "What are you upset about, brother?" asked his sister.

He revealed his misfortune to her, told her his grief.

"What odd kind of ring is this?" asked the sister. "Let me try it on." She put it on her slender finger—and the ring tightened, shone, and fit on her hand as if it had been poured on purpose just for her.

"Ah, sister, you're my intended, it's you who'll be my wife!"

"What are you saying, brother? Think about God, think about sin! Do people marry their own sisters?"

But her brother wouldn't listen. He danced with joy and ordered the wedding preparations. She dissolved in bitter tears, left the sunlit room, and sat on the threshold. Her tears poured like a river!

Some old pilgrim women were passing by. She invited them in to have some food and drink. They asked: what was troubling her, what was her sorrow? There was no point hiding it, so she told them everything.

"Well, don't cry, don't grieve, but listen to us. Make four dolls, set them in the four corners. When your brother starts calling you to join him under the marriage crown, go. When he starts to call you into the sunlit room, don't be in a hurry. Hope in God. Farewell." The old women went away.

The brother and sister got married. He went into the sunlit room and said, "Sister Katerina, come to bed!"

She answered, "In a moment, brother. Let me take off my earrings."

And the dolls in the four corners began to lament:

Cuckoo, Prince Danila!
Cuckoo, Govorila!
Cuckoo, you want to marry,
Cuckoo, your own sister.
Cuckoo, earth split open,
Cuckoo, sister fall through!

The earth began to split open, and the sister began to fall in.

The brother shouted, "Sister Katerina, come to bed!"

"In a moment, brother! Let me untie my belt!"

The dolls kept on lamenting:

Cuckoo, Prince Danila!
Cuckoo, Govorila!
Cuckoo, you want to marry,
Cuckoo, your own sister.
Cuckoo, earth split open,
Cuckoo, sister fall through!

By now you couldn't see anything but her head. Her brother called again. "Dear sister Katerina, come to bed!"

"Right away, brother! Let me take off my slippers."

The dolls kept on lamenting, and the earth closed over her.

Her brother called again. He called even louder—no answer! He got angry, came running, slammed into the doors, and the doors flew open. He looked everywhere—but it was as if his sister had never been there. Only the dolls sat in the corners, and they kept on lamenting: "Earth split open, sister fall through!" He grabbed an axe, cut off their heads, and threw them all into the stove.

But the sister walked and walked under the ground, and she saw a house standing on chicken legs. It stood there and turned around. "Little house, little house! Stand with your back to the forest and your front to me." The house stood still, and the doors opened.

In the little house sat a lovely maiden. She was embroidering a piece of cloth with silver and gold. She greeted her guest kindly, sighed and said, "My dear, my little sister! My heart is glad to see you. I'll welcome you and treat you well, as long as my mother isn't here. But when she flies home, then woe to you and me both. My mother's a witch!"

Her guest was frightened to hear such words, but she had nowhere else to go. She sat down with her hostess at the piece of cloth. They sewed and chatted. For a long time or a short time, the hostess knew what time it was, she knew when her mother would come flying home. She turned her guest into a little needle, stuck it into a garland, and stood the garland in the corner.

No sooner had she put everything away than the witch was lurking at the door: "My good daughter, my comely daughter! It smells of bones from Rus'!"

"My lady mother! People were walking by. They came in to have a drink of water."

"Why didn't you make them stay?"

"They were old, my dear, not to your taste."

"From now on see to it—call everyone into the yard, don't let anyone out of the yard. And I'll pick up my heels and go back out after plunder."

She went away, and the girls sat down at the length of cloth, sewed, talked, and laughed.

The witch came flying. Sniff, sniff through the house. "My good daughter, my comely daughter! It smells of bones from Rus'!"

"Some old men just came in to warm their hands. I tried to make them stay, but they wouldn't."

The witch was hungry. She gave her daughter a tongue-lashing and flew away again. Her guest had been sitting hidden in the garland. They set right back to sewing the cloth. They sewed and made haste, and tried to figure out how they could escape from misfortune, run away from the wicked witch.

They hadn't even managed to look at each other or whisper to each other when she was at the door, speak of the devil, and caught them by surprise. "My good daughter, my comely daughter! It smells of a bone from Rus'!"

"Well, you see, Mother, a fair maiden is waiting for you."

The fair maiden took a look at the old woman and was horror struck! There stood a Baba Yaga, bony leg, nose grown into the ceiling. "My good daughter, my comely daughter! Stoke the stove as hot as can be!" They brought firewood of oak and maple and built a fire. Flames flickered from the stove.

The witch took a wide paddle and began to entreat the guest, "Sit down, my beauty, on the paddle." The beauty sat down. The witch pushed her toward the oven, but she put one leg into the oven and the other onto the stove. "What, girl, don't you know how to sit? Sit down properly!" She changed her position and sat down properly. The witch moved her into the opening, but once again she put one leg into the oven and the other under the stove.

The witch flew into a rage and pulled her back out. "You're playing around, playing around, young lady! Sit still, like this. Watch me!"

She flopped down on the paddle and stuck out her legs. The maidens quickly shoved her into the oven, set her down there, closed the latches, piled up logs, smeared and sealed it with pitch, and set off at a run, taking along the embroidered cloth, a brush, and a comb.

They ran and ran, and then they took a look behind them. The evil woman had fought her way out. She caught sight of them and started to whistle: "Hi, hi, hi! You over there!"

What could they do? They threw down the brush, and it grew up into a thick, thick patch of reeds. She wouldn't be able to crawl through. The witch put out her claws, pinched a path through, and she drew closer to them again . . . Where could they hide? They threw down the comb—it grew up into a dark, dark oak wood. A fly couldn't have flown through it.

The witch sharpened her teeth and got to work. Whatever she grabbed, she'd pull a tree up by the roots! She tossed them in all directions, cleared a path and started chasing again . . . She got even closer!

They ran and ran, but there was nowhere to go. They had used up all their strength! They threw the gold-embroidered cloth, and it poured out into a wide sea, deep and fiery. The witch rose high up. She wanted to fly over it, but she fell down into the fire and burned up.

The two maidens were left alone, homeless doves. They had to go somewhere, but where? They didn't know. They sat down to rest.

Then a man came over to them, asked who they were, and reported to his master that there were not two migratory birds, but two young maidens, as beautiful as if they had been painted, sitting in his lands. They were just alike in height and nobility, brow for brow, eye for eye. "One of them must be your sister, but which one? We can't figure it out."

The master went to take a look and called them to him. He saw that one of them was his sister, the servant hadn't lied, but which one? He couldn't make it out, and she was angry and wouldn't tell him. What was he to do?

"Well, here's what, my lord! I'll fill a ram's bladder with blood and put it under your arm. You chat with your guests, and I'll come up and catch you in the side with a knife. The blood will flow, and your sister will reveal herself!"

"All right!"

They did this just as they had planned it. The servant caught his master in the side, the blood spurted, and the brother fell down. The sister ran to embrace him, and she cried and lamented, "My dear, my incomparable one!"

But the brother jumped up neither burned nor hurt. He hugged his sister and gave her in marriage to a good man, while he married her friend, whose hand fit the ring perfectly. And they all lived marvelously ever after.

(Afanas'ev, no. 114)

Prince Ivan and Beloy Polyanin

In a certain kingdom, in a certain state there once lived a tsar. This tsar had three daughters and one son, Prince Ivan. The tsar grew old and died, and Prince Ivan took the crown. As soon as the neighboring kings learned about this, they immediately gathered numberless armies and set off to make war against him. Prince Ivan didn't know what to do. He went to his sisters and asked, "My dearest sisters, what can I do? All the kings have risen in war against me."

"Oh, such a brave warrior! What are you frightened of? How is it that Beloy Polyanin[42] makes war against Baba Yaga, golden leg? For thirty years he hasn't dismounted from his horse, and he knows no rest. But you're frightened, even though you haven't seen anything yet!"

Prince Ivan at once saddled his good horse, put on his battle harness, took his sword, his long-measuring spear, and his silken lash, said a prayer to God, and rode out against the enemy. He didn't strike with his sword so much as he trampled with his horse. He battered through all the enemy forces, returned to the city, lay down to sleep, and slept for three days without waking. On the fourth day he woke up, went out onto the balcony, and looked at the open field. The kings had gathered an even larger force and had come back up to the very walls.

The prince was sad, and he went to his sisters. "Ah, my sisters! What can I do? I wiped out one force, but now another one stands beneath the city walls, threatening us even more than the first."

"What kind of warrior are you? You fought for one day, and then you slept for three days without waking. How is it that Beloy Polyanin fights against Baba Yaga, golden leg, and hasn't dismounted from his horse for thirty years, and knows no rest?"

Prince Ivan ran into the white-stoned stable, saddled up his good *bogatyr* horse, put on his battle harness, girded on his sword, took his long-aiming spear in one hand, his silken lash in the other, said a prayer to God, and went out against the enemy. It was not a bright falcon flying at a flock of geese, swans, and gray ducks—it was Prince Ivan attacking the enemy force. He himself didn't strike as much as his horse trampled. He beat down the forces of the great host, returned home, lay down to sleep, and slept for six days without waking. On the seventh day he awoke, came out onto the balcony, and looked at the open field. The kings had collected an even larger army and had once again surrounded the whole city.

Prince Ivan went to his sisters. "My dearest sisters! What can I do? I wiped out two armies, but a third one stands at the walls, threatening us even more."

"Ah, you brave warrior! You fought for one day, then you slept for six without waking. How is it that Beloy Polyanin fights with Baba Yaga, golden leg? For thirty years he hasn't dismounted from his horse, he knows no rest."

This seemed bitter to the prince. He ran to the white-stoned stables, saddled his good *bogatyr* horse, put on his battle harness, girded on his sword, took his long-aiming spear in one hand, his silken lash in the other, said a prayer to God, and rode out against the enemy. It was not a bright falcon flying at a flock of geese, swans, and gray ducks; it was Prince Ivan attacking the enemy army. He himself didn't strike so much as his horse trampled. He beat down the forces of the great host, returned home, lay down to sleep, and slept without waking for nine days. On the ninth day he awoke and called all the ministers and senators. "Gentlemen, my ministers and senators! I have decided to travel to distant lands, to take a look at Beloy Polyanin. While I'm away, I ask you to judge and keep order, to resolve all matters of justice." After that he said good-bye to his sisters, mounted his horse, and set out on his way.

For a long time or a short time, he rode in a thick forest. He saw a little house standing. An old man lived in that house. Prince Ivan dropped in to see him. "Hello, granddad!"

"Hello, Russian prince! Where is God carrying you?"

"I'm seeking Beloy Polyanin. Do you happen to know where he is?"

"I don't know myself, but wait a moment. I'll gather all my faithful servants and ask them." The old man stepped out onto the porch, began to play a silver horn, and suddenly all the birds came flying to him from all directions. A visible and invisible number of them flew; they covered the whole sky in a black cloud. The old man shouted in a loud voice and whistled a heroic whistle. "My faithful servants, flying birds! Have you seen or heard anything about Beloy Polyanin?"

"No, we haven't seen or heard anything!"

"Well, Prince Ivan!" said the old man. "Now go see my older brother; perhaps he'll be able to tell you. Here, take this ball of thread and let it go before you. Wherever the ball of thread rolls, you turn your horse that way." Prince Ivan mounted his good horse, rolled the ball of thread, and rode off after it, and the forest got darker and darker.

The prince came to a little house, and he went in the door; in the house sat an old man, his hair white as snow. "Hello, granddad!"

"Hello, Russian prince! Where does your road lead you?"

"I'm seeking Beloy Polyanin. Do you happen to know where he is?"

"Now, wait here while I gather my faithful servants, and I'll ask them." The old man stepped out onto the porch and began to play a silver horn, and suddenly all kinds of animals came running over from all directions. He shouted to them in a loud voice and whistled a *bogatyr* whistle. "My faithful servants, leaping beasts! Have you seen or heard anything about Beloy Polyanin?"

"No," answered the beasts, "we haven't seen or heard anything."

"Well then, count yourselves. Perhaps not everyone is here."

The beasts counted themselves, and one lame she-wolf came up missing. The old man sent runners to look for her, and they went right out and brought her. "Tell me, crooked she-wolf! Do you happen to know where Beloy Polyanin is?"

"Of course know I, because I always live near him. He wins battles, and I feed on the corpses."

"Where is he now?"

"In the open field. He's asleep in a tent on a great burial mound. He was fighting with Baba Yaga, golden leg, and after the battle he lay down to sleep for twelve days."

"Well, then, take Prince Ivan there." The she-wolf ran off, and the prince galloped after her. Soon he came to the great burial mound and went into the tent. Beloy Polyanin was sleeping soundly. "There, my sisters told me that Beloy Polyanin fought without rest, but he lay down and went to sleep for twelve days! Shouldn't I sleep for a while, too?" Prince Ivan thought and thought, and then he lay down beside him.

Just then a little bird flew into the tent, hovered at the very head of the bed, and said these words: "Get up, wake up, Beloy Polyanin, and hand my brother, Prince Ivan, over to an evil death. Otherwise, he'll get up and kill you!"

Prince Ivan leapt up, caught the bird, tore off its right leg, threw it outside the tent, and lay back down next to Beloy Polyanin. He hadn't had time to go back to sleep when another little bird flew in, hovered at the head of the bed, and said, "Get up, wake up, Beloy Polyanin, and turn my brother Prince Ivan over to an evil death. Otherwise, he'll get up and kill you!"

Prince Ivan leapt up, caught the bird, tore off its right wing, threw it out of the tent, and lay back down in the same place.

Right after that a third little bird flew in, hovered at the head of the bed, and said, "Get up, wake up, Beloy Polyanin, and hand my brother Prince Ivan over to an evil death; otherwise, he'll get up and kill you!"

Prince Ivan jumped up, caught that bird, and tore off its beak. He threw the bird outside, lay down, and fell sound asleep.

The time came and Beloy Polyanin woke up. He looked and saw who knows what kind of *bogatyr* lying next to him. He grabbed his sharp sword and wanted to hand him over to an evil death, but he stopped himself in time. "No," he thought. "He came upon me while I was asleep, and he didn't want to bloody his sword. It would be no honor and no praise to me, a handsome young man, if I slew him! A sleeping man is like a dead man! Better I should wake him." He woke up Prince Ivan and said to him, "Good man or evil man! Tell me, what is your name and why have you stopped by here?"

"They call me Prince Ivan, and I came here to see you, to test your strength."

"You're mighty brave, prince! You came into my tent without asking, and you went to sleep without announcing yourself. You could have met your death for that!"

"Eh, Beloy Polyanin! You haven't jumped over the trench yet, but you're bragging. Wait and see, perhaps you'll stumble! You have two arms, but I don't have only one either, as my mother bore me."

They mounted their *bogatyr* horses, rode toward each other, and struck each other so hard that their spears shattered into fragments, and the good horses fell to their knees. Prince Ivan knocked Beloy Polyanin out of his saddle and lifted his sharp sword over him.

Beloy Polyanin began pleading with him. "Don't hand me over to death! Grant me my life! I'll call myself your younger brother, and I'll honor you like a father!"

Prince Ivan took him by the hand, raised him from the ground, kissed him on the lips, and called him his younger brother. "I heard, brother, that you've been fighting for thirty years against Baba Yaga, golden leg. Why are you at war?"

"She has a beautiful daughter, and I want to win her for my wife."

Baba Yaga riding a pig and fighting the infernal Crocodile, early seventeenth century, anonymous. This satirical *lubok* (popular woodcut print) depicts Baba Yaga, dressed in traditional Estonian costume, mounted on a pig as she battles the infernal Crocodile. Sometimes interpreted as a satire by the religious Old Believers on the secularizing Peter the Great, whom they dubbed Crocodile, and his second wife, Catherine, a native of Estonia, the scene likely dramatizes a marital squabble. Since no fairy tale mentions Baba Yaga's conjugal status, despite her role of mother, this *lubok* draws on her reputation not as a quarrelsome spouse, but as a termagent. Artist unknown, possibly by Korenj Wassilij circa 1700, http://en.wikipedia.org/wiki/File:Babayaga_lubok.jpg.

"Well," said the prince, "if we're going to be friends, then we should help each other in misfortune! Let's go to battle together."

They mounted their horses and rode out into the open field. Baba Yaga, golden leg, had raised an uncountable host and force. It was not bright falcons that swooped upon a flock of doves, but mighty and powerful *bogatyrs* who flew at the enemy army! They didn't so much cut with their swords as they trampled with their horses. They slashed and trampled whole thousands. Baba Yaga hurried to run away and escape, but Prince Ivan went off after her. He was about to catch right up to her when suddenly she came to a deep hole in the ground, lifted an iron board, and disappeared under the ground.

Prince Ivan and Beloy Polyanin gathered a great number of bulls, killed them, flayed their hides, and cut straps. From those hides they wove a cable—and such a long one that if you had one end here, the other could reach all the way to the other world. The prince said to Beloy Polyanin, "Lower me right away into the hole, and don't pull the cable back out, but wait. When I tug on the cable, then pull it!" Beloy Polyanin lowered him into the hole, to the very bottom. Prince Ivan took a look around and set off to search for Baba Yaga.

He walked and walked, looked, and saw some tailors sitting behind a grating. "What are you doing?"

Titled **Baba Yaga and the Epic Hero**, this contemporary response to the eighteenth-century *lubok* is by Sergei Tyukanov, an artist who works in various media and is strongly influenced by Hieronymus Bosch. Illustration by Sergei Tyukanov, http://www.tyukanov.com/.

"Here's what, Prince Ivan. We're sitting and sewing an army for Baba Yaga, golden leg."

"How do you sew it?"

"Here's how: as soon as you stick in a needle, you get a Cossack with a pike. He mounts a horse, they get into formation, and then they go to make war against Beloy Polyanin."

"Eh, brothers! Your work's quick, but not strong. Line up, I'll show you how to sew stronger." They immediately got into a single line, but that very moment Prince Ivan swung his sword, and their heads went flying. He killed all the tailors and went farther along. He walked and walked, looked, and saw some cobblers sitting behind a grating. "What are you doing here?"

"We're sitting and putting together an army for Baba Yaga, golden leg."

"How do you make an army, brothers?"

"Well, here's how: whenever we poke with the awl, we get a soldier with a rifle. He mounts a horse, gets into formation, and goes to make war against Beloy Polyanin."[43]

"Hey, lads! Your work's fast, but not careful. Line up, I'll show you how to do it better." So they stood in a line. Prince Ivan swung his sword, and their heads went flying. He killed the cobblers and got back on the road.

For a long time or for a short time, he made his way to a large, splendid city. Royal chambers stood in that city, and in those chambers sat a maiden of indescribable beauty. She saw the handsome young man in the window; she fell in love with his black curls, his falcon eyes, his sable brows, his *bogatyr* movements. She called the prince to her, asked him who he was and where he was going. He told her that he was looking for Baba Yaga, golden leg.

"Ah, Prince Ivan! Why, I'm her daughter. She's sound asleep now. She lay down to rest for twelve days."

She led him out of the city and showed him the way. Prince Ivan went to Baba Yaga, golden leg, found her asleep, struck her with his sword, and cut her head off. The head rolled and said, "Strike again, Prince Ivan!"

"One blow from a *bogatyr* is enough!" answered the prince. He returned to the chamber and the fair maiden, and sat down with her at the oak tables, by the laden tablecloths. He ate and drank his fill, and he began to ask her, "Is there anyone in the world stronger than I and more beautiful than you?"

"Ah, Prince Ivan! What kind of beauty am I? Over thrice-nine lands, in the thrice-tenth kingdom there is a queen who lives with the dragon tsar. That one's truly an indescribable beauty. I've just washed my face with the water she used to wash her feet!"

Prince Ivan took the fair maiden by her white hand, led her to the place where the cord was hanging, and gave the sign to Beloy Polyanin. He grabbed the cable and began to lift. He pulled and pulled, and he hauled out the prince with the fair maiden.

"Hello, Beloy Polyanin!" said Prince Ivan. "Here's your bride. Live and be happy, may you know no sorrow! And I'm off to the dragon kingdom."

He mounted his *bogatyr* horse, said farewell to Beloy Polyanin and his bride, and rode off over thrice-nine lands. For a long time or for a short time, low or high—speedily a tale is spun, but not so fast a deed is done—he came to the dragon kingdom, slew the dragon tsar, freed the beautiful princess from captivity, and married her. After that he returned home and began to live and live well with his young wife and to earn great wealth.[44]

(Afanas'ev, no. 161)

The Bear Tsar

Once there lived a tsar and his wife, and they had no children. One day the tsar rode out to hunt beautiful beasts and to shoot at migratory birds. It got hot, and he wanted a drink of water. He saw a well to one side, went up to it, bent over and was about to drink his fill—but the Bear Tsar[45] grabbed him by the beard.

"Let me go," begged the tsar.

"Give me the thing you have at home that you don't know. Then I'll let go."

"What would I not know at home?" thought the tsar. "It seems I know everything . . ."

"I'd rather give you a herd of cattle," he said.

"No, I don't even want two herds."

"Well, then, take a herd of horses."

"I don't need even two herds. Give me the thing in your house that you don't know."

The tsar agreed, freed his beard, and rode home. He walked into his palace, and his wife had just given birth to twins: Prince Ivan and Princess Mar'ia.[46] That's what he didn't know in his house. The tsar threw up his hands and started crying bitterly.

"What's the matter? Why are you crying like that?" the tsaritsa asked him.

"How can I help but cry? I've given my own children away to the Bear Tsar."

"And how did that happen?"

"Like this and like that," the tsar explained.

"But we won't give them up!"

"Oh, that's impossible! He'll ruin the whole kingdom, but he'll take them in the end."

So they thought and thought about what they could do. And they came up with an idea. They dug a very deep hole, furnished it, and decorated it as if it were a palace. They brought in all kinds of provisions, so there'd be something to eat and drink. After they put their children into the hole, they made a ceiling on the top, covered it with earth, and scraped it until it was completely even.

Not long after that the tsar and tsaritsa died, but their children grew and grew. Finally the Bear Tsar came for them. He looked here and there, but there was nobody there! The palace was empty. He walked, walked, walked around the whole house and thought, "Who can tell me about the tsar's children, where they're hiding?" He looked and saw an awl stuck into the wall. "Awl, awl," asked the Bear Tsar. "Tell me, where are the tsar's children?"

"Take me out into the yard and throw me to the ground. Where I fall and stick in the earth, dig there."

The Bear Tsar took the awl, went out into the yard, and threw it to the ground. The awl spun, twisted, and stuck right in the place where Prince Ivan and Princess Mar'ia were hidden. The bear dug through the dirt with his paws, broke through the ceiling, and said, "Ah, Prince Ivan, ah, Princess Mar'ia, there you are! They thought they could hide you from me! Your father and mother tricked me, so for that I'll eat you up."

"Ah, Bear Tsar, don't eat us, our father left a lot of chickens and geese and all kinds of goods. There are things to whet your appetite."

"All right, let it be so! Climb up on my back. I'll take you to serve me."

They climbed up on his back, and the Bear Tsar took them to mountains so steep and high that they went up to the very sky. No one lived there; it was all deserted. "We're hungry and thirsty," said Prince Ivan and Princess Mar'ia.

"I'll run and bring you something to eat and drink," answered the bear. "You stay here for now and rest."

The bear ran off to get food, but the prince and princess stood and cried many tears. Out of nowhere a bright falcon[47] appeared, flapped his wings and said these words, "Ah, Prince Ivan and Princess Mar'ia, what kind of fate has brought you here?" They told the story. "Why did the bear take you?"

"To serve him in every way."

"Do you want me to take you away? Climb up on my wings."

They climbed up. The bright falcon rose up higher than a standing tree, lower than a passing cloud, and was about to fly away to distant lands. At that moment the Bear Tsar ran back, caught sight of the falcon high in the sky, struck his head against the damp earth, and burned the bird's wings with flame. The falcon's wings were singed, and he dropped the prince and princess to the ground.

"Ah," said the bear. "You wanted to leave me. For that, I'll eat you up, even your bones!"

"Don't eat us, Bear Tsar. We'll serve you faithfully."

The bear forgave them and took them toward his kingdom; the mountains got higher and higher, steeper and steeper.

Time passed, neither much nor little. "Ah," said Prince Ivan. "I want something to eat!"

"Me, too!" said Princess Mar'ia.

The Bear Tsar ran off to get food, but he gave them strict orders not to leave that spot. They sat on the green grass and tears fell from their eyes. Out of nowhere an eagle appeared, soared down from above the clouds, and asked, "Ah, Prince Ivan and Princess Mar'ia, by what fates have you wound up here?" They told the story. "Do you want me to take you away?"

"How could you! The bright falcon tried to take us away, but he couldn't do it, and you won't be able to either!"

"The falcon is a small bird. I'll fly off higher than he can. Climb up on my wings."

The prince and princess climbed on. The eagle flapped his wings and flew up even higher. The bear came running, caught sight of the eagle high in the sky, struck his head against the damp earth, and singed the bird's wings. The eagle dropped Prince Ivan and Princess Mar'ia to the ground.

"Ah, you tried to run away again!" said the bear. "I'll eat you up for that!"

"Don't eat us, please. The eagle tempted us! We'll serve you in faith and truth."

The Bear Tsar forgave them for the last time, fed them and gave them something to drink, and took them on farther.

Time passed, neither a lot nor a little. "Ah," said Prince Ivan, "I want something to eat!"

"Me, too!" said Princess Mar'ia.

The Bear Tsar left them and ran off to get food. They were sitting on the green grass and crying. Out of nowhere a little shitty bullock appeared, shook his head, and asked, "Prince Ivan, Princess Mar'ia! By what fates have you turned up here?" They told the story. "Do you want me to take you away from here?"

"How could you! The falcon-bird and the eagle-bird tried to carry us away, and they couldn't do it. You won't be able to for sure!" and they burst into tears—they could hardly say a word in their weeping.

"The birds couldn't take you away, but I'll take you away! Climb up on my back." They climbed up, and the shitty bullock ran off, not terribly fast. The bear caught sight of the prince and princess trying to escape, and he raced after them in pursuit. "Ah, shitty bullock!" shouted the tsar's children, "the bear is chasing us."

"Is he far away?"

"No, he's close!"

No sooner had the bear jumped close—he was about to grab them!—but the little bullock strained a bit . . . and pasted both his eyes shut. The bear ran to the blue sea to wash out his eyes, but the shitty bullock kept going on and on! The Bear Tsar washed himself off and started back in pursuit.

"Ah, little shitty bullock! The bear's after us!"

"Is he far?"

"Oh, he's close!"

The bear jumped up, but the little bullock strained again . . . and pasted both his eyes shut. While the bear was running to wash out his eyes, the little bullock kept going on and on! And he pasted the bear's eyes shut for a third time. After that he gave Prince Ivan a comb and a towel and said, "If the Bear Tsar starts to get too close to us, first throw down the comb, and the next time wave the towel."

The little shitty bullock ran on and on. Prince Ivan looked back, and the Bear Tsar was chasing after them: he was just about to grab them! Prince Ivan took the comb and threw it down behind them. Suddenly it grew up into such a great, thick forest that even a bird couldn't fly through it, a beast couldn't pick its way through, a man couldn't walk through on foot, and a horseman couldn't ride through it. The bear chewed and chewed, he barely managed to chew a narrow path through it for himself. He made his way through the deep forest and raced after in pursuit. But the tsar's children were far, far away! The bear started to catch up to them. Prince Ivan looked back and waved the towel behind them. Suddenly there was a fiery lake, so very wide! The waves ran from one end of it to the other.

The Bear Tsar stood and stood for a while on the bank and then went back home. But the shitty little bullock, Prince Ivan, and Princess Mar'ia ran all the way to a clearing.[48]

In the same clearing stood a large, wonderful house. "There's a house for you!" said the little bullock. "Live there and don't be sad. Make a bonfire in the yard right now, slaughter me, and burn me in that bonfire."

"Oh no," said the tsar's children, "why should we slaughter you? Better live with us. We'll take care of you, we'll feed you with fresh grass and give you spring water to drink."

"No, burn me, and sow my ashes in three vegetable rows. A horse will jump up from one row, a dog from the second, and an apple tree will grow up on the third. You'll go riding on the horse, Prince Ivan, and you'll go hunting with that dog."[49] So they did everything as he had told them.

One day Prince Ivan decided to go out hunting. He said good-bye to his sister, mounted the horse, and rode off into the forest. He killed a goose, killed a duck, and caught a live wolf cub and brought it home. The prince saw that he was good at hunting, and he rode out again, shot all kinds of birds, and caught a live bear cub. The third time Prince Ivan went out hunting, he forgot to bring his dog along.

At the same time Princess Mar'ia had gone out to do the washing. She walked along, but on the other side of the fiery lake a six-headed dragon flew down to the bank, took on the form of a handsome man, caught sight of the princess, and spoke so sweetly, "Hello, fair maiden!"

"Hello, good young man!"

"I've heard from old people that in earlier times this lake did not exist. If they built a high bridge above it, I would cross over to that side and marry you."

"Wait! There'll be a bridge there in a moment," Princess Mar'ia answered him, and she threw up the towel. That very moment the towel bent into an arch and stopped over the lake as a beautiful bridge. The dragon crossed over the bridge, turned back into its original form, locked up Prince Ivan's dog, and threw the key into the lake. Then he grabbed the princess and carried her away.

Prince Ivan came home from hunting and found his sister missing and the dog howling, locked up. He saw the bridge over the lake and said, "A dragon must have carried off my sister!" He set off to search for her. He walked and walked, and in the open field he saw a hut standing on chicken legs, on dogs' heels. "Little hut, little hut! Turn your back to the forest, and your front to me!" The hut turned, and Prince Ivan went in. In the hut lay Baba Yaga, bony leg, from corner to corner, nose grown into the ceiling. "Fie, fie!" she said. "Until now I couldn't smell the Russian spirit, but now the Russian spirit appears before my eyes, throws itself into my nose! Why have you come, Prince Ivan?"

The Dancing Hut of Baba Yaga by Lisa Smedman. Fantasy Roleplaying. TSR Inc. 1995. http://tinyurl.com/azp6eaq.

"If only you could ease my grief!"

"And what is your grief?" The prince told her. "Well, go home. You have an apple tree in your yard. Break three green twigs off it, braid them together, and there where the dog is locked up, hit the lock with them. The lock will immediately fly apart into little pieces. Then bravely go find the dragon; he won't be able to stand against you."

Prince Ivan went home and freed the dog—she ran out angry as could be! He took the wolf cub and the bear cub along with him, too, and set out to fight the dragon. The beasts threw themselves on it and tore it to shreds. But Prince Ivan took Princess Mar'ia, and they began to live and live well, to earn riches.

(Afanas'ev, no. 201)

The Bogatyrs Soska, Usynia, Gorynia, and Duginia

Once there lived an old woman who had no children. One day she went out to collect wood chips, and she found a block of pine. She took it back home, went in, heated up her house, put the block on the stove, and said to herself, "Let it dry out, and it will make good splinters for light."

But the old woman's house had no windows. Soon the chips started to burn, and the whole house filled with smoke. Suddenly the old woman heard what seemed like the pine block on the stove shouting, "Mother, it's smoky! Mother, it's smoky!"

She said a prayer, went over to the stove and picked up the block, took a look, and—what marvel was this? The block of wood had turned into a little boy. The old woman rejoiced, "God has given me a little son!" And that boy began to grow not by the year, but by the hour, rising like yeasted dough. He grew up and started to go to the boyars' yards and play *bogatyr* tricks. If someone grabbed his arm, he'd pull their arm off. If someone grabbed his leg, he'd pull their leg off. If someone grabbed his head, he'd pull their head off! The boyars started to complain to the old woman. She called her son and told him, "What's the idea? Live a bit more quietly, sir."

But he answered her, "If I'm making things awkward for you, I'll just go away!"

He left the city and set out along the road. Toward him came the *bogatyr* Duginya; take any tree, he could bend it into a bow![50] Duginya asked, "Where are you going, *bogatyr* Soska?"[51]

"I'm following my nose!"

"Take me along with you."

"Let's go."

They set out together, and they ran into *bogatyr* Gorynya.[52] "Where are you going?"

"We're following our noses!"

"Take me along with you."

"All right, come along."

Another few *vyorsts* went by. They ran into the *bogatyr* Usynya beside a big river.[53] He was sitting on the bank, with half his mustache stretched across the river, and people were walking across on his mustache. Horses were riding, wagons were driving, just as if it were a bridge.

Usynya asked, "Where are you going, *bogatyr* Soska?"

"I'm following my nose!"

"Take me with you, too."

"All right, be our comrade."

So they walked along as a foursome, for a long time, for a short time, and they came up to the blue sea. They wanted to get to the other side, but how could they? They didn't know. But *bogatyr* Usynya stretched out his mustache, and they all made it across to the other side on the mustache.

They walked and walked and wound up in a deep, dark forest. "Stop, boys!" said *bogatyr* Soska. "Why should we go wandering through the whole world? Wouldn't it be better to stay and live here?"

They got to work, cut down logs for a house, and started to go out hunting. Every time, one of them would take turns staying home to make the dinner and to look after the housekeeping. The first day it was Duginya's turn. He got food and drink ready and lay down on the bench to rest a bit.

Knock-knock! In came a Baba Yaga. "Give me some dinner," she said. "I want something to eat and drink." Duginya put bread and salt and some roast duck on the table. She gobbled it all down and asked for more.

"There's nothing else," answered Duginya. "We're visitors here ourselves."

The Baba Yaga grabbed him by the hair and started to drag him across the floor. She dragged him and dragged him and left him barely alive.

His comrades came back from hunting. "Why are you lying there, Duginya?"

"I got faint breathing the fumes from the smoke, brothers! It's a new house, the wood is raw . . ."

The next day the same thing happened with Gorynya, and on the third day with Usynya.

It got to be *bogatyr* Soska's turn. Baba Yaga came to see him and demanded, "Give me something to eat and drink!" He put some bread and salt on the table and some roast goose. Baba Yaga ate it all and asked for more.

"There's nothing else, we're visitors here ourselves."

She threw herself at the *bogatyr*, but *bogatyr* Soska was strong himself. He grabbed her by her gray braids, dragged her around, and threw her out of the house barely alive. Baba Yaga crawled off on all fours and went under a big stone.

When the comrades came back from hunting, *bogatyr* Soska took them to that stone and said, "We have to lift it, lads." They tried and tried. The others couldn't move it, but when *bogatyr* Soska hit it with his fist the stone flew off and landed a *vyorst* away. They took a look, and where the stone had been lying it turned out there was a deep hole. "Well, lads, we need to kill some beasts and twist ropes!" They killed some beasts, cut up their skins, tied together a long strap, and fastened a net to it. In that net they lowered *bogatyr* Soska into the underground kingdom.

He started walking through the underground kingdom. He came to a little house and went into it. Baba Yaga's daughter sat in the house, embroidering a carpet. She saw her guest and cried out, "Ah, *bogatyr* Soska! My mother's about to come home. Where can I hide you from her?" She up and turned him into a pin and stuck him into her embroidery.

Baba Yaga came in and asked, "Who do you have in the house?"

"No one, Mother!"

"Why does it smell of Russian spirit?"

She rushed around looking, searched and searched, but didn't find anyone. The moment Baba Yaga left, the fair maiden threw the pin on the floor, and out of the pin appeared *bogatyr* Soska. She took him into a shed. Two jugs were standing in that shed. The blue one was full of strengthening water, and the white one was full of weakening water. "When you fight with mama, jump out the door as fast as you can and into the shed, drink all the water from the blue jug, and fill it up with water from the white one."

No sooner had she managed to tell him this than Baba Yaga came running up. She wanted to get her claws into the *bogatyr*. "Wait, Mother!" her daughter said to her. "First you have to agree. If he knocks you down, let him give you a chance to catch your breath, and if you knock him down, then he may ask for a rest."

Soska *bogatyr* and Baba Yaga agreed on that and jumped at each other. Baba Yaga threw him against the floor. The fair maiden shouted at once, "Mother! Give him a chance to catch his breath." *Bogatyr* Soska ran into the shed, drank all the water from the blue jug, and poured the water from the white one into it. Then he grabbed Baba Yaga and threw her onto the floor.

"Let me catch my breath!" shouted the old woman. She jumped up, ran into the shed, and drank her fill of weakening water. They started to fight again. *Bogatyr* Soska hit her so hard that he killed her. He put her dead into the fire, burned her, and let the ashes scatter in the wind. Then he took the fair maiden, put her into the net, and tugged on the belt. The *bogatyrs* Duginia, Gorynia, and Usynia hauled her right out. They lowered the cable again, lifted *bogatyr* Soska halfway, and then tore the belt.[54]

(Afanas'ev, no. 142)

The Brother

Once there lived a lady. She had three daughters and a little son. She took very great care of her son and wouldn't let him out of the house. One splendid summer day the daughters came to their mother and asked her to let them take their brother to walk in the garden. For a long time the mother wouldn't agree, then finally she let him go. They walked for a long time in the garden. Suddenly a strong wind came up. The sand and dust rose up in a cloud, and the child was torn out of the nanny's arms and carried off to who knows where. They looked and looked for him in the garden, but they couldn't find him. They cried a bit, then went and told their mother that their little brother had disappeared.

The mother sent the oldest daughter to look for him. She went out into a meadow, where three paths lay in front of her. She set off along the one that went straight ahead. She walked and walked, until she came to a birch tree. "Birch tree, birch tree! Tell me, where's my little brother?"

"Pick leaves from me, take half of them for yourself, and leave half for me. I'll come in handy to you in time!"

The girl didn't listen. She said, "I don't have time!" and she went on farther. She came to an apple tree. "Apple tree, apple tree! Did you happen to see my little brother?"

"Pick all the apples off me; take half for yourself, and leave half for me. I'll come in handy to you in time."

She said, "No, I don't have time! How can I pick fruit? I'm going to look for my very own blood brother!" She walked and walked. She came to a stove. And the stove had been lit, it was very hot. "Stove, stove! Did you happen to see my own little brother?"

"Fair maiden! Sweep out the stove, bake a wafer, take half for yourself, and leave half for me. I'll come in handy to you in time."

"How can I sweep and bake? I'm on my way to take care of my brother!"

She went on farther. A house was standing on chicken legs, on spindle heels; it stood there and spun around. She said, "Little house, little house! Stand with your back to the woods, your front to me!" The house turned around, and she went up into it. She said a prayer to God and bowed in all four directions.

A Baba Yaga was lying on the bench, with her head in the wall, her legs sticking up into the ceiling, and hungry as anything. Baba Yaga said, "Fie, fie, fie! Until now there was no smell or sight of a Russian soul. You, maiden! Are you doing a deed or fleeing a deed?"

She said, "Granny! I've walked over mosses and over swamps. I got all soaked through, and I've come to you to warm up."

"Sit down, fair maiden! Look for things on my head!"

She sat down to look and saw her brother sitting on a chair, while the tomcat Yeremei told him stories and sang songs. The old woman, the Baba Yaga, fell asleep. The girl took her brother and ran off to take him home.

She came to the stove. "Stove, stove! Hide me!"

"No, fair maiden, I won't hide you."

She came to the apple tree. "Apple tree, apple tree! Hide me!"

"No, fair maiden, I won't hide you."

She came to the birch tree. "Birch tree, birch tree! Hide me!"

"No, fair maiden, I won't hide you!" She walked on farther.

But then the cat started to purr, and Baba Yaga woke up and saw the boy was missing. She shouted, "Gray eagle! Fly off at once. The sister's been here, and she's taken the boy!" (This eagle was the one who had carried the boy away from his mother.)

The gray eagle flew off. "Stove, stove! Did you happen to see, did a girl pass by here with a little boy?"

"Yes, she did."

The eagle flew farther. "Apple tree, apple tree! Did you happen to see, did a girl pass by here with a little boy?"

"She just went by!"

The eagle flew on to the birch tree. It caught right up to the girl, took away her brother, and scratched her all up, scratched her all over with its claws.

She came home to her mother. "No, Mother, I didn't find my own dear brother!"

Then the middle sister asked, "Will you let me go search for our brother?" They let her go. She set off and everything happened just the same way. She came home all tattered, scratched all over.

The youngest sister started asking to go. They told her, "Your two sisters went out and didn't find him, and you won't find him either!"

"God knows, maybe I will find him!" She set off. She came to the birch tree. "Birch tree, birch tree! Tell me where my little brother is!"

"Pick leaves off me. Take half for yourself and leave half for me. I'll come in handy to you some time!"

She picked the little leaves, and she took half for herself and left half for the tree. She went on farther, and she came to the apple tree. "Apple tree, apple tree! Did you happen to see my own little brother?"

"Fair maiden, pick apples from me. Take half for yourself, leave half for me. I'll come in handy to you some time!" She picked the apples. She took half for herself and left half for the tree, and she went on farther. She came to the stove. "Stove, stove! Did you happen to see my own little brother?"

"Fair maiden! Sweep me out and bake a wafer. Take half for yourself, leave half for me!" So she swept out the stove, baked a wafer, took half for herself, and left half for the stove.

She went along farther. She came close and saw a little house standing on chicken legs, on spindle heels, spinning around. She said, "Little house, little house! Stand with your back to the forest, with your front to me!" The house turned. She went inside and said a prayer to God. (And she had brought along from home a piece of butter, some pretzels, some of everything.)

The Baba-Yaga said, "Until now there was no smell or sight of a Russian soul, but now a Russian soul appears before my eyes! Why are you here, fair maiden, are you doing a deed or fleeing a deed?"

"No, granny! I was walking through the forest, through the swamps, and I got soaked through, chilled through. I've dropped by your place to warm up!"

She said, "Sit down, fair maiden! Look for things on my head!"

She began to look and kept saying, "Fall asleep one eye, fall asleep other eye. If you don't fall asleep I'll pour pitch over you, I'll stop you up with cotton balls!" Baba Yaga fell asleep. The girl took some cotton and dipped it in pitch, smeared Baba Yaga's eyes with pitch. Right away she gave the cat Yeremei a piece of butter, and a doughnut, and some pretzels, and some apples, some of everything. And she took her brother. The cat ate his fill, lay down, and took a nap.

She left with her brother. She came to the stove and said, "Stove, stove! Hide me!"

"Sit down, fair maiden!" Right away the stove spread out, it got much wider. She sat down in it. And the Baba Yaga woke up, but she couldn't pull her eyes open, so she crawled to the door and shouted, "Tomcat Yeremei! Claw my eyes open!"

But he answered her, "Purr, purr! I've lived with you so long, and I never saw so much as a burned crust. But the fair maiden came for only an hour, and she gave me a lump of butter!"

Then Baba Yaga crawled to the threshold. She shouted, "Gray eagle! Fly at once, the sister's been here, she's taken her brother away!"

He flew off. He flew up to the stove. "Stove, stove! Did you happen to see, did a girl happen to pass here with a little boy?"

"No, I haven't seen anything."

"And why, stove, have you gotten so wide?"

It said, "It's just for a time. I was stoked not long ago!"

Then the eagle went back again, scratched and scratched at the Baba Yaga's eyes, scratched her all over. The sister and brother came to the apple tree. "Apple tree, apple tree! Hide me!"

"Sit down, fair maiden!"

The apple tree made itself fluffy, curly.

She sat right down in a crevice in the trunk. Then the gray eagle came flying again and flew to the apple tree. "Apple tree, apple tree! Did you happen to see, did a girl happen to pass here with a little boy?"

It answered, "No."

"Why have you, apple tree, gotten so curly, lowered your branches right down to the ground?"

"The time has come," it said. "I'm standing here all curly."

The eagle went back to Baba Yaga. It clawed and clawed, but it couldn't scratch her eyes open.

And the girl came to the birch tree. "Birch tree, birch tree! Hide me!"

"Sit down, my dear!" it said. It made itself fluffy, curly, like the apple tree.

The gray eagle came flying again. "Birch tree, birch tree! Did you happen to see, did a girl happen to pass by here with a little boy?"

"No, she didn't."

The eagle went back again. The girl came home, and she brought the little boy with her. Everyone rejoiced.

I was there, and I drank mead and beer. It dripped down my mustache, but none got into my mouth.

(Khudiakov, no. 53)

The Daughter-in-Law

Once there lived an old man and an old woman. They had a son, and they married the son to a young woman.

The mother-in-law sent her daughter-in-law to shear the sheep. But she didn't have sheep, she had bears. So the daughter-in-law sat down on an oak and called, "My teddies, my gray ones, come shear yourselves!" They came and they sheared themselves. Then she went back, and she took the wool to her mother-in-law.

Then the mother-in-law sent her to milk the cows. But she didn't have cows, she had wolves. She sat down on an oak and called, "Bossies and brownies! Come milk yourselves!" They came and they milked themselves. Then she took the milk to her mother-in-law.

Then the mother-in-law sent her to see her sister, who was a witch, to ask for some loom reeds. She came to that witch's house. "Auntie!" she said, "Give my mother some reeds!"

"Niece! Sit down, do some weaving for me."

Then the witch went into the cellar to sharpen her teeth. She sharpened and sharpened for a while and said, "Niece! Are you here?"

"I'm here, auntie!" Then she (the niece) spat in all four directions.

The witch asked, "Niece! Are you here?"

"Here, auntie." Then the niece left for home. She gave the cat a lump of butter, she put a stag-beetle[55] in the house with a prayer. She sprinkled the door with water and closed it with a prayer. And she gave a piece of beef to the dog, and she left.

Baba Yaga came. She saw that the girl was gone. "Cat, why did you let her go?"

He said, "She gave me a lump of butter. I've lived with you so long, and I've never seen even a burnt crust."

Then she said, "Stag-beetle, why did you let her go?"

It said, "I've lived an age with you, and I never saw a burnt crust. But she put me here with a prayer!"

"Door, why did you let her go? You could have slammed on her!"

It said, "I've lived with you for an age, I never saw a burned crust; but she closed me with a prayer!"

"You, dog, why didn't you bite her?"

It said, "I've lived for an age with you, I've never seen a burnt crust; but she gave me a piece of meat!"

So the daughter-in-law got away.

(Khudiakov, no. 59)

The Enchanted Princess

Once in a certain kingdom there was a soldier who served in the king's horse guard. He served out his twenty-five years in faith and truth. For his honest conduct, the king ordered him discharged and granted him full retirement. As a reward, he gave the soldier the same horse he used to ride in his regiment with the saddle and all the gear. The soldier said farewell to his comrades and rode off to his homeland. He rode for a day, a second, and a third. Soon a whole week had passed, and a second week, and a third. The soldier didn't have enough money. He had no way to feed himself or his horse, and his home was still far, far away! Things looked very bad for him. He wanted very much to get something to eat. He started to look around, and he saw a great castle off to one side. "Well, now," he thought. "Shouldn't I head that way? Perhaps at least they'll take me into service for a short time, and I can earn a little something."

He turned toward the castle, rode into the courtyard, put his horse in the stable, and gave her some feed. He himself went into the chambers. In the chambers stood a laden table, and on the table both food and wine, everything your soul could desire! The soldier ate and drank his fill. "Now I can have a bit of a nap, too!" he thought.

Suddenly a she-bear came in. "Don't be afraid of me, fine young man. It's good that you've come here. I'm not a wild bear, but a fair maiden—an enchanted princess. If you can stand to stay here for three nights, then the enchantment will be broken. I'll turn into a princess as I was before, and I'll marry you."[56]

The soldier agreed. The she-bear went out, and he was left there alone. Here such a longing fell upon him that he would rather have died, and the longer it lasted the stronger it got. If it weren't for the wine, it seemed, he wouldn't have been able to hold out for a single night! On the third day it got to the point where the soldier decided to give it all up and run out of the castle, but no matter how he struggled, no matter how he tried, he couldn't find any way out. There was nothing he could do: he had to stay there against his will. He spent the third night, too. In the morning a queen of indescribable beauty appeared, thanked him for his service, and told him to get dressed for the wedding. Then they held the wedding and began to live together, and they had nothing to complain of.

After a certain time the soldier started to think about his native land, and he felt the desire to spend a bit of time there.

The queen tried to talk him out of it. "Stay here, my friend, don't go away. What do you lack here?"

No, she couldn't talk him out of it. She said good-bye to her husband and gave him a little sack; it was full of seed. She said, "Whatever road you ride on, toss this seed to either side. Wherever it falls, trees will grow up that very minute. Rare fruits will begin to glow on the tree branches, all kinds of birds will sing songs, and cats from overseas will tell fairy tales." The fine young man mounted the horse he had served on and set off on his way. Wherever he rode, he threw seeds to both sides, and forests rose up in his tracks as if they were crawling up out of the damp earth!

He rode for one day, a second, a third, and he saw a caravan standing on the grass in an empty field. There were merchants sitting on the ground and playing cards, while a cauldron hung beside them. Even though there was no fire under the kettle, the broth was boiling hard. "What a marvel!" thought the soldier. "There's no fire, but broth's boiling up in the kettle like a spring. Let me take a closer look." He turned his horse to the side, rode over to the merchants, and said, "Hello, honest gentlemen!"

But he didn't realize that they weren't merchants, they were unclean spirits. "That's a good trick, a kettle that boils without fire! But I have a better one." He pulled one grain of the seed out of his little bag and threw it to the ground—and that instant a thousand-year tree grew up, precious fruits glowed on the tree, all kinds of birds sang songs, and cats from overseas told tales.

The unclean ones recognized him by his boasting. "Ah," they said among themselves. "Why, this must be that same one who rescued the queen. Let's put him to sleep with a potion, brothers, and let him sleep for half a year." They started offering him food and drink, and they plied him with magical herbs. The soldier fell down on the grass and fell into a sound, unwaking sleep, but the merchants, the caravan, and the kettle disappeared in an instant.

Not long after that the queen went out to take a walk in her garden. She looked and saw that all the tops of the trees had begun to wither. "That's a

Illustration by Viktor Zamirailo (1898–1939).

bad sign!" she thought. "I can tell something bad has happened to my husband. Three months have passed, it's time for him to be coming back, but there's no sign of him!" The queen prepared her things and set off to find him. She rode along the same road where the soldier had made his way, with trees growing on both sides, and birds singing, and the cats from overseas meowing. She came to a place where the trees stopped and the road wound off through the open field. She thought, "Where could he have gotten to? The earth can't have swallowed him up!" She looked to one side and saw the same kind of wondrous tree, with her dear friend lying under it.

She ran up to him and began to shake and poke him, but no, he wouldn't wake up. She started to pinch him, to prick his side with pins, she pricked and pricked him, but he didn't feel the pain either, he lay there as if he were dead and didn't stir.

The queen got angry, and in her anger she spoke a curse. "You worthless sleepy-head, may the wild whirlwind pick you up and carry you off to unknown lands!" No sooner had she said it than suddenly the winds began to rustle and whistle, and in one moment they had picked up the soldier with a wild whirlwind and carried him out of her sight. The queen realized too late that she had said a bad thing. She went back home and started to live all on her own.

But the whirlwind carried the poor soldier far, far away, over thrice-nine lands, and it threw him onto a neck of land between two seas. He fell on the narrowest spit of land. If he had rolled to the left or if he had turned over to the right in his sleep, he would have fallen right into the sea, and that would have been the end of him! The fine young man slept for half a year without moving even a finger. But when he awoke he jumped right to his feet and took a look: on either side he saw waves rising, and there was no end in sight to the wide sea. He stood there deep in thought and asked himself, "What miracle brought me here? Who lugged me all this way?" He walked along the spit of land and came out onto an island. There was a steep, high mountain on that island. Its summit reached up to the clouds, and on the mountain lay a great boulder.

He walked over to that mountain and saw three devils brawling. Blood was pouring from all of them, and tufts of fur were flying! "Wait, you evil ones! What are you fighting about?"

"Well, you see, our father died three days ago, and he left us three marvelous things, a flying carpet, seven-league boots, and an invisible hat. So we can't divide them up."

"Oh, you cursed ones! You've started a battle over such trifles. If you want, I'll divide everything for you. You'll be satisfied—I won't slight anyone."

"Well then, countryman, divide it all, please!"

"All right! Run off right now to the pine forests, gather a hundred poods[57] of pitch, and bring it here."

The devils raced off to the pine forests, gathered three hundred poods of pitch, and brought it to the soldier.

"Now bring the very biggest cauldron in hell."

The devils dragged up a huge cauldron—forty barrels would have fit inside it!—and they poured all the pitch into it.

The soldier started a fire, and as soon as the pitch was melted he ordered the devils to drag the cauldron up the mountain and pour the pitch down it from top to bottom. The devils did this at once. "Well, then," said the soldier. "Now tip over that boulder there. Let it roll down the mountain, and you three go running after it. The first of you to catch it will be the first to choose one of these three marvelous things. The second one to catch it will be the second to have his choice of the two objects left. And then the last marvelous thing will go to the third."

The devils tipped over the boulder, and it went rolling off down the mountain. All three raced after it. One devil caught up with it and grabbed the boulder, but the boulder turned right over, flipped him under it, and smashed him down into the pitch. The second devil caught up to it, and then the third, and the same thing happened to them! They were stuck to the pitch, firmly as could be! The soldier took the seven-league boots and the invisible hat under his arm, took a seat on the flying carpet, and flew off to look for his own kingdom.

After a long time or for a short time, he flew up to a little house and went inside. In the house sat a Baba Yaga, bony leg, old and toothless. "Hello, granny! Tell me, how can I find my beautiful queen?"

"I don't know, dear! I haven't seen any sight of her, nor heard any news of her. Off you go and cross over so many seas, over so many lands; my middle sister lives there. She knows more than I do, perhaps she'll be able to tell you."

The soldier took a seat on the flying carpet and flew off. He had to wander for a long time through the white world. If he started to get hungry and thirsty, he'd put on the invisible hat right away, fly down into some city, go into the shops, take whatever his heart desired, get back on the carpet, and fly on farther. He flew up to another little house and went in. A Baba Yaga was sitting there, bony leg, old and toothless. "Hello, granny! You don't happen to know where I could find my beautiful queen?"

"No, dear, I don't know. You must travel over so many seas, over so many lands. My older sister lives there, perhaps she knows it."

"Eh, you old grouch! You've lived in the world so many years, all your teeth have fallen out, but you don't know anything useful." He took a seat on the flying carpet and flew off to see the oldest sister.

He wandered for a long, long time, saw many lands and many seas, and finally flew to the end of the world. There was a little house standing there, but there was nowhere farther to go—nothing but pitch darkness, you couldn't see a thing! "Well," he said. "If I can't get an answer here, there's nowhere else to fly!"

He went into the little house, and there he saw a Baba Yaga, bony leg, gray and toothless. "Hello, granny! Tell me, where's my beautiful queen!"

"Wait a bit, let me call all the winds together, and I'll ask them. After all, they blow all over the world, so they ought to know where she's living now." The old woman went out on the porch, shouted in a loud voice, and whistled a *bogatyr* whistle. Suddenly the restless winds appeared and started to blow from all directions, so that the house started to shake! "Softer, softer!" shouted Baba Yaga. And as soon as the winds had gathered she started asking them, "My wild winds, you blow over the whole world. Have you seen the beautiful queen?"

"No, we haven't seen her anywhere!" the winds answered in unison.

"And are you all present?"

"All of us, except the south wind."

The south wind came flying a little bit later. The old woman asked it, "Where were you all this time? We almost stopped waiting for you!"

"I'm to blame, granny! I dropped by a new kingdom, where a beautiful queen lives. Her husband disappeared without a trace, so now she's being courted by all kinds of tsars and tsars' sons, kings and princes."

"And how far is it to the new kingdom?"

"On foot you'd have to go thirty years, on wings you would have to fly for ten, but if I blow I can get you there in only three hours."

The soldier began to plead tearfully for the south wind to take him to the new kingdom. "Certainly!" said the south wind. "I'll take you there, if you give me leave to stroll as much as I wish in your kingdom for three days and three nights."

"Stroll for three weeks if you want!"

"All right. I'll just rest for a day or two, to gather my strength, and then we'll be on the road."

The south wind rested, gathered his strength, and said to the soldier, "Well, brother, get ready, we're leaving now. And listen, don't be afraid. You won't get hurt!" Suddenly a fierce whirlwind began to rustle and whistle; it lifted the soldier into the air and carried him over mountains and seas beneath the very clouds, and after exactly three hours he was in the new kingdom, where his beautiful queen lived. The south wind said to him, "Farewell, fine young man! I've taken pity on you, I won't go strolling in your kingdom."

"Why is that?"

"Because, if I started strolling, not a house would be left in the city, and not a tree would be left in the gardens. I'd turn everything upside-down!"

"Farewell then! Thank you!" said the soldier. He put on his invisible hat and went into the white stone chambers.

Now, while he was away from the kingdom all the trees in the garden had stood with withered leaves, but as soon as he appeared they came to life at once and started to flower. He came into the great room, and there at the table sat all kinds of tsars and tsars' sons, kings and princes, who had come to pay court to the beautiful queen. They sat there and treated themselves to sweet wines. Whenever a suitor poured a glass, the moment he lifted it to his lips the soldier would immediately *whap!* the glass with his fist and knock it right away. All the guests were surprised at this, but the beautiful queen guessed at once. "It must be that my friend has returned!" she thought.

She looked out the window. All the treetops had come to life in the garden, and she began to tell a riddle to her guests. "I had a handmade casket with a golden key. I lost the key and had no hope of finding it, but now that key has shown up by itself. Whoever can guess that riddle, I will marry him." The tsars and tsars' sons, the kings and princes cracked their heads over this riddle for a long time, but there was no way they could solve it. The beautiful queen said, "Show yourself, my friend!"

The soldier took off the invisible hat, took her by the white hands and began to kiss her sugared lips. "And there's the solution for you!" said the beautiful queen. "The handmade casket—that's me, and the little golden key—that's my faithful husband." The suitors had to turn their carriages around. They all drove off to their own homes, but the queen began to live with her husband and to earn riches.

(Afanas'ev, no. 272)

The Feather of Finist the Bright Falcon

Once there lived an old man who had three daughters.[58] The eldest one and the middle one were fancy dressers, but the youngest one cared only about keeping house.

The father got ready to go to town and he asked his daughters what he should buy for each of them.

The eldest asked, "Buy me a dress!"

And the middle one said the same thing.

"And what for you, my beloved daughter?" he asked the youngest.

"Buy me a feather of Finist the bright falcon, Father."

The father said good-bye to them and left for the city. He bought material for dresses for the older daughters, but he couldn't find a feather of Finist the bright falcon anywhere.

He returned home and made the eldest and middle daughter glad with the new clothes. "But I didn't find a feather of Finist the bright falcon for you," he said to the youngest.

"So be it," she said. "Perhaps another time you'll have the good fortune to find it."

The older sisters cut and sewed new dresses for themselves. They laughed at her, but she knew how to keep her peace.

Once again as the father was getting ready to go to the city he asked, "Well, daughters, what should I buy you?"

The eldest and the middle one asked for kerchiefs, but the younger one said, "Buy me a feather of Finist the bright falcon, Father."

The father went to the city and bought two kerchiefs, but he didn't see any feathers. He returned home and said, "Ah, daughter! You know, I didn't find a feather of Finist the bright falcon this time either!"

"It's nothing, Father. Perhaps next time you'll have better luck."

The father was getting ready to go to the city a third time and he asked, "Tell me, daughters, what should I buy you?"

The older ones said, "Buy us earrings."

But the youngest kept on with her "Buy me a feather of Finist the bright falcon."

The father bought the golden earrings and hurried off to search for the feather, but no one had even heard of it. He was sad and left the city. No sooner had he gone through the gates, when an old man came toward him carrying a little box. "What do you have there, old man?"

"A feather of Finist, the bright falcon."

"What are you asking for it?"

"Give me a thousand."

The father paid the money and galloped home with the little box. His daughters met him. "Well, my dear daughter," he said to the youngest, "at last I've bought you a present. Here, take it!"

The youngest daughter almost jumped for joy, took the little box, began to kiss and caress it, and pressed it tightly to her heart.

After dinner they all parted to go sleep in their own rooms. She too went into her bedroom. She opened the little box, and the feather of Finist the bright falcon flew out at once, struck against the floor, and a handsome prince appeared before her. They exchanged words that were sweet and good.

The sisters heard and asked, "Who's that you're talking with, sister?"

"Just with myself," answered the fair maiden.

"Well then, open up!"

The prince struck the floor and turned into a feather. She picked it up, put the feather in the little box, and opened the door. Her sisters looked this way and peered that way—no one was there!

No sooner had they left than the fair maiden opened the window, took out the feather, and said, "Fly away, my feather, into the open field; stroll around there until the time comes!" The feather turned into a bright falcon and flew away into the open field.

The next night, too, Finist the bright falcon came flying to his maiden. They began to have merry conversations.

The sisters overheard and ran to their father. "Father! Someone is visiting our sister at night. Even now he's sitting and talking with her."

The father got up and went to see his youngest daughter, but when he went into her chamber the prince had long ago turned into a feather and was lying in the little box. "You naughty girls!" the father laid into the older daughters. "Why are you telling false tales about her? Better keep an eye on yourselves!"

The next day the sisters turned to cunning. In the evening, when it was completely dark in the yard, they put up a ladder, gathered many sharp knives and needles, and fastened them outside the window of the fair maiden.

At night Finist the bright falcon came flying, and he struggled and struggled. He couldn't get into the room; he only cut his wings all over. "Farewell, fair maiden!" he said. "If you wish to search for me, then seek me over thrice-nine lands, in the thrice-tenth kingdom. You'll wear out three pairs of iron shoes, break three iron staffs, and gnaw through three stone loaves before you find me, the fine young man!" But the maiden kept on sleeping. Even though she heard these unwelcoming words through her dream, she couldn't wake or get up.

In the morning she woke up and looked. Knives and needles were fastened to her window, and blood kept dripping from them. She threw up her hands. "Oh, my God! That means my sisters have wounded my dear friend!"

That very hour she got ready and left the house. She ran to the smithy and had them forge her three pairs of iron shoes and three iron staffs. She packed away three stone loaves and set off on her way to find Finist the bright falcon.

She walked and walked, wore out one pair of shoes, broke an iron staff, and gnawed through a stone loaf. She came to a little house and knocked. "Master and mistress of the house! Shelter me from the dark night."

An old woman answered, "Welcome, fair maiden! Where are you going, my dove?"

"Ah, granny! I'm looking for Finist the bright falcon."[59]

"Well, fair maiden, you'll have a long way to search."

In the morning the old woman said, "Now go see my middle sister, she'll give you good advice. And here's my gift to you: a silver distaff and a golden spindle. If you start to spin fleece, it stretches out into a golden thread." Then she took a ball of thread, rolled it along the path and told the maiden to follow after it. Wherever the ball rolled, she should follow that road!

The maiden thanked the old woman and set off after the ball of thread.

For a long time or a short time, the second pair of iron shoes was worn out, the second staff broken, and one more stone loaf gnawed away. Finally the ball of thread rolled up to a little house. She knocked. "Good hosts! Keep a fair maiden from the dark night!"

"Welcome!" answered an old woman. "Where are you going, fair maiden?"

"I'm looking for Finist the bright falcon, granny."

"You'll have to search a long way!"

In the morning the old woman gave her a silver saucer and a golden egg and sent her along to her eldest sister. She would know where to find Finist the bright falcon!

The fair maiden said good-bye to the old woman and set off on her way. She walked and walked. The third pair of iron shoes was worn out, the third staff broken, and the last stone loaf gnawed away when the ball of thread rolled up to a little house. She knocked. "Good owners! Protect a fair maiden from the dark night!"

Again an old woman came out. "Come in, my dear! Welcome! Where do you come from and where are you going?"

"I'm looking for Finist the bright falcon, granny."

"Oh, it's very, very hard to find him! Now he lives in such and such a city, he's married to the wafer-baker's daughter there."

In the morning the old woman said to the fair maiden, "Here's a present for you: a golden embroidery frame and a needle. You just hold the frame, and the needle will embroider by itself. Well, go with God. Ask the wafer-baker to hire you as a servant."

No sooner said than done. The fair maiden came to the wafer-baker's yard and got herself hired as a worker. Her hands did the work quickly: she stoked the stove, brought the water, and prepared dinner.

The wafer-baker watched and rejoiced. "Thank God!" she said to her daughter. "We have a worker who's both obliging and good. She does everything with no reward!"

But when the fair maiden had finished her domestic tasks around the house, she took the silver distaff and the golden spindle and sat down to spin. She spun, and a thread stretched from the fleece, not a plain thread but pure gold.

The wafer-baker's daughter saw this. "Ah, fair maiden! Won't you sell me your toy?"

"Perhaps I will!"

"And what's the price?"

"Let me spend the night with your husband."

The wafer-baker's daughter agreed. "It's no trouble," she thought. "I can get my husband drunk with a sleeping potion, but that spindle will cover me and my mother with gold!"

But Finist the bright falcon was not at home. The whole day he roamed the skies, and he only returned toward evening. They sat down to dine; the

Baba Yaga and the Black Sunflower, The Raleigh Little Theatre 2007–2008 Season. Ellen Landau, http://tinyurl.com/2f3anmt. Photo by Stuart Wagner.

fair maiden served the food at the table and kept looking at him, but he, the handsome young man, did not recognize her.

The wafer-baker's daughter mixed some sleeping-potion into Finist the bright falcon's drink, put him to bed, and said to the maidservant, "Go in to his bedroom and chase the flies away!"

So the fair maiden chased away the flies, but she herself cried tearfully, "Wake up, wake up, Finist, bright falcon! It's me, the fair maiden—I've come to you. I broke three iron staffs, I wore through three pairs of iron shoes, I gnawed away three stone loaves and kept on searching for you, my dear!"

But Finist slept and didn't hear anything. So the night passed.

The next day the servant took her silver dish and rolled a golden egg from it. She rolled many golden eggs!

The wafer-baker's daughter saw this. "Sell me your toy," she said.

"All right, buy it."

"And what's the price?"

"Let me spend one more night with your husband."

"Very well, I agree!"

But Finist the bright falcon once again spent the whole day roaming the skies and flew home only toward evening. They sat down to dine, the fair maiden served the food and kept looking at him, but it was as if he had never even known her.

Again the wafer-baker's daughter put him to sleep with a potion, tucked him into bed, and sent in the servant to chase the flies away. This time too, no matter how she cried, no matter how the fair maiden tried to wake him, he slept until morning and didn't hear a thing.

On the third day the fair maiden was sitting, holding the golden embroidery frame in her hands, while the needle embroidered by itself, and such marvelous patterns!

The wafer-baker's daughter could not stop watching. "Sell it to me, fair maiden, sell me your toy!" she said.

"All right, buy it!"

"And what's the price?"

"Let me spend a third night with your husband."

"All right, I agree!"

In the evening Finist the bright falcon came flying back. His wife plied him with a sleeping potion, put him to bed, and sent in the servant to chase away the flies.

So the fair maiden chased away the flies, but all the while she cried tearfully. "Wake up, wake up, Finist, bright falcon! I, the fair maiden, have come to you. I broke three iron staffs, I wore out three pairs of iron shoes, I gnawed through three stone loaves—as I kept searching for you, my dear!" But Finist the bright falcon slept soundly, he didn't hear anything.

For a long time she cried, for a long time she tried to wake him. Suddenly the fair maiden's tear fell onto his cheek, and at that very moment he woke up.

"Ah," he said, "something burned me!"

"Finist, bright falcon!" the maiden answered him. "I have come to you. I broke three iron staffs, I wore out three pairs of iron shoes, I gnawed away three stone loaves—I kept looking for you! And for three nights I've been standing here over you, while you go on sleeping—you don't wake up, you don't answer my tears!"

Only then did Finist recognize her, and he was so glad that words can't tell it. They agreed about what to do, and they left the home of the wafer-baker.

In the morning when the wafer-baker's daughter went to get her husband, neither he nor the maidservant was there! She complained to her mother. The wafer-baker ordered horses and raced off to chase them. She drove and drove, and she drove by the three old women's houses, but she didn't catch Finist the bright falcon: even his tracks were long faded!

Finist the bright falcon found himself with his intended beside her parents' house. He struck the damp earth and turned into a feather; the fair maiden took him, hid him inside her blouse, and went to her father. "Ah, my beloved daughter! I thought that you were no longer among the living. Where were you for so long?"

"I went to pray to God."

This happened just around Holy Week. The father and the older daughters were getting ready to go to morning mass. "What is it, my dear daughter?" he asked the youngest. "Get ready and let's go. Today is such a joyous day."

"Father! I don't have anything to wear."

"Put on our fine clothes," said the older sisters.

"Ah, my sisters! Your dresses aren't made to fit me.[60] I'd better stay at home."

The father and two of his daughters left for morning mass. Then the fair maiden pulled out her feather. It struck the ground and turned into a handsome prince. The prince whistled out the window, and all at once fine clothes, and finery, and a golden carriage all appeared. They dressed, got into the carriage, and set off. They went into the church and stood there in front of everyone. The people marveled: such-and-such a prince with his princess has deigned to pay a visit! At the end of the service they went out before everyone else and drove off home. The carriage disappeared, the dresses and finery vanished as if they had never been, and the prince turned into a feather.

The father returned home with his daughters. "Ah, dear sister! You didn't come with us, but in the church there was a handsome prince with an unimaginably beautiful princess."

"It's all right, sisters! You told me, so it's just as if I'd been there myself."

The next day the same thing happened. On the third day, as the prince and princess were getting into the carriage, the father left the church, and with his own eyes he saw the carriage drive up to his house and disappear. The father came home and began to question his youngest daughter. She said, "There's nothing to be done, I have to confess!"

She took out the feather. The feather struck against the floor and turned into the prince. They were married immediately, and it was a rich wedding!

I was at that wedding. I drank wine, it ran down my mustache, but it didn't get into my mouth. They put a cap on my noggin and got their elbows going. They put a basket on me and said, "Now, kiddo, don't you delay, out of the yard with you right away!"

(Afanas'ev, no. 234)

The Firebird

In a certain kingdom, but not in our country, there lived a tsar. This tsar had three sons, Prince Pyotr, Prince Dimitrii, and Prince Ivan. They had an orchard, too. An apple tree grew in that orchard with golden apples on it. Only the tsar began to notice that every night one apple would disappear. A certain amount of time passed, and a lot of the apples were already missing. So he called his sons together and said, "My dearest children! If you love me, then stand guard and catch this thief. If one of you catches this thief, I'll give that one half the kingdom."

On the first night the eldest brother went out. He sat until twelve o'clock, but after twelve he fell asleep. When he woke up in the morning, he looked and saw that one more apple was missing. He went to his father and told him about everything in detail. On the second night the middle brother went out. The very same thing happened with him.

On the third night the youngest brother started to ask to go out, but his father would not agree to let him go. He said, "You're very small," and "Something could frighten you." But the prince begged persuasively to be let out. At last his father agreed and let him go, so he went out to the garden and sat down under the apple tree.

He had been sitting for only a little while when the whole garden was lit up. Prince Ivan saw the Firebird flying. He hid beneath the tree, and the bird flew up and sat on a branch. Just as she was about to peck at an apple, the youngest brother crept up to her and grabbed her by the tail. She tore loose and flew away, but one feather was left in his hand. He wrapped the feather right up in a handkerchief and stayed there until morning.

In the morning he went to his father. His father asked, "What then, my dear son—did you see the thief?"

"I saw it," said Prince Ivan, and then he unwrapped the handkerchief. The feather just lit up the whole room. "Ah, my dear son!" said the tsar. "What kind of bird was it?"

After that the father called the other two sons. "Well, my good children," he said. "We've seen the thief but we haven't caught it. But now I beg you: go out on a journey and find me this Firebird. If one of you finds it, I'll give that one the whole kingdom."

The older two got ready to set out, but the father wouldn't let the youngest go. He started to beg. His father didn't agree for a long time, then finally he agreed, blessed them all, and they all set out on the journey.

They rode for a long or a short time, and they rode up to a pillar. Three roads led away from this pillar, and on the pillar was written: "If you ride to the right, you'll be killed; if you ride to the left, you'll be hungry yourself; if you take the middle road, your horse will be hungry." They thought over who should go which way. The youngest brother went to the right, and the other two took the other roads.

Finally the youngest brother was riding along for a while, and he saw a little house on chicken legs standing by the road; it was turning around by itself. Prince Ivan said, "Little house, little house! Turn your face to me and your back to the woods!" The little house turned its face toward him.

He stepped up into the house. On the stove lay Baba Yaga, bony leg, she had her nose stuck in the ceiling, and she yelled from there, "What is it here that smells of Russian spirit?"

And he shouted at her, "Here! I'll knock you off your seat on the stove, you old she-devil!"

She jumped down off the stove and began to beg him, "Young man, don't beat me. I'll come in handy to you."

He said to her, "Instead of yelling at me, you'd do better to feed me, give me something to drink, and put me to bed."

She began to ask him, "Who are you?"

He said, "I'm Prince Ivan."

Then she fed him, gave him something to drink, and made up a bed for him.

In the morning Prince Ivan woke up, washed, dressed, prayed to God, and asked her, "Do you happen to know where the Firebird is?"

She answered him, "I don't know, but you ride on farther. My middle sister will be there, she'll tell you. And here, take this ball of thread. When you take away the Firebird, they'll chase after you, so you say, 'Little ball, little ball, turn into a mountain!' It'll turn into a mountain, and you'll ride on farther." Then he thanked her and rode on farther to her sister's house.

He rode for a while, and on the road stood a little house on chicken legs, turning around by itself. Prince Ivan said, "Little house, little house! Turn your face toward me, and your back to the woods." The little house turned its face toward him.

He went into the house. On the stove lay a Baba Yaga, the middle sister, bony leg, her nose stuck into the ceiling, and she shouted from there, "What is it here that smells like Russian spirit?"

"Here," he said, "I'll knock you off the stove, you old she-devil!"

She jumped down off the stove, fed Prince Ivan, gave him something to drink, and put him to bed. In the morning he got up and asked the Baba Yaga, "Where's the Firebird?"

She told him, "Ride on farther to my older sister!" Here she gave him a comb. "When you ride off with the Firebird," she said, "they'll chase after you, and you say, 'Little comb, little comb! You turn into an impassible forest!' It'll turn into a forest, and you'll ride away." So he thanked her and rode on to see the oldest sister.

He rode along for a while, and then he saw another little house on chicken legs. "Little house, little house! Turn toward me with your front, but to the woods with your back!"

He went into the house. On the stove lay a Baba Yaga, bony leg, with her nose poked up into the ceiling, and she yelled from there, "What is it here that smells of Russian spirit?"

"Here," he said, "you old she-devil, I'll knock you off the stove!"

She jumped down off the stove, fed Prince Ivan, gave him something to drink, and put him to bed. In the morning Prince Ivan got up, prayed to God, and started asking her about the Firebird.

She gave him a brush and said, "When they chase after you, you say: 'Little brush, little brush, you turn into a fiery river!' And it will turn into a fiery river, and you'll ride farther. And when you come close to such-and-such a kingdom, there'll be a fence, and in that fence there'll be a gate. Behind that gate three cages are hanging. There's a raven in the golden cage, a rook in the silver one, and the Firebird in the copper one. But you keep this in mind: don't take the silver cage, and don't take the golden or the copper ones either, but open the little door, pull out the Firebird, and tie it up inside a handkerchief."

Prince Ivan thanked her and set off on his way.

He rode up to the kingdom and saw a stone wall. There was no way to climb over it and no way to pass through the gates: there were lions standing there. He just took a look and said, "Ah, my horse, my true horse! Jump over the wall and let me get the Firebird!" He rode back a bit, broke into a gallop,

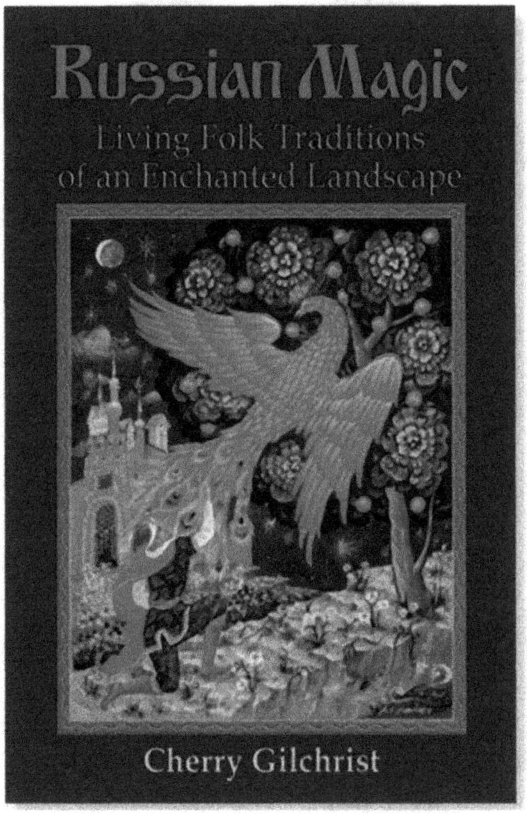

Russian Magic: Living Folk Traditions of an Enchanted Landscape by Cherry Gilchrist. Publisher: Quest Books, 2009.

and jumped over the wall. Then he saw that the Firebird was very big, there was no way to tie it in a handkerchief. He thought a bit and then took the whole copper cage. Suddenly little bells began to jingle, and the lions started to roar. Then he was afraid they would catch him; he broke into a gallop, jumped over the wall, and galloped on with the Firebird.

He had ridden only a little way when he saw them chasing after him. He took out the ball of thread. "Little ball, little ball, turn into a mountain!" The ball of thread turned into a mountain, and he went on. The army galloped up to the foot of the mountain and saw that the mountain was impassible, so they (the army) turned back, took spades, rode up to the mountain, and dug it up. They went back to chasing after Prince Ivan.

As soon as Prince Ivan saw they were after him, he took the comb and said, "You, little comb, turn into an impassible forest!" It turned into one. The army galloped into the forest and saw that it was an impassible forest. They turned back, got axes, and chopped a road through for themselves. They galloped off again after him.

Prince Ivan saw them chasing him, so he took the brush and said, "Little brush, you turn into a fiery river!" The army galloped up and saw that it was a fiery river. But just past the river Prince Ivan lay down to take a rest. The army found that no matter which of them tried to cross over, they would get scalded right away. There was nothing they could do, so the army headed back. Prince Ivan got his rest and then set off on his way.

He'd been riding for a only a little while when he came up to that very same pillar. A tent was pitched by the pillar, and in that tent sat two fine young men. He walked up to them and saw that it was his brothers. He was very glad at this chance, greeted them, and told them about everything in detail. Then he lay down to rest with them. But the brothers were envious that he, the youngest brother, would bring the Firebird home to their father. "Then we, the older ones, will ride home and without bringing anything." They agreed to throw him into a ditch. They threw him all sleepy into the ditch: there were all kinds of vermin in that ditch, beasts, and you couldn't even see the light of the sun from down there. But when he had nothing to eat and drink, he fed himself on dirt, and he got the idea of digging and climbing upward. As soon as he started to climb, he dug with his hands and climbed higher and higher. Finally he climbed higher and higher and saw from there a ray of sunlight. Then he climbed farther and came out at the top. He rested for a while next to the ditch and then he went on.

As soon as he came close to one city, he saw a crowd of people standing in the city. He went up to the people and asked, "What does this mean—you're standing by the lake?"

They answered him, "We're waiting for a six-headed dragon to come out of there. We're supposed to throw him a maiden, but he's eaten up all our maidens one after the other, so now we have to throw in the tsar's daughter."

But he said to them, "Ah, that makes me so sorry! But show me, where are the tsar and his daughter?" When the tsar and his daughter came out, he went up to them. "I can save your daughter!" he said.

The tsar said, "That's impossible now, because of that dragon!"

But Prince Ivan said again, "I'll save your daughter for you, just order them to bind up three bundles of honeysuckle sticks!"

When they were done binding them, they brought them. Suddenly the dragon came swimming, it whistled and roared in all kinds of voices. The moment it opened its mouth, Prince Ivan cut off two of its heads with one bundle, two more with the second bundle, and two more with the third. He cut off all six heads.

Then the tsar began right away to rejoice, he hurried to kiss him and asked him to visit his palace. All the residents were overjoyed that he had conquered the dragon, and they held a feast right away. And that princess, his daughter, was such a raving beauty that there are few like her in the world. The tsar suggested that Prince Ivan should marry her. They had the wedding. After marrying them, the tsar began to ask Prince Ivan, "What kingdom are you from?"

He answered, "From such-and-such a kingdom, the son of such-and-such a tsar."

The tsar began to suggest, "Wouldn't it be good to go see your father? And if you'd like to go see your father, I'll give you two ravens. Take a seat on those ravens, and once you're on them then say, 'To such-and-such a kingdom,' and they'll take you straight there." So the tsar gave them the ravens. They climbed on them and flew off.

But the two older brothers took the Firebird and brought it straight to their father. Their father was happy to see the Firebird. The day after that the Firebird turned into a crow. They were so surprised, and their father was surprised, too. "What could something like this mean?"

However, their father hung the crow up in his room. It hung there looking just like a crow. When Prince Ivan began flying closer to his father's palace, then it suddenly turned from a crow back into the Firebird. The father was very surprised to see that it had suddenly turned from a crow back into the Firebird. Then he saw two ravens flying, and a man and a young woman riding on the ravens. The father was very frightened at this. He thought, "Can they have come after the Firebird, and did she turn from a crow into the Firebird because her own people were coming?"

But suddenly Prince Ivan came in with his spouse, threw himself on his father's neck, and begged forgiveness for marrying without his permission. The father didn't recognize him at all. "Ah, you're my son! Why were you gone for so long? Your brothers came back, they got the Firebird."

"No," he said. "It wasn't my brothers. I was the one who got the Firebird. I rode out with them, they threw me into a deep ditch while I was sleeping, and they took the Firebird away from me." And then he told his father everything in detail.

Then the father made his two older sons herd cattle, and he gave his whole kingdom to the youngest. Then they had a great feast. I was there, I drank wine and beer, it ran down my mustache, but it didn't go into my mouth.[61]

(Khudiakov, no. 1)

The Frog and the Bogatyr

In a certain kingdom, in a certain state there lived a king who had three sons. One day he called his sons to him and said, "Dear children! Now you're of age, it's time for you to think about marriage. Each of you make an arrow, go out into the secluded meadows, and shoot in different directions. Each one's arrow will land by a house, and the one who shot the arrow will find his bride in that house."

Each prince made himself a bow, went out into the secluded meadows, and took his shot. The eldest brother shot to the right, the middle one to the left, and the youngest one, who was called Ivan-*Bogatyr,* let his arrow go straight ahead. After that they went in the different directions to search for their arrows. The big brother found his arrow at a court minister's house, while the middle one found his at a general's house. The princes married their beautiful daughters.

But for a long time Ivan-*Bogatyr* couldn't find his arrow, and he was exceedingly sorrowful. For two whole days he walked through the forests and mountains, but on the third day he went through a swamp and saw a big white frog, holding in its mouth the arrow he had shot. Ivan-*Bogatyr* wanted to run off and get away from what he had found, but the frog cried out, "Kvaa-kvaa, Ivan-*Bogatyr*! Come here and take your arrow, or else you'll be trapped in the swamp forever."

After saying these words, the frog flipped over, and at that very moment a decorated gazebo appeared. Ivan-*Bogatyr* went into the gazebo. "I know you've had nothing to eat for three days," said the frog. "Wouldn't you like something to eat?" Then the frog flipped over again, and all at once a table appeared with all kinds of dishes and drinks. Ivan-*Bogatyr* sat down at the table, ate and drank his fill.

"Listen," the frog told him. "I'm the one who found your arrow, so you have to marry me. And if you don't marry me you'll never get out of this swamp!" Ivan-*Bogatyr* grew sorrowful and didn't know what to do. He thought a bit and took the frog with him back to his own state. The brothers and their brides started to laugh at him.

The day came when Ivan-*Bogatyr* was to get married. He set off in a carriage, but the frog was carried to the palace on a golden saucer. When night came and the bride and groom went into their rooms, the frog took off her frog skin and became a beautiful woman, but by day she turned into a frog. Ivan *Bogatyr* lived with her in good fortune and happiness.

After a certain time the king ordered his sons to come to him and said to them, "Dear children! Now all three of you are married. I'd like to wear shirts made by each of your wives, my daughters-in-law." He gave each of them a piece of linen and said that the shirts must be ready by the next day. The elder brothers took the cloth to their wives, and they started to call their nannies, their nurses, and the lovely chambermaids, to help them sew a shirt. Their nannies and their nurses came running right away and got to work. One would cut, while another would sew.

At the same time they sent a scullery maid to see how the frog would sew the shirt. The girl came to Ivan-*Bogatyr*'s rooms as he brought in the cloth and put it on the table with a sorrowful look.

"Why are you so sad, Ivan-*Bogatyr?*" asked the frog.

And he answered her, "How can I help being sad? My father has ordered that a shirt be sewn for him from this cloth by tomorrow."

"Don't cry, don't grieve," said the frog. "Lie down and go to sleep; morning's wiser than the evening. Everything will be done properly!" She grabbed the scissors, cut all the cloth up into tiny scraps, then opened the window, threw them into the wind and said, "Wild winds! Take away these scraps and sew my father-in-law a shirt." The scullery maid went and told the princesses that the frog had cut all the cloth into little pieces and thrown them out the window. They laughed at the frog and said, "And what will her husband bring the king tomorrow!"

The next day Ivan-*Bogatyr* woke up, and the frog gave him a shirt. "Here, my dear Ivan-*Bogatyr*! Take this shirt to your father."

Ivan-*Bogatyr* took the shirt and brought it to his father. The older brothers brought their shirts, too. The first to present his shirt was the big brother. The king took a look and said, "This shirt is sewn the way people usually sew." He looked at the second son's shirt and said that shirt was sewn no better. But when his youngest son handed him the shirt, the king could not marvel enough. You couldn't see a single stitch in the shirt, and he said, "Bring me this shirt for the greatest holidays."

The king called his sons a second time and said to them, "My dear children! I want to know whether your wives know how to sew with gold and silver. Take some silk, some gold and silver thread, and let each of you have a carpet ready by tomorrow."

The wives of the elder brothers began to call nannies, nurses, and lovely chambermaids to help them embroider the carpets. Right away the nannies, nurses, and lovely chambermaids came and began to embroider the carpets, one with silver, one with gold, and another with silk. They sent the scullery maid again to take a look at what the frog would do.

Ivan-*Bogatyr* brought the gold, silver, and silk to his rooms and was most sorrowful. The frog, sitting on a chair, said, "Kvaa-kvaa-kvaa! Why are you sorrowing so, Ivan-*Bogatyr?*"

"How could I help being sorrowful?" he answered. "Father has ordered that a carpet be embroidered with this silver, gold, and silk by tomorrow."

"Do not weep and do not grieve," said the frog. "Lie down to sleep. Morning's wiser than the evening!" She herself took the scissors, cut up all the silk, tore up the silver and gold, threw it all out the window, and said, "Wild winds! Bring that carpet my father used to cover the windows." The daughters-in-law, hearing all that from the scullery maid, got the idea of doing the same thing themselves. They waited for a long time, but once they saw that the winds were not bringing them any carpets, they sent out to buy gold, silver, and silk and began embroidering carpets the way they had been doing it before.

In the morning, as soon as Ivan-*Bogatyr* got up, the frog gave him the carpet. So all three brothers brought their carpets to their father. He took the carpet first from the eldest, looked at it, and said, "This carpet would do to cover a horse from the rain." He took a look at the middle son's and said, "This carpet could be put in the entryway, for people to wipe their feet on." Then he took the carpet from the youngest son, marveled at it, and said, "But this carpet may be spread on my table on the most festive days." The king ordered that Ivan-*Bogatyr*'s carpet be put away and carefully kept, but he gave the carpets back to the other sons. "Take them to your wives," said the king, "and tell them to keep them for themselves."

For a third time the king spoke to his sons. "Now, my dear children, I want to have a loaf of bread made by your wives' hands." When the princesses heard this from their husbands, they immediately sent the scullery maid to see what the frog would do. Just then, Ivan-*Bogatyr* came into his rooms most sorrowful.

"Kvaa-kvaa-kvaa! Why are you sorrowing?" the frog asked him.

Baba Yaga paper hut.

"How could I not be sorrowful? Father has ordered you to bake a loaf of bread."

"Don't weep, don't grieve, everything is done!" and she ordered yeast, flour, and water brought. She poured the flour into the yeast, poured in the water, opened the oven door, poured it into the cold stove, closed the oven door, and said, "Bake, bread, clean, delicate, and white as snow!"

The scullery maid went back to the daughters-in-law and said, "I don't know why the king keeps praising the frog. It doesn't know how to do anything!"

Once they heard all this, the daughters-in-law thought they would do the same thing as the frog. They dissolved the flour in cold water and poured it into cold stoves. But, seeing that their mixtures had poured flat, they ordered still more flour, mixed their dough with warm water, and put it into heated stoves. They were afraid they wouldn't finish in time and they hurried, so one's bread burned, while the other's came out half-baked. The frog pulled her bread out of the stove, and it was clean and delicate, white as snow.

The brothers went to their father and brought their loaves. The king took the loaf from his big son, took a look, and said, "You'd eat that kind of bread only in great poverty!" He took the middle son's loaf and said, "This bread is no better!" Then he took the bread from the youngest son and ordered that this bread be served at his table when he had guests. "My dear children!" the king continued. "Your wives have done everything for me that I ordered, and therefore I ask you and your wives to come to the palace tomorrow for dinner." The princes went back to their wives.

Ivan-*Bogatyr* was greatly sorrowed, and he thought, "How will I take a frog with me?"

But the frog, sitting in a chair, asked, "Kvaa-kvaa-kvaa! Ivan-*Bogatyr*, what are you so sorrowful about?"

Ivan-*Bogatyr* answered, "How could I help being sorrowful? Father has ordered us all to come to his palace tomorrow and bring their wives. But how can I bring you?"

"Do not weep, do not grieve," said the frog. "Morning's wiser than the evening. Lie down and sleep!"

The next day Ivan-*Bogatyr* got ready and went to the palace, but the daughters-in-law sent the scullery maid again to watch. What would the frog be traveling in? Just then the frog opened the window and called out in a loud voice. "Ah, you wild winds! Fly to my country and tell them to send a rich carriage, with the whole set, with lackeys, with haiduks,[62] with heralds and with horsemen." After that she slammed her window shut and sat down on the chair.

Everyone had already ridden to the palace; they were only waiting for the frog. Suddenly they saw footmen running, horsemen galloping, and up drove an extremely rich carriage. The king thought some other king or queen must be coming to visit him, and he went out to meet them. "Don't trouble yourself, Father!" said Ivan-*Bogatyr*. "That just means my froggie's dragging along in a box."

The carriage drove up, and Ivan-*Bogatyr*'s wife got out, such a beauty that everyone began to marvel. They sat at the table. Whatever the frog didn't finish drinking, she poured into her sleeve, and she put the bones in her other sleeve. The other daughters-in-law saw and started to do the same thing. Whatever they didn't finish drinking, they would pour into one sleeve, and whatever they didn't finish eating they put into the other. When they got up from the table, music began to play, and the frog went to dance. She waved one sleeve, and suddenly water stood one *arshin* high,[63] she waved the other sleeve, and geese and swans sailed off across the water. When they saw this, no one could marvel enough at her cunning. But when she stopped dancing, it all disappeared—the water, the geese, and the swans.

Then the other daughters-in-law went to dance, and when they waved their sleeves they slopped and sprayed on everyone and almost knocked people's eyes out with the bones!

Just then Ivan-*Bogatyr* headed home, took the frog's skin, and burned it right away. His wife came home and ran to find her frog skin. She couldn't find it, and she said, "Well, Ivan-*Bogatyr*! Since you couldn't wait for even a little time, then search for me over thrice-nine lands, in the thrice-tenth kingdom, in the sunflower kingdom, and know that I am called Vasilisa the Wise." She said this, and then she suddenly disappeared.

Ivan-*Bogatyr* began to cry inconsolably and set off to search for Vasilisa the Wise. He walked for a long time or a short time, near or far—quickly may a tale be spun, but not so fast a deed is done!—and he came to a little house that stood on chicken legs and spun around by itself. Ivan-*Bogatyr* said, "Little house, little house! Stand with your back to the woods, your front to me!" And at his words the little house stopped.

Ivan-*Bogatyr* went into the house and saw a Baba Yaga sitting in the front corner. She spoke up in an angry voice. "Until now the Russian spirit was unheard by the hearing and unseen by the sight, but nowadays the Russian spirit appears before my eyes! What are you doing, Ivan-*Bogatyr*? By free will or by compulsion?"

Ivan-*Bogatyr* answered that it was this much by free will, but twice as much by compulsion, and he told her everything that had happened.

"I'm sorry for you," said the Baba Yaga. "Be my guest, I'll do you a good turn, I'll show you Vasilisa the Wise. She comes flying to see me every day to take a rest. When she comes flying, you try to catch her by the head. When you catch her she'll start to turn into a frog, a toad, a snake, and other kinds of unclean creatures, and last of all she'll turn into an arrow. You take that arrow and break it in two, and she'll be yours forever. Just take care: once you catch your wife don't let her go!"

Then Baba Yaga hid the prince, and hardly had she managed to hide him when Vasilisa the Wise came flying. Ivan-*Bogatyr* went over to her softly and grabbed her by the head. She began to turn into a frog, a toad, and finally a snake. Ivan-Bogatyr was frightened and loosened his grip. That very moment Vasilisa the Wise disappeared.

Baba Yaga said to him, "If you couldn't hold her, you'll never see her here again. But if you wish, go see my sister. Vasilisa the Wise goes to visit her, too, to rest." Ivan-*Bogatyr* set off to see the second Baba Yaga, and there too he couldn't keep hold of Vasilisa the Wise. He went to see the third Baba Yaga sister.

"If you let Vasilisa the Wise go this time, then you'll never find her again," she said. This time, no matter what Vasilisa the Wise turned into, Ivan-*Bogatyr* didn't let her out of his hands. Finally she turned into an arrow. Ivan-*Bogatyr* took the arrow and broke it in two. That very moment Vasilisa the Wise appeared before him and said, "Well, Ivan-*Bogatyr*, now I give myself to your will!"

The Baba Yaga gave them a flying carpet, and they flew off on the flying carpet to their own state. Three days passed, and on the fourth the carpet landed right in the palace. The king met his son and daughter-in-law with great joy, held a great feast, and afterward made Ivan-*Bogatyr* king after him.[64]

(Afanas'ev, appendix 8 to tales no. 267–69)

The Frog Princess

In a certain kingdom, in a certain state there lived a tsar with his tsaritsa. He had three sons, all young and unmarried, such brave men that it's not possible to tell it in a tale or write it with a pen. The youngest one was called Prince Ivan.

One day the tsar said to them, "My dear children, each of you take an arrow, draw your bows tight, and shoot in different directions. Wherever your arrow falls, go to that household to find a bride."

The eldest brother shot his arrow, and it fell in the yard of a boyar, just outside the maidens' chambers.[65] The middle son shot; his arrow flew into a merchant's yard and landed by the main porch, and on that porch stood a fair maiden, the merchant's daughter. The youngest son shot, and the arrow landed in a muddy swamp, where a croaking frog picked it up.

Prince Ivan said, "How can I take a croaker for a wife? A croaking frog's not a match for me!"

"Marry her," the tsar answered him. "It means that this is your fate."

So the princes were married: the eldest to the boyar's daughter, the middle one to the merchant's daughter, and Prince Ivan to the croaking frog.

The tsar called them together and ordered, "Let each of your wives bake me a loaf of soft white bread by tomorrow."

Prince Ivan returned to his chambers, sorrowful, with his wild head hanging lower than his shoulders.

"Kvaa-kvaa, Prince Ivan! Why have you grown so sad?" the frog asked him. "Or have you heard an unkind word from your father?"

"How can I not be sad? The lord my father orders you to prepare a loaf of soft white bread by tomorrow."

"Don't grieve, prince! Go to sleep and rest; morning is wiser than the evening!" She put the prince to bed and threw off her frog skin, and she turned into a fair maiden, Vasilisa the Wise. She went out on the main porch and called in a loud voice, "Nurses and nannies! Gather here, get ready, and make a soft, white loaf of bread, like the ones I ate and tasted in my own father's house."

In the morning, when Prince Ivan woke up, the frog had the bread long ready, and it was so wonderful that you couldn't imagine it or guess, but only tell of it in a tale! The bread was decorated with all kinds of clever designs; on the sides you could see the tsar's cities with banners.

The tsar thanked Prince Ivan for the bread and right away gave another order to his three sons: "Let each of your wives weave me a carpet in a single night."

Prince Ivan came back, sorrowful, with his wild head hanging lower than his shoulders.

"Kvaa-kvaa, Prince Ivan! Why have you grown so sad? Or have you heard a harsh word, an unkind word from your father?"

"How can I help but be sad? The lord my father has ordered that you must weave him a silken carpet in a single night."

"Don't grieve, Prince! Lie down to sleep and rest. Morning's wiser than the evening!" She put him to bed, but she threw off her frog skin and turned into a fair maiden, Vasilisa the Wise. She went out on the main porch and cried in a loud voice, "Nurses and nannies! Gather here, prepare yourselves to weave a silken carpet—let it be like the one I sat on in my own father's house!"

No sooner said than done. In the morning Prince Ivan awoke, and the frog had her carpet long finished. It was so marvelous that you couldn't imagine it or guess at it, but perhaps only tell of it in a tale. The carpet was decorated with silver and gold, with clever patterns.

The tsar thanked Prince Ivan for the carpet and right away gave a new order: all three princes should come to visit him for inspection, together with their wives. Again Prince Ivan came back home sorrowful, with his wild head hanging lower than his shoulders.

"Kvaa-kvaa, Prince Ivan! Why are you grieving? Or have you heard an unwelcoming word from your father?"

"How can I help but be sad? The lord my father demands that I bring you to an inspection. But how can I show you to people!?"

"Don't grieve, prince! Go by yourself to visit your father, and I'll come along after you. When you hear knocking and thunder, just say: that's my froggie riding in a little box."

So the older brothers went to their father for inspection with their wives, all dressed up and decked out. They stood there and laughed at Prince Ivan. "Why did you come without your wife, brother? You could at

Baba Yaga as the queen of hearts (ironically, though she does aid loving couples) appears on the face of a post-Soviet pack of cards, designed by Palekh artist Aleksei Orleanskii in the 1990s. The ace of hearts depicts her hut on chicken legs, with skulls (and mushrooms—never mentioned in Russian fairy tales), whereas the back of the box shows the hut as a four-suit image. The face cards were later reproduced by Orleanskii in the form of postcards. The deck in its entirety showcases Russian lower mythology—leshii (forest spirit; king of hearts), *rusalka* (mermaid; queen of clubs), Koshchei the Deathless (king of spades), and so forth.

least have brought her in a handkerchief! And where did you find such a beauty? You must've searched through all the swamps!"

Suddenly there was a great knocking and thunder—the whole palace started to shake. The guests were mighty scared; they jumped up from their places and didn't know what to do.

But Prince Ivan said, "Don't fear, ladies and gentlemen! It's my froggie, riding in a little box."

A gilded carriage drawn by six horses flew up to the tsar's porch, and Vasilisa the Wise stepped out of it. Well, you can't imagine or guess what a beauty she was, but only tell of it in a tale! She took Prince Ivan by the hand and led him to the oak tables, to the laden tablecloths.

The guests began to eat and drink, to make merry. Vasilisa the Wise drank from her glass and poured the last drops into her left sleeve. She ate some swan and hid the little bones in her right sleeve. The wives of the older brothers saw her tricks and started doing the same things themselves.

Later, when Vasilisa the Wise went to dance with Prince Ivan, she waved her left sleeve and a lake appeared, waved her right sleeve and white swans swam across the water. The tsar and his guests were astounded.

But when the older daughters-in-law went to dance, they waved their left sleeves and spattered the guests. They waved their right sleeves and a bone flew right into the tsar's eye! The tsar got angry and sent them away without honor.

Meanwhile, Prince Ivan chose a good moment, ran home, found the frog skin, and burned it in a great fire.

When Vasilisa the Wise returned, she took a look, but her frog skin wasn't anywhere. She grew dejected and sad, and she said to the prince, "Oh, Prince Ivan! What have you done? If you had waited just a little bit longer I would have been yours forever; but now farewell! Seek me beyond thrice-nine lands, in the thrice-tenth kingdom, with Koshchei the Deathless." She turned into a white swan[66] and flew out the window.

Prince Ivan started crying bitterly, prayed to God in all four directions and set out—heading wherever his eyes looked.

He walked quickly or slowly, for a long time or a short time, and he came upon an old, old man. "Hello, you fine young lad!" he said. "What do you seek and where are you going?"

The prince told him about his misfortune.

"Eh, Prince Ivan! Why did you burn the frog skin? You weren't the one who put it on her, so it wasn't your place to take it off! Vasilisa the Wise was born craftier and more clever than her father. He got angry with her for that and turned her into a croaker for three years. Here's a ball of thread for you, follow it bravely wherever it rolls."

Prince Ivan thanked the old man and set off after the ball of thread. He was walking through an open field when he met a bear. "Here, let me kill this beast!" he said.

But the bear spoke to him, "Don't strike me, Prince Ivan! Some day I'll be of use to you."

He went on and saw a drake flying over him. The prince aimed his rifle and was ready to shoot the bird, when suddenly it spoke to him in a human voice. "Don't shoot me, Prince Ivan! I'll be of use to you some day."

He took pity on it and went on. A crooked hare ran by. The prince took his rifle again and began to aim, but the hare spoke to him in a human voice. "Don't shoot me, Prince Ivan! I'll come in handy to you some day."

Prince Ivan took pity on him and went along farther, up to the blue sea,[67] and he saw a pike-fish lying on the sand, unable to breathe. "Ah, Prince Ivan," the fish spoke up. "Take pity on me, let me back into the sea." He threw the fish into the sea and set off along the shore.

After a long time or a short time, the ball of thread rolled up to a little house. The little house stood on chicken legs and spun around. Prince Ivan said, "Little house, little house! Stand in the old way, as your mother set you—with your face to me, your back to the sea."

The little house turned its back to the sea and its front to him. The prince went into the house and saw on the stove, on the ninth brick shelf, a Baba Yaga, bony leg, nose grown into the ceiling, her snot hanging across the threshold, her tits slung up on a hook, and she was sharpening her teeth.[68] "Hail, good young man! Why have you come to see me?" the Baba Yaga asked Prince Ivan.

"Ah, you old hag! You'd do better to feed me first, give me a drink, and steam me in the bathhouse, fine young man that I am, and then you could ask questions."

Baba Yaga fed him, gave him a drink, and steamed him in the bathhouse.

The prince told her he was looking for his wife, Vasilisa the Wise.

"Ah, I know!" said the Baba Yaga. "Now she's with Koshchei the Deathless. It's hard to get to her, and not easy to handle Koshchei. His death is on the tip of a needle, that needle's in an egg. The egg's inside a duck, the duck's inside a hare, the hare's in a trunk, and the trunk's at the top of a tall oak tree, and Koshchei cares for that tree like the apple of his eye."

Yaga pointed out the place where the oak tree grew. Prince Ivan went there and didn't know what to do: how could he get the trunk down? Suddenly, out of nowhere, a bear ran up and tore the tree up by the roots; the trunk fell down and broke into little pieces. A hare dashed out of the trunk and ran off at full speed. Before he could take a second look, another hare ran after it, caught up with it, seized it, and tore it into little pieces. A duck flew up out of the hare and rose high into the sky. As she flew, the drake raced after her. When he hit the duck, she immediately dropped an egg, and the egg fell into the sea. Prince Ivan, seeing inevitable disaster, dissolved in tears. Suddenly the pike-fish swam to the shore, holding the egg in its teeth.

Prince Ivan took the egg, broke it, got the needle out, and snapped off its tip. No matter how Koshchei struggled, no matter how he thrashed here and there, still the time had come for him to die![69]

Prince Ivan went to Koshchei's house, took Vasilisa the Wise and returned home. After that they lived together long and happily.

(Afanas'ev, no. 269)

The Geese and Swans

There once lived an old man and an old woman. They had a daughter and a baby son. "Daughter, daughter!" said her mother. "We're going to work. We'll bring you a bread-roll, we'll sew you a dress and buy you a handkerchief. Be good, take care of your little brother, and don't go out of the yard."

The parents left, but the daughter forgot what they had told her. She set her brother down on the grass under the window, and she herself ran out onto the street and lost track of the time, playing and running around. The geese and swans flew over, grabbed the boy, and flew away with him.

The girl came back and looked, and her brother wasn't there! She gasped and ran here and there, but he wasn't anywhere! She called, she sobbed, she lamented—she was going to be in trouble with her father and mother—but her brother didn't answer! She ran out into the empty field. She caught sight of the geese and swans far away, and then they disappeared beyond the dark forest. These geese and swans had had a bad reputation for a long time; they did a lot of harm and would steal little children. The girl guessed that they were the ones who had taken away her brother, and she ran off after them.

She ran and ran and saw a stove standing there. "Stove, stove! Tell me, where did the geese fly?"

"Eat my rye pastry, and I'll tell you."

"Oh, in my dad's house we don't even eat wheat ones!"

The stove wouldn't tell her. She ran farther and saw an apple tree standing there. "Apple tree, apple tree! Tell me where the geese flew?"

"Eat some of my wild apple, and I'll tell you."

"Oh, in my dad's house we don't even eat orchard apples!"

She ran farther, and there was a river of milk, with banks of custard. "Milk river, custard banks! Where did the geese fly?"

"Eat some of my simple custard with milk, and I'll tell you."

"Oh, at my dad's we don't even eat cream!"

Baba Yaga / Geese and Swans, by Katherine Bykova. A lacquer box illustrating Geese and Swans by the young Palekh artist Katherine Bykova, who also produces art for children. The owl and the flying bats in the background betray a Western influence, for they are not part of the Russian folkloric tradition. Artist: Katherine Bykova, from the village of Palekh, http://www.russianlacquerart.com/gallery/Mstera/0000/001000.

And she would have run through the fields and wandered in the forest for a long time, but fortunately she ran into a hedgehog. She wanted to give him a poke, but she was afraid of pricking herself, so she asked, "Hedgehog, hedgehog, did you happen to see where the geese flew?"

"Right that way," he showed her.

She ran off, and there stood a little house on chicken legs: it stood there and turned around. Inside the house sat a Baba Yaga, sinewy snout, leg made of clay. She was sitting there, and the little brother was on a bench playing with golden apples. The sister saw him, stole up, grabbed him, and

A lacquer box titled Geese and Swans by Dobrin Evgeny Yurievich, a contemporary Kholui specialist in miniatures. The green-dominated and somewhat eerie image illustrates one of the many sibling plots in Russian fairy tales. As so often, the heroine (Alenushka) rescues her little brother, Ivanushka, who is kidnapped by Baba-Yaga's servants, the geese and swans. Baba Yaga, with her customary mortar and broom, hut, and so forth, plus the owl and walking stick that are a recent innovation, threatens the boy while her obedient geese soar overhead. Artist: Dobrin Evgeny Yurievich, from the village of Kholuy, http://tinyurl.com/bqtdfvk.

carried him away. But the geese flew after them and chased her. The villains were about to catch her; where could she hide?

The milk river was flowing by, with its banks of custard. "Mother river, hide me!"

"Eat some of my custard!"

The girl had no choice, so she ate it. The river set her down under its bank, and the geese flew past.

She came out and said, "Thank you!"

Again she went running with her little brother, but the geese had turned around and were flying toward her. What could she do? Oh no! There stood the apple tree. "Apple tree, mother apple tree! Hide me!"

"Eat my sour apple!" She ate it on the double. The apple tree shielded her with its branches, covered her with its leaves, and the geese flew by.

She came out and ran again with her brother, but the geese saw them and took off after her. They were ever so close, already hitting her with their wings—just look, any second they would pull him out of her arms! Fortunately, the stove was just ahead of her. "My lady stove, hide me!"

"Eat my rye pastry!"

The girl popped the pastry right into her mouth, and she herself jumped into the stove and sat down in its mouth. The geese flew and flew, called and called, and flew away with nothing. But the girl ran home, and it's a good thing she managed to run home, because her father and mother had just come back.

(Afanas'ev, no. 113)

The Stepdaughter and the Stepmother's Daughter

There lived an old man and an old woman. They had only one daughter. The old woman died, and the old man married another woman. He had a daughter with the second wife as well. The old woman didn't like her stepdaughter and was always trying to hurt her. Once the old woman sent her to the river to wash thread and told her, "Watch out! If you let the threads sink to the bottom, then don't bother coming home!"

The girl went to the river and laid the thread on the water. The thread floated along the river, and she walked slowly along the bank after it. The thread floated all the way to the forest and sank.

She went into the forest and saw a little house on chicken legs. She said, "Little house, little house! Stand with your back to the woods, your front to me!" The little house obeyed.

The stepdaughter went into it and saw a Yaga-Baba. Her head lay in one corner of the house, her feet in another. The Baba Yaga saw her and said, "Fie, fie, fie! I can smell a Russian soul. What are you up to, girl, doing a deed or fleeing a deed?"

The girl told her that her mother had sent her to wash thread and said that if she let it sink, she shouldn't come home.

Baba Yaga made her heat up the bathhouse. The girl asked the Yaga-Baba, "Where's your firewood?"

And the Yaga-Baba answered, "My firewood is behind the bathhouse!" But the fuel stacked there was really human bones.

The girl went to heat up the bathhouse, hauled in lots of bones, and put them in the stove, but no matter how she tried she couldn't make them catch fire. The bones only smoldered. Then she sat on the ground and cried, and she saw a sparrow come flying up to her. The sparrow said, "Don't cry, girl! Go into the woods, gather firewood there, and use it to stoke the stove!"

The Feather of Finist the Falcon by Ivan Bilibin, 1900. Illustration by Ivan Bilibin (1876–1942).

The girl did just that. Then she went and told the Yaga-Baba that the bathhouse was heated. But the Yaga-Baba said, "Now go and bring water in a sieve!"

She went and thought, "How am I going to bring water in a sieve?"

The sparrow flew up again and said to her, "Why are you crying? Smear the sieve with clay!"

The girl did just that. She brought plenty of water and went to call the Yaga-Baba to the bathhouse, but the Yaga-Baba answered, "You go to the bathhouse! I'll send you my children now!" The girl went into the bathhouse.

Suddenly she saw worms, frogs, rats, and all sorts of insects come crawling up to her in the bathhouse. She washed all of them and gave them a good steaming. Then she went to get Baba Yaga and washed her, too. Then she washed herself. She came out of the bathhouse, and the Yaga-Baba told her to heat up the samovar. She did, and they drank tea.

Baba Yaga sent her into the cellar, too.

"There are two trunks in my cellar," she said. "A red one and a blue one. Take the red one for yourself!" So the girl took the red trunk and went home to her father. Her father was glad to see her. He opened the trunk, and the trunk was full of money.

The stepmother started to envy her and sent her own daughter to the Baba Yaga, who told the girl to stoke the bathhouse with bones. The sparrow flew down to her and said, "Go into the woods and gather firewood!"

But she swatted the bird with her hand. "Go away," she said. "I don't need you to tell me that." Yet she herself couldn't get the bathhouse heated. Then the Baba Yaga told her to bring water in a sieve.

The sparrow flew up to her again and said, "You could smear the sieve with clay."

She hit it again. "Go away," she said. "I don't need you to tell me that." But then she saw that rats and frogs and all sorts of vermin were coming into the bathhouse. She squashed half of them, but the others ran home and complained about her to their mother. The stepmother's daughter went back to the Baba Yaga. Baba Yaga told her to heat up the samovar, and she did. After tea Baba Yaga sent her to the cellar and told her to take the blue trunk. The girl was very happy. She ran into the cellar, grabbed the trunk, and ran off home. Her father and mother were waiting for her at the front gate. She and her mother went into the shed and opened the lid of the trunk. But there was fire in it, and it burned them both up.[71]

(Khudiakov, no. 14)[70]

The Tale of the Daring Young Man and the Apples of Youth

Once there lived a tsar with his tsaritsa, and he had three sons. One day he sent out his sons to find the water of youth. So the princes set out on their way. They rode up to a pillar where the road split in three, and on the pillar it said: if you go to the right, the fine young man will be sated, but his horse hungry. If you go to the left, the young man will be hungry, but his horse sated. If you go straight, there's no way you'll stay alive. The eldest prince set off to the right, the middle one to the left, and the youngest went straight ahead.[72] For a long time, for a short time, the youngest brother rode, and he came upon a deep ditch. He didn't think long about how to cross it. He blessed himself, whipped his horse, jumped across to the other side, and saw a little house beside a deep forest—it stood on chicken legs. "Little house, little house! Turn your back to the forest, your front to me."

The little house turned around. The prince went inside, and there sat a Baba Yaga. "Fie, fie!" she said. "Until now there was no sight of the Russian spirit, no sound of it, but now the Russian spirit appears before my eyes, puts itself into my mouth! What is it, good young man, are you fleeing a deed or doing a deed?"

"Ah, you old hag! You shouldn't be talking, and I shouldn't be listening. First bring me something to drink and eat, and then ask me questions." She gave him something to drink and eat, asked for his news, and gave him her winged horse. "Off you go, sir, to see my middle sister."

He rode for a long time or a short time and then saw a little house. He went inside, and there was a Baba Yaga. "Fie, fie!" she said. "Until now the Russian spirit wasn't to be seen by the eyes, wasn't to be heard with the hearing, but now the Russian spirit appears before my eyes, puts itself into my mouth! What is it, young man, are you doing a deed or fleeing a deed?"

"Eh, auntie! Give me something to drink and eat, and then ask me questions."

A Baba Yaga matryoshka. The matryoshka, otherwise known as a stacking doll, pioneered in the 1890s during Russia's concerted push to create a traditional national identity through folk culture, symbolized the country's robust fecundity (matryoshka/mater/mother), reified in the womblike construction of the item. For decades the matryoshka functioned as tourists' favorite memento and empirical proof of their visit to Russia. One of many Baba Yaga matryoshkas, this set comprises her pear-shaped figure, the hut, the egg, and an ambiguous-looking "needle."

She gave him something to drink and eat and started to ask, "What fates have brought you to these distant lands?"

"My father sent me to search for the water of youth."

"Well, take my best horse for a change and go see my oldest sister."

The prince set off on his road without delay. For a long time or for a short time he rode, and again he saw a little house on chicken legs. "Little house, little house! Stand with your front to me, your back to the forest."

The little house turned around. He went in, and there sat a Baba Yaga. "Fie, fie! Until now the Russian spirit wasn't to be seen or heard, but now the Russian spirit appears before my eyes, puts itself into my mouth! Well, young man, are you doing a deed or fleeing a deed?"

"Eh, you old hag! You haven't fed me, haven't given me anything to drink, but you're asking for news."

The Baba Yaga gave him food, gave him something to drink, asked him for his news, and gave him a horse better than the first two. "Go with God! There's a kingdom not far away. Don't you ride in at the gates. There are lions on guard at the gates,[73] but give my horse a good lashing and jump right over the fence. Watch out, don't snag on the strings. If you do, the whole kingdom will rise up, and then you won't remain alive! And once you jump over the fence, open the door softly, and you'll see the Tsar-Maiden sleeping.

She has a vial with the water of youth hidden under her pillow. You take the vial and hurry back. Don't look too long upon her beauty."

The prince did everything as the Baba Yaga had told him. There was only one thing he could not resist—he looked too long at the maiden's beauty . . . He mounted the horse, and the horse's legs were shaky. He went to jump over the fence, and he hit one of the strings. In a moment the whole kingdom awoke; the Tsar-Maiden got up and ordered her horse saddled. But the Baba Yaga already knew what was happening to the young man, and she was preparing for the response. She barely had time to let the prince come in, when the Tsar-Maiden flew up and found the Baba Yaga all disheveled.

The Tsar-Maiden said to her, "How dare you allow such a rascal into my kingdom? He lay with me, he drank some kvass and didn't cover up the pitcher."

"My lady, Tsar-Maiden! You must see how my hair is messed up. I fought with him for a long time, but I couldn't overcome him." The other two Baba Yagas said the same thing.

The Tsar-Maiden raced off in pursuit of the prince and was just about to grab him when he leapt over the ditch. The Tsar-Maiden called after him, "Wait for me in three years' time. I'll come on a ship."

The prince was so happy that he didn't notice he had come back to the pillar and turned to the left. He came to a silver mountain, where a tent was pitched. Beside the tent stood a horse, eating bright white wheat and drinking honeyed ale, and in the tent lay a fine young man—his very own brother. The younger prince said to him, "Let's go and find our older brother."

They saddled their horses and rode off to the right. They rode up to a golden mountain, where a tent was pitched. Beside the tent a horse was eating bright white wheat, drinking honeyed ale; inside the tent lay a fine young man—their older brother. They woke him up and set off all together toward the pillar where the three roads came together. They sat down there to rest. The two older brothers began to question the younger one: "Did you find the water of youth for our father?"

"I found it."

"How and where?"

He told them everything that had happened, then lay down on the grass and fell asleep. The brothers cut him up into tiny pieces and threw them all around the empty field. They took the vial with the water of youth with them and set off back to their father's palace.

Suddenly a firebird flew up, collected all the scattered pieces, and put them together, the way a person is supposed to be. Then she brought dead

The Red Horseman or **The Sunrise Horseman** by Forest Rogers. http://www.forestrogers.com/.

water in her mouth, sprinkled it, and all the pieces grew together. She brought living water, sprinkled it, and the prince came back to life, stood up, and said, "I was asleep for such a long time!"

The firebird answered, "You would have slept forever without waking, if not for me!"

The prince thanked the bird and set off for home. His father felt no love for him and refused to have him within his sight, so for three whole years he wandered around in various corners.

But once three years had passed, the Tsar-Maiden came sailing on a ship and sent the tsar a letter, asking him to send out the guilty man. If he resisted, she would burn and slash his whole kingdom to the ground. The tsar sent out his oldest son, and he went to the ship. Two little boys, the Tsar-Maiden's sons, saw him and asked their mother, "Isn't this our father?"

"No, that's your uncle."

"Then how should we welcome him?"

"Each of you take a whip and send that one back."

The older brother went back home, looking as if he had tasted something unsalted! But the Tsar-Maiden made the same threats and demanded that the tsar hand over the guilty party. The tsar sent out his second son, and the same thing happened to him as to the first one.

Then the tsar ordered that the youngest prince be found, and as soon as they found him, his father started to send him to the ship to the Tsar-

Maiden. But he said, "I'll go only when there is a crystal bridge built, reaching all the way to the ship, and all kinds of food and wines laid out on the bridge."

There was nothing to be done: they built the bridge, prepared lots of dishes, and stocked up on wine and mead. The prince gathered his comrades and said, "Come along with me as my company, eat and drink, don't stint yourselves!"

Then he walked over the bridge, and the boys shouted, "Mother! Who's that?"

"That is your dad."

"How should we welcome him?"

"Take him by the hands and bring him to me."

Here they kissed, embraced, caressed, and afterward they went to the tsar and told him everything that had happened. The tsar drove his older sons away from the court, but he began to live and live well with the youngest, and to earn riches.

(Afanas'ev, no. 172)

The Tale of the Fine Young Man and the Apples of Youth

Over the waters, over the lands, over the Russian cities there was a tsar. He had three sons, and the youngest son was Prince Ivan. Near that kingdom was a mountain no one could climb, on foot or on horseback. The tsar heard a knock that knocked and a thunder that thundered on the mountain, but what could it be? No one knew, and he sent his first son to find out why a knock was knocking and thunder thundering on the mountain. The first son rode up only one third of the mountain and came back. He went to his father and said, "My lord father! I rode as you ordered, but I could barely get a third of the way up the mountain." After some time the tsar sent off his middle son, who rode halfway up the mountain but could do no more and turned back. Then the tsar sent his youngest son, Prince Ivan.

Prince Ivan chose a good horse for himself in the tsar's stables, said farewell to his father, and in a moment he had disappeared. He rode up to the top of the mountain, as if a falcon had flown up it, and he saw a palace standing there. Prince Ivan got off his good horse and went into the house. In the house an old Baba Yaga was sitting on a chair and spinning fine silk. "Hello, old Baba Yaga!" said Prince Ivan.

"Hello, young man! Until now a Russian bone wasn't to be seen or smelled, but now it's come into my yard by itself." And she began to ask him, "What families are you from, and what cities, and whose father's son are you?"

Prince Ivan answered her, "I'm Prince Ivan, the son of the Russian tsar. I rode into your mountains to find out what kind of knock is knocking and what kind of thunder is thundering."

The Baba Yaga told him, "The knock is knocking and the thunder's thundering in our mountains because the black-braided Tsar-Maiden, the beautiful beauty, is riding."

"Is that Tsar-Maiden far away?" asked Prince Ivan.

The Adventures of Baba Yaga: Little Girl Stew, Messenger Theatre Co. Adapted and directed by Emily Davis, produced by Agathe David-Weill, http://tinyurl.com/c4vsajp. Photo by Stuart Wagner.

"Twice as far as you've already ridden!" said the Baba Yaga. She gave him a drink, fed him and put him to sleep. And in the morning Prince Ivan got up early-early, said farewell to the old Baba Yaga, and rode onward.

He'd ridden for exactly four months when he saw a castle standing. He got off his horse, went into the house, and in the house sat an old Baba Yaga. "Hello, Baba Yaga!" said Prince Ivan.

"Hi, boy! Is your road a long one? How has God brought you this way?"

He told her everything. The Baba Yaga gave him drink and food and put him to bed, and in the morning Prince Ivan got up early-early, said farewell to the Baba Yaga, and rode onward. Again he rode for exactly four months, and then he saw a courtyard standing there. He got off his good horse and went into the house, and in the house sat a Baba Yaga. "Hello, old Baba Yaga!" said Prince Ivan.

"Hello, Prince Ivan! How has God brought you here?"

He told her everything, where and why he was riding. "Many tsars and princes have come to see our Tsar-Maiden," said the Baba Yaga, "and they didn't ride back out alive! The walls around her city are high, and there are strings tightened on the walls, and if you touch even one string, then all of a sudden the strings sing out, the drums begin to beat, all the *bogatyr* men will be disturbed, and the guards will kill you, too."

Vasilisa goes into the Woods, to borrow light from Baba Yaga by Forest Rogers. Image by the versatile contemporary American artist Forest Rogers, who specializes in fantasy art, favors female subjects, and obviously was influenced by the renowned fairy-tale illustrations of Arthur Rackham and Edmund Dulac. Inspired by the most popular version of "Vasilisa the Beautiful" (Afanas'ev, no. 104), the visual depicts Vasilisa's journey through the forest to obtain light from Baba Yaga. As conceived by Rogers, this scene resembles a sequence in Aleksandr Rou's film *Vasilisa the Beautiful* (1939), based on motifs from sundry fairy tales, including the best-known version of "The Frog Princess" (Afanas'ev, no. 150). Rogers's dense forest recalls the mysterious, dark domain of Baba Yaga and the three-headed dragon Zmei Gorynych, from whom the on-screen simpleton Ivan must rescue his beloved. Illustration by Forest Rogers, http://www.forestrogers.com/.

Prince Ivan waited for the dark of night, mounted his horse, and galloped on his good horse over the high walls. He didn't touch a single one of the strings. Prince Ivan got off his horse, but at that time the *bogatyr* men and sentries were all sleeping, so he went right into the royal palace—into the bedroom of the Tsar-Maiden. The Tsar-Maiden was sleeping, too. The fine young man looked a long time at her indescribable beauty, and forgetting that death was just over his shoulder he sweetly kissed her. He left the bedroom, mounted his good horse, and rode out of the city. The horse leapt up and caught on the tight strings. At once the strings sang out, the drums thundered, the *bogatyr* men, guards, and the whole army awoke, and the beauteous beauty, the black-braided Tsar-Maiden, awoke and realized that someone had been in her bedroom and that she was pregnant from him. She ordered her carriage prepared, took along provisions for a whole year, and set off after Prince Ivan. She rode up to the old Yaga-Baba and said to her very angrily, "Why didn't you catch a man like that? He rode into my kingdom, dared to come into my bedroom and kiss me."

The Baba Yaga answered her, "I couldn't restrain that man, and even you will have trouble catching him!"

The Tsar-Maiden went off farther to catch up and drove up to the middle Baba Yaga, "Why didn't you catch a man like that?"

The old Baba Yaga answered her, "How is an old woman like me supposed to hold onto a fine young man? Even you will hardly be able to catch up to him!"

Again the Tsar-Maiden set out on the road. A little while before she reached the oldest Baba Yaga she gave birth to a son. Her son grew not by the year, but by the hour. At three hours her child looked the way a child looks at three months, and at three months hers looked the way a child looks at three years. She came to the last Yaga-Baba and asked, "Why didn't you hold onto the good young man?"

"How is an old woman like me supposed to stop a fine young man like that?"

Without waiting at all the Tsar-Maiden rushed ahead, rode as far as the mountain, and saw that Prince Ivan was halfway down the mountain, and she herself set off down the mountain after him. She drove to the border of his kingdom. There she pitched her white tents, spread the whole road to the city with red cloths, and sent an emissary to the tsar with the request: "Whoever it might be from his kingdom who came into her chambers at night-time, let the tsar give that one up to her. If you don't give him up, then I'll capture your kingdom, burn it down with fire, and roll it like a charred log."

The tsar summoned his oldest son and sent him out to answer to the Tsar-Maiden. The prince set off and came to the place where the red cloths were spread out, washed his feet until they were white as could be, and went along barefoot. The Tsar-Maiden's son saw him and said to his mother, "Here comes my dad!"

"No, darling son! That's your uncle."

As soon as the oldest prince came to the Tsar-Maiden, she gave him one blow with her lash[74] and knocked two bones out of his spine: why was an innocent person coming to answer? The next day she once again demanded the guilty one from the tsar. The tsar sent out his middle son. The prince came to the red cloths, took off his boots and went barefoot. The Tsar-Maiden gave him a blow of her lash and knocked two bones out of his spine.

On the third day the tsar sent out his youngest son, Prince Ivan. Prince Ivan mounted his good horse, rode up to the red cloths, and trampled all the cloths into the mud. When the Tsar-Maiden's son saw him he said to his mother, "What kind of fool is that riding?"

"Darling son, it's your father riding," the Tsar-Maiden answered. She went out herself to meet him, took him by his white hands, kissed his sugared lips and led him into the white tents, sat him down at oak tables, and gave him all the food and drink he wanted. Then they went to see the tsar and receive lawful marriage and, after spending a little while in that kingdom, they set out on ships to the realm of the Tsar-Maiden. There they ruled long and with good fortune.

(Afanas'ev, no. 178)

The Tale of the Fine Young Man and the Apples of Youth II

Once there lived a tsar. The tsar had three sons, Fyodor, Yegor and Ivan. Ivan was not quite all there in the head. The tsar sent his oldest son out to get living water, and to get the sweet apples of youth. He set out and rode until he came to a fork in the road. Here stood a pillar, and on the pillar was an inscription: "If you go to the right, you'll drink and eat; if you go to the left, you'll lose your head." He headed to the right and came to a house. He went into the house, and there a maiden said to him, "Prince Fyodor! Come sleep with me." He lay down, and she up and shoved him into who knows where. The tsar didn't wait for him long but sent out his second son. This one set off and came to the same place. He went into the house. The maiden took care of this one as well. The tsar sent his third son: "You go!"

The youngest son set off, rode up to the same fork in the road, and said, "For the sake of my father I'll go and lose my head!" And he rode to the left.

He came to a house, went in, and in the house was a yagishna.[75] She was sitting at a spinning wheel, spinning silk thread on a gold spindle, and she said, "Where, Russian bone Prince Ivan, have you set out to go?"

He answered, "Give me something to drink and eat, then ask me about everything."

She gave him something to eat and drink and asked him questions. He said, "I've set off to get living water, and the sweet apples of youth—there, where White Swan Zakhar'evna lives."

Yagishna said to him, "You're not likely to get them! Perhaps I'll help you," and she gave him her horse.

He mounted and rode off, and he came to the house of a second yagishna sister. He went into the house, and she said to him, "Fie-fie, there was no scent or sight of Russian bone, but now it's come right into my yard. Where are you headed, Prince Ivan?"

He answered, "First give me something to eat and drink, then ask me questions." She gave him something to drink and eat, and he said, "I've set off to get hold of living water and the sweet apples of youth—there where White Swan Zakhar'evna lives."

"You're not likely to get them!" said the old woman, and she gave him her horse.

The prince set off to see the third yagishna. He went into the house, and she said, "Fie, fie, there was no smell and no sight of Russian bone, but now Russian bone has come into the yard by itself. Where are you headed, Prince Ivan?"

"First give me something to eat and drink, then ask me questions." She gave him something to eat and drink, and then he said, "I'm off to get living water and the sweet apples of youth."

"That's hard, prince! You're not likely to get them." Then she gave him her horse and a seven-hundred club, and she told him, "When you ride up to the city, hit the horse with the club so he'll jump over the fortress wall."

So that's what he did. He leapt over the fortress wall, hitched his horse to a pillar, and went into the palace of White Swan Zakhar'evna. The servants did not want to let him pass, but he pushed his way through them. "I'm bringing a message for White Swan Zakhar'evna," he said. He fought his way to the chambers of White Swan Zakhar'evna. At that time she was sound asleep, stretched out on a feather bed, and the living water was under her pillow. He took the water, kissed the maiden, and wickedly had his way with her. Later, after he had gathered some of the apples of youth, he set off to go back. His horse leapt over the fortress wall and clipped its edge. Suddenly all the bells sounded, all the gongs, and the whole city awoke. White Swan Zakhar'evna ran about—first she beat this nurse, then she pounded that one, and she shouted, "Get up! Someone was in the house and drank some water, but he didn't close the well."

Meanwhile, the prince rode up to the house of the first yagishna and changed horses. But Swan Zakhar'evna was chasing him. She came to the yagishna at the house where the prince had just changed horses, and asked her, "Where did you go riding? Your horse is all in a lather."

She answered, "I rode out into the field to drive the livestock."

Prince Ivan changed horses at the second yagishna's house. But Swan Zakhar'evna arrived right after him and said, "Where, yagishna, have you been riding? Your horse is in a lather."

"I rode into the field to drive out the livestock, that's why my horse is sweaty."

Prince Ivan came to the last yagishna and changed horses. But Swan Zakhar'evna was still chasing, and she came up just after him. She asked the yagishna, "Why is your horse sweaty?"

She answered, "I rode out in the field to drive the livestock out."

After that, White Swan Zakhar'evna returned home, but Prince Ivan rode to find his brothers. He came to where they were. The maiden leapt out onto the porch and said, "Welcome!" Then she invited him to sleep with her.

The prince said, "Give me something to drink and eat, then put me to bed."

She gave him something to drink and eat and said again, "Come to bed with me!"

The prince answered, "You lie down first!"

She lay down first, and he shoved her. The maiden flew who knows where. Prince Ivan thought, "Well, let's open up this trap. Could this be where my brothers are?" He opened it—and they were sitting right there. He said to them, "Come out, my brothers! What are you doing here? Aren't you ashamed?"

They got their things together and set out homeward to see their father. Along the way the older brothers got the idea of killing the younger one. Prince Ivan realized what they were thinking and said, "Don't strike me, I'll give you everything!"

They didn't agree to that. Instead, they killed him and scattered his bones over the empty field. Prince Ivan's horse gathered his bones into one place and sprinkled them with the water of life. His bones and joints healed back together. The prince came back to life and said, "I slept a long time, but woke up quickly!"

He came to his father wearing a rude canvas caftan,[76] and his father said, "Where have you been? Go and clean the latrines."

At the same time White Swan Zakhar'evna rode out onto the hereditary meadows of the tsar and sent the tsar a letter, telling him to hand over the guilty one. The tsar sent his oldest son.

White Swan's little children, catching sight of him, shouted, "Here comes our father! How should we welcome him?"

But their mother said, "No, that's not your father, it's your uncle. Treat him to what you have in your hands."

And each of them was holding an oak club. They gave his sides such a drubbing[77] that he could hardly walk back home.

Then the tsar sent his second son. When that one arrived, the children rejoiced and shouted, "Here comes our father!"

But their mother said, "No, that's your uncle."

"How should we welcome him?"

"Why, treat him to what you have in your hands!"

They gave his sides a drubbing just like the one they had given to the oldest brother.

Then White Swan Zakhar'evna sent a message to the tsar saying that he must send out the guilty one. The tsar finally sent his youngest son. He wandered over—he was wearing ragged bast shoes[78] and a ragged canvas caftan. The children shouted, "Here comes some kind of beggar!"

But their mother said, "No, that's your father!"

"And how should we treat him?"

"To whatever God has sent!" When Prince Ivan came up, she put good clothing on him,[79] and they went to see the tsar. When he got there Prince Ivan told his father about his adventure: how he had rescued his brothers from the trap, and how they had killed him. His father was so angry that he up and disinherited them and made them take up low duties, but he made the youngest son his heir.

(Afanas'ev, no. 174)

The Three Kingdoms

In a certain kingdom, in a certain state there lived a tsar named Bel Belyanin;[80] he had a wife, Nastasia Zlatokos,[81] and three sons: Prince Pyotr, Prince Vasilii, and Prince Ivan. The tsaritsa went out to walk in the garden with her nurses and nannies. Suddenly a strong whirlwind arose and—oh my God!—grabbed the tsar's wife and carried her off, no one knew to where. The tsar was sorrowful and mournful and he didn't know what to do. The tsar's sons grew up, and he said to them, "My dear children! Who among you will go to seek and find your mother?"

The two older sons got together and set out, and after that the youngest began to ask his father to go. "No," said the tsar, "don't you go away, my son! Don't leave me alone, an old man."

"Permit me, Dad! I have a terrible desire to go wander through the white world and to search out my mother."

The tsar tried and tried, but he couldn't talk him out of it. "Well, there's nothing to be done. Go, and may God be with you!"

Prince Ivan saddled his good horse and set off on his way. He rode and rode, for a long time or a short time; quickly may a tale be spun, but not so soon a deed is done. He came to a forest. In that forest stood a very rich palace. Prince Ivan rode into the broad courtyard; he saw an old man and said, "May you be well for many years, old man!"

"Welcome! Who may you be, good lad?"

"I am Prince Ivan, son of tsar Bel Belyanin and tsaritsa Nastasia Zlatokos."

"Ah, my own nephew! And where is God taking you?"

"Well, it's like this and like that," he said. "I'm traveling to search out my mother. Can you not tell me, dear uncle, where to find her?"

"No, nephew, I don't know. I'll be of service to you as much as I can. Here's a ball for you, toss it in front of you, and it will roll and lead you to steep, high mountains. In those mountains there's a cave. Go inside it, take the iron claws, put them on your hands and feet, and climb up on the mountains. Mayhap you'll find your mother Nastasia Zlatokos there."

So very well. Prince Ivan said good-bye to his uncle and let the ball go ahead of him. The ball rolled and rolled, while he rode after it, for a long time or for a short time, and then he saw his brothers Prince Pyotr and Prince Vasilii standing in the open field in a camp, and they had a multitude of soldiers with them. The brothers met him, "Bah! Where are you going, Prince Ivan?"

"What do you think?" he said. "I got lonely at home and got the idea of riding out to look for our mother. Send the armies home, and let's go together."

That's what they did; they let the army go and rode off all three together after the ball. They caught sight of the mountains from far away—so steep, so high, that oh my God! their summits pierced the clouds. The ball rolled right up to the cave. Prince Ivan dismounted and said to his brothers, "Here you are, brothers, take my good horse. I'm going into the mountains to look for our mother, and you remain here; wait for me exactly three months, and if I'm not back here in three months there's nothing to wait for!"

The brothers thought, "How can you climb up on these mountains, you could crack your head open here!"

"Well," they said, "go with God, and we'll wait for you here."

Prince Ivan went up to the cave. He saw an iron door and pushed it with all his might, and the door opened. He went inside; the iron claws put themselves onto his hands and his feet. He began to make his way onto the mountains, climbed and climbed; he labored for a whole month and barely made it to the top. "Well," he said, "God be praised!"

He rested a little bit and then set off through the mountains. He walked and walked, walked and walked, and looked: there stood a copper palace. At the gates terrible dragons were shackled on copper chains, they were just teeming! But a bronze dipper was hanging at the well on a fine bronze chain. Prince Ivan took the dipper, dipped some water, and gave a drink to the dragons. They calmed down and lay down, and he passed through into the palace.

The tsaritsa of the copper kingdom jumped out to meet him: "Who are you, good lad?"

"I am Prince Ivan."

"What," she asked, "by your own will, or have you come here unwillingly, Prince Ivan?"

"By my own will; I'm searching for my mother, Nastasia Zlatokos. Some Whirlwind snatched her out of our garden. Do you happen to know where she is?"

"No, I don't know; but not far from here lives my middle sister, the tsaritsa of the silver kingdom; perhaps she will tell you." She gave him a copper ball and a little copper ring. "The ball," she said, "will lead you to my middle sister, and that ring contains the whole copper kingdom. After you vanquish the Whirlwind, who keeps me here too and flies to see me every three months, then don't forget poor me. Rescue me from here and take me with you to the free world."

"Very well," said Prince Ivan. He took the copper ball and threw it. The ball rolled off, and the prince set off after it.

He came to the silver kingdom and saw a palace better than the first one—all made of silver. Frightful dragons were shackled on silver chains at the gates, and beside them was a well with a silver dipper. Prince Ivan dipped some wine and gave the dragons a drink; they lay down and let him into the palace. Out came the tsaritsa of the silver kingdom. "For almost three years," she said, "since the mighty Whirlwind started keeping me here, I've had neither sight nor sound[83] of the Russian spirit, but now the Russian spirit takes its place in plain view. Who are you, good lad?"

"I'm Prince Ivan."

"How did you make your way here—by your own will or under compulsion?"

"By my own will; I'm searching for my mother. She went out into the green garden to take a stroll, when a Whirlwind arose and rushed her off, no one knows where. Do you happen to know where to find her?"

"No, I don't know; but not far from here lives my oldest sister, the tsaritsa of the golden kingdom, Elena the Beautiful. Perhaps she'll be able to tell you. Here's a silver ball for you. Roll it ahead of you and follow after it; it will lead you to the golden kingdom. But look, when you kill the Whirlwind, don't forget poor me; rescue me from here and take me with you into the free world. The Whirlwind keeps me in captivity and flies to see me every two months." Then she gave him a little silver ring. "This ring contains the whole silver kingdom!"

Prince Ivan rolled the sphere; wherever the sphere rolled, he would follow in that direction.

For a long time, or for a short time, he saw a golden palace standing there; it burned like fire. Frightful dragons teemed at the gates, shackled on

Artist unknown.

golden chains, but a well stood nearby, and at the well hung a golden dipper on a golden chain. Prince Ivan dipped some water and gave the dragons a drink; they lay down and got peaceful. The prince went into the palace; Elena the Beautiful greeted him, "Who are you, good lad?"

"I'm Prince Ivan."

"How did you make your way here—by your own will, or under compulsion?"

"I came of my own will; I'm looking for my mother, Nastasia Zlatokos. Do you happen to know where to find her?"

"How could I not know! She lives not far from here, and the Whirlwind flies to see her once a week, but he comes to me once a month. Here's a golden ball for you, roll it ahead of you and follow after it: it will lead you where you need to go. And take this little golden ring, too. This little ring contains the whole golden kingdom! Look, prince: when you conquer the Whirlwind, don't forget poor me. Take me with you into the free world."

"Very well," he said, "I'll take you!"

Prince Ivan rolled the sphere and set out after it: he walked and walked and came to such a palace that, oh my Lord God! It's as if it was on fire with diamonds and precious gemstones. At the gates, six-headed dragons hissed;

Prince Ivan gave them a drink, and the dragons calmed down and let him go into the palace. The prince passed through large chambers, and in the very farthest he found his mother: she was sitting on a high throne, dressed up in royal garb, crowned with a precious crown. She took a look at her guest and cried out, "Ah, my God! Is it you, my darling son? How did you get here?"

"Like this and like that," he said. "I've come to get you."

"Well, my son! It won't be easy for you. For a cruel, mighty Whirlwind rules here in the mountains, and all the spirits are subject to him; he's the one who carried me away. You must fight with him! Let's go to the cellar right now."

So they went down to the cellar. There stood two tubs with water, one on the right hand, the other on the left. Tsaritsa Nastasia Zlatokos said, "Drink some of the water that stands on the right."

Prince Ivan drank some.

"So, well, how much strength is in you?"

"Why, I'm so strong that I could turn the whole palace over with one hand."

"Ah then, drink some more."

Prince Ivan drank up some more.

"How much strength is in you now?"

"Now if I wanted to I could turn the whole world over."

"Oh, that's already a great deal![84] Switch these tubs into each other's places: move the one on the right to the left side, and move the one on the left to the right."

Prince Ivan took the tubs and switched their places.

"Do you see there, my dear son: one tub has strengthening water, and the other has weakening water. Whoever drinks from the first will be a strong and powerful *bogatyr*, but whoever drinks from the second will lose all his strength. The Whirlwind always drinks the strong water and keeps it on the right side; so we have to fool him, or else there's no way to handle him!"

They went back into the palace. "Soon the Whirlwind will come flying," said the tsaritsa to Prince Ivan. "Sit here under my purple robes, so he won't see you. But when the Whirlwind flies up and rushes to hug and kiss me, then you grab his cudgel. He'll fly up high-high; he'll carry you over seas and over abysses. You watch out, don't let go of the cudgel. The Whirlwind will get tired, he'll want to drink some of the strengthening water, he'll go down into the cellar and throw himself on the tub on the right side; but you drink from the tub on the left side. Then he'll lose all his strength. You take away his sword and cut off his head with one stroke. Once you cut his head off, voices behind you will shout, 'Cut again! Cut again!' But you, my son, don't cut, instead say: 'The hand of a *bogatyr* doesn't strike twice, but all the first time!'"

No sooner had Prince Ivan managed to hide under the purple robe than suddenly it got dark in the yard, and everything around began to shake. The Whirlwind had come flying up; he struck the ground, turned into a goodly young man, and walked into the palace. In his hands he had a cudgel.

"Fie-fie-fie! What is it here that smells of Russian spirit? Has someone been visiting?"

The tsaritsa answered, "I don't know why it seems that way to you."

The Whirlwind rushed to hug and kiss her, but Prince Ivan went straight for the cudgel. "I'll eat you up!" the Whirlwind shouted at him.

"Well, maybe you will and maybe you won't:[85] either you'll eat me or else you won't!"

The Whirlwind leapt up—through the window and up into the skies; he carried Prince Ivan farther and farther. Over the mountains, he said, "Do you want me to crush you?" And over the seas, he threatened, "Do you want me to drown you?" But no, the prince didn't let go of the cudgel.

The Whirlwind flew through[85] the whole world, got tired out, and began to fly lower. He went down right into the cellar, ran over to the tub that was standing on the right, and started to drink the weakening water, while Prince Ivan went to the left, drank his fill of strengthening water, and became the most powerful *bogatyr* in the world. He saw that the Whirlwind had lost all his strength, snatched his sharp sword away, and cut off his head with one blow. Voices started to shout behind him, "Strike again! Strike again! Or else he'll come back to life."

"No," answered the prince, "the hand of a *bogatyr* doesn't strike twice, but finishes everything the first time!"

Then right away he made a fire, burned both the body and the head, and scattered the ashes in the wind.[86]

Prince Ivan's mother was so glad! "Well," she said, "my darling son! Let's celebrate, let's have something to eat, and then can we go right home; it is boring here, there are no people."

"But who serves you here?

"You'll see."

The moment they thought about eating something, right away the table set itself: various dishes and wines appeared by themselves on the table. The tsaritsa and the prince ate, and invisible music played wonderful songs for them. They ate and drank their fill, and they rested; then Prince Ivan said, "Let's go, Mother; it's time! For my brothers are waiting for us below the

The Dream World of Aleksandr Pushkin by the Palekh miniaturist Fedor Kritov. Observing the conventions of narrative icons, this lacquer box places its "sacred subject"—Russia's premier poet, Pushkin (1799–1837)—at the center, framed by illustrations of the various folkloric works he penned. These included fairy tales in verse, short lyrics, and mock epic poems that drew on popular lore and inspired graphic artists, filmmakers, and composers. The relegation of Baba Yaga to the upper right corner of the visual is doubtless motivated by her absence from Pushkin's cast of magical characters apart from a brief mention in his narrative poem "Ruslan and Ludmila" (1820). Artist: Fedor Kritov, from the village of Palekh, http://catalog.instaplanet.com/PALEKH_Russian_Lacquer_Pushkin.html.

mountains, and on our way I have to rescue the three tsaritsas who were living here with the Whirlwind."

They took everything they needed and set out on their way. First they stopped by for the tsaritsa of the golden kingdom, then for the tsaritsa of the silver kingdom, and then for the tsaritsa of the copper kingdom. They took them along, grabbed some canvas and all kinds of things, and in a short time they came to the place where they had to go down from the mountains. Prince Ivan used the canvas to lower first his mother, then Elena the Beautiful and her two sisters. The brothers were standing down below, waiting, but they thought to themselves, "Let's leave Prince Ivan up above, and we'll take Mother and the tsaritsas to our father and tell him that we're the ones who found them."

"I'll take Elena the Beautiful for myself," said Prince Pyotr. "You take the tsaritsa of the silver kingdom, Vasilii, and perhaps we'll leave the tsaritsa of the copper kingdom for a general."

So when it was time for Prince Ivan to come down from the mountains, his older brothers grabbed the canvas, pulled on it, and tore it off completely. Prince Ivan was left behind in the mountains. What could he do? He started to cry bitterly and headed back; he walked and walked through the copper kingdom, and through the silver kingdom, and through the gold kingdom—there wasn't a soul! Well, what could he do alone? Deadly boredom! He looked, and he saw a whistle lying on one window.[87]

The moment he whistled, a lame man and a crooked man jumped out. "What is your will, Prince Ivan?"

"I want to eat."

Right away from who knows where a table was set, and on the table both wines and dishes of the very first sort. Prince Ivan ate and thought, "Now it wouldn't be a bad thing to have a rest."

He whistled into the whistle, and the lame man and the crooked man appeared. "What is your will, Prince Ivan?"

"For a bed to be prepared." Before he finished speaking, a bed was spread—nothing could be better.

So he lay down, slept wonderfully, and then once again blew into his whistle. "What is your will?" the lame man and the crooked man asked him.

"So, could it be that you can do anything?" asked the prince.

"We can do anything, Prince Ivan! Whoever blows into this whistle, we'll do everything for him. Just as we served the Whirlwind before, now we're happy to serve you; all you need to do is keep this whistle always with you."

"Very well," said Prince Ivan, "I want to be in my own kingdom now!" He had only just said it, and that moment he found himself in his own kingdom in the middle of a market. He was walking along through the bazaar, and a shoemaker came toward him, such a merry man! The prince asked him, "Where are you going, my man?"

"I'm taking slippers[88] to sell; I'm a shoemaker."

"Take me as your apprentice."

"And do you really know how to sew slippers?"

"Yes, I can do anything you like; not just slippers, I can sew clothes."

"Well, then, let's go!"

They came home, and the shoemaker said, "So then, make something! Here's some first-class material; I'll take a look to see what you can do."

Prince Ivan went into his room, pulled out his pipe, and whistled—and the lame man and the crooked man appeared. "What is your will, Prince Ivan?"

"To have a pair of slippers ready by breakfast."

"Oh, that's a little task, not a real task!"

"Here's the material."

"What kind of material is that? Trash—that's all! We should throw it out the window." The next morning when the prince woke up a pair of magnificent slippers, the finest, stood on the table.

The master got up as well: "So, young man, have you sewed the slippers?"

"They're ready."

"Well then, show me!"

The shoemaker took a look and gasped. "See what a master-craftsman I've found for myself! Not a master, but a miracle!" He took those slippers and went to the market to sell them.

At that very time there were three weddings at the tsar's palace: Prince Pyotr was preparing to marry Elena the Beautiful, Prince Vasilii to marry the tsaritsa of the silver kingdom, and they were marrying the tsaritsa of the copper kingdom to a general. They began to buy up fancy clothes for the wedding; Elena the Beautiful needed a pair of slippers. Our shoemaker turned out to have the best slippers of all; they brought him into the palace.

Elena the Beautiful took one look. "What's that," she said to herself, "they know how to make slippers like that only in the mountains." She paid the shoemaker well and ordered, "Make me another pair of slippers without measuring, and let them be marvelously embroidered, decorated and set with precious gems, diamonds. And let them be ready tomorrow by breakfast, or else—to the gallows!"

The shoemaker took the money and the precious stones, and he went home so gloomy! "Oh woe," he said. "What can I do now? How could I sew slippers like that by tomorrow, and what's more without measuring? It's clear they're going to hang me tomorrow! Let me at least have some fun with my friends first, to ease my grief."

He stopped into a tavern. He had many friends there, and they all asked him, "What are you so gloomy for, brother?"

"Ah, my dear friends, tomorrow they're going to hang me!"

"For what?"

The shoemaker told them about his misfortune. "How can I think about work like that? Better just to enjoy this last evening."

So they drank and drank, reveled and reveled, and the shoemaker was already staggering. "Well," he said, "I'll take a cask of wine home and go to bed. And tomorrow, when they come for me to hang me, I'll drink half a bucket at once; let them hang me unconscious."

He came home. "Well, damn you!" he said to Prince Ivan, "Here's what your slippers have done, it's like this and like that . . . in the morning, when they come for me, wake me up at once."

That night Prince Ivan pulled out his whistle, blew into it, and the lame and crooked men appeared: "What is your will, Prince Ivan?"

"To have this sort of slippers made."

"We hear and obey!"

Prince Ivan lay down to sleep; in the morning when he woke up the slippers were standing there on the table, burning like fire. He went in and woke his host. "Master! Time to get up!"

"What, have they come for me? Give me the cask of wine right away, there's a mug, pour some; let them hang me drunk."

"But the slippers are ready."

"Ready how? Where are they?" The master ran in and looked. "Ah, when did you and I make those?"

"Why, last night; can it be, master, that you don't remember how we cut and sewed?"

"I overslept entirely, brother; I barely-barely remember!"

He took the slippers, wrapped them up, and ran to the palace. Elena the Beautiful saw the slippers and guessed, "It must be the spirits who made them for Prince Ivan."

"How did you do this?" she asked the shoemaker.

"Well," he said, "I can do anything!"

"If that's so, then make me a wedding gown, and let it be embroidered in gold, set with diamonds and precious stones. And let it be ready tomorrow, or else—off with your head!"

The shoemaker again walked along, all gloomy, but his friends had been waiting for him for a long time. "So, what happened?"

"Well, what," he said. "A damned mess! A leader of the Christian people has appeared; she ordered me to sew her a wedding dress by tomorrow, with gold and precious stones. But what kind of tailor am I!? Tomorrow they'll take my head off for sure."

"Eh, brother! Morning's wiser than the evening: let's go and have a party."

They set out for the tavern, drank and reveled. The shoemaker slurped up his fill again, dragged a whole cask of wine home, and said to Prince Ivan, "Well, laddie! When you wake me up tomorrow, I'll snort a whole bucket; let them cut off my head when I'm drunk! But I couldn't make a gown like that in all my life."

The master lay down to sleep, while Prince Ivan blew into his pipe, and the lame and the crooked men appeared. "What is your will, Prince?"

"Let a gown be ready by tomorrow—just the sort Elena the Beautiful wore when she was with the Whirlwind."

"We hear you and obey! It will be ready."

As soon as it was light Prince Ivan woke up, and the gown lay on the table, burning like fire; it lit up the whole room. He went to wake the master.

He opened his eyes: "What, have they come for me, to cut off my head? Give me the wine right now!"

"But the gown's ready . . ."

"Oh really! When did we manage to sew it?"

"Why at night. Do you really not remember? You did the cutting yourself."

"Ah, brother, I remember just a little bit; it's as if I see it in a dream." The shoemaker took the gown and ran to the palace.

Then Elena the Beautiful gave him a lot of money and ordered, "See to it that tomorrow by dawn, seven miles from here toward the sea, a golden kingdom be standing, and that a golden bridge be made from it to our palace. The bridge must be spread with costly velvet, and marvelous trees must be growing around the railings on both sides and songbirds singing in various voices. If you don't have this done by tomorrow, I'll order you drawn and quartered!"

The shoemaker left Elena the Beautiful and hung his head. His friends met him. "What is it, brother?"

"Here's what! I'm ruined; tomorrow they're going to draw and quarter me. She ordered such a task that no devil could do it."

"Eh, that's enough! Morning's wiser than the evening; let's go to the tavern."

"Yes, let's go! I should at least enjoy myself a bit in the end."

So they drank and drank; by evening the shoemaker was so drunk that they had to hold him up as he walked home. "Farewell, laddie!" he said to Prince Ivan. "Tomorrow they're executing me."

"So is there some new task assigned?"

"Yes, and such and such a task!"

He lay down and started to snore; but Prince Ivan went right into his room, blew in the whistle, and the lame man and the crooked man appeared. "What is your will, Prince Ivan?"

"Can you do such and such a task for me?"

"Yes, Prince Ivan, that is a task indeed! Well, but there's nothing to be done—it will all be ready by morning."

The next morning the moment it started to get light Prince Ivan woke up, looked out the window—and holy godfathers! everything was done in that very way: a golden palace was burning just like fire. He woke the master.

He jumped up. "What? Have they come for me? Give me some wine right away! Let them execute me when I'm drunk."

"But the palace is ready."

"What are you saying!" The shoemaker glanced out the window and gasped with surprise. "How was that done?"

"Do you really not remember how you and I put it together?"

"Ah, I must have overslept, I remember just a little bit!"

They ran to the golden palace, and it was full of unseen and unheard-of richness. Prince Ivan said, "Here, master, is a bird's wing for you. Go, dust off the railings of the bridge, and when they come to ask who is it that lives in the palace, don't you say anything, just hand over this note."

Very well, the shoemaker went and started to dust off the railings of the bridge. In the morning Elena the Beautiful woke up, saw the golden palace, and ran straight to the tsar. "Look, your highness, what has happened here! Someone has built a golden palace near the sea; a bridge seven miles long leads to it, and around the bridge marvelous trees are growing, and song-birds singing in various voices."

The tsar sent at once to ask, "What could this mean? Has some *bogatyr* come into my kingdom?"

The emissaries came to the shoemaker, and they started to ask him questions. He said, "I don't know, but I have a note for your tsar." In that note Prince Ivan told his father everything as it had happened: how he rescued his mother and won Elena the Beautiful, and how his older brothers had deceived him. Along with the note Prince Ivan sent a golden carriage and asked the tsar and tsaritsa to come to him, with Elena the Beautiful and her sisters; but he asked them to let his brothers be brought behind in simple peasant sledges.

Everyone immediately got ready and set out. Prince Ivan met them with joy. The tsar wanted to punish his older sons for their lie, but Prince Ivan interceded with his father, and they were forgiven. Then there was a great feast; Prince Ivan married Elena the Beautiful, Prince Pyotr married the tsaritsa of the silver kingdom, Prince Vasilii married the tsaritsa of the copper kingdom, and the shoemaker was promoted to general. I was at that feast too; I drank mead and beer, and it ran down my mustache but didn't go into my mouth.

(Afanas'ev, no. 129)

The Three Kingdoms—Copper, Silver, and Gold

Once upon a time there happened to live an old man and an old woman who had three sons. The first was Egorushko Zalët,[89] the second Misha Kosolapoy,[90] and the third was Ivan Zapechnik.[91] The father and mother decided to marry them off, and they sent the oldest son to find a bride. He walked and walked for a long time. No matter where he took a look at the girls, he couldn't find a bride for himself; none of them caught his eye.

Then on the road he met a dragon with three heads. He was frightened, but the dragon said to him, "Where are you headed, good man?"

Egorushko said, "I've set out to find a wife, but I can't find myself a bride."

The dragon said, "Come with me. I'll show you how to find a bride."

So they walked and walked, and they came up to a big boulder. The dragon said, "Move the stone. Whatever you want, you'll get it there."

Egorushko tried to move the stone, but he couldn't do anything. The dragon said to him, "So, no bride for you!" And Egorushko went back home and told his father and mother about everything.

His father and mother thought and thought again, what to do and how to live, and they sent their middle son, Misha Kosolapoy. The very same thing happened with him. Then the old man and woman thought and thought, and they didn't know what to do. If they sent Ivashko[92] Zapechnik, he wouldn't be able to do anything!

But Ivashko Zapechnik himself started asking to go and have a look at the dragon. At first his father and mother wouldn't let him go, but then they let him. Ivashko too walked and walked, and he met the dragon with three heads. The dragon asked him, "Where are you headed, good man?"

He said, "My brothers wanted to get married, but they couldn't find brides. Now my turn has come."

"If you please, let's go, and I'll show you if you'll be able to get a bride."

So the dragon set out with Ivashko. They came to the same boulder, and the dragon ordered him to move it from its place. Ivashko seized it, and it was as if there was no boulder: it flew away. Underneath it there was a hole in the ground with straps fastened beside it.

Then the dragon said, "Ivashko! Sit down on the straps, I'll lower you. There you'll come to three kingdoms, and in each kingdom you'll see a maiden."

Ivashko went down and set off walking. He walked and walked, and he came to the copper kingdom. He dropped in there and saw a maiden who was splendidly beautiful. The maiden said, "Welcome, unknown guest! Come here and sit down wherever you see an empty place. Tell me, where are you coming from and where are you going?"

"Ah, lovely maiden!" said Ivashko, "you haven't fed me, you haven't given me a drink, but you've started to ask for news."

Then the maiden brought together all kinds of food and drink on the table. Ivashko ate and drank and began to tell her how he was traveling to find himself a bride. "If you'll be so kind, I'll ask you to marry me."

"No, good man," said the maiden. "You keep on going. You'll come to the silver kingdom, and there's a maiden there even more beautiful than I am!" And she gave him a silver ring.

So the good young man thanked the maiden for her bread and salt,[93] said good-bye and set off. He walked and walked, and he came to the silver kingdom. He dropped in there and saw a maiden sitting who was even more beautiful than the first one. He said a prayer to God and bowed down to the ground. "Hi there, fair maiden!"

She answered, "Welcome, traveler! Sit down and boast: whose are you, where do you come from, and what task has brought you this way?"

"Ah, fair maiden!" said Ivashko. "You haven't given me a drink, you haven't fed me, but you've started to ask for news."

So the maiden got the table together, brought all kinds of food and drink. Then Ivan[94] took a drink and ate a bit, as much as he wanted, and he began to tell the story of how he'd set off to seek a bride. Then he asked her to marry him.

"Keep going," she said. "The golden kingdom's still there ahead, and in that kingdom there's a maiden even more beautiful than I am." And she gave him a golden ring.

Ivashko said good-bye and sent off again. He walked and walked until he came to the golden kingdom, dropped in, and saw a maiden more beautiful than anyone else. So he said a prayer to God and greeted the maiden in the proper manner. The maiden began to ask him where he came from and where he was going. "Ah, fair maiden!" he said. "You haven't given me a drink, haven't fed me, but you've started asking for news."

So she put all kinds of food and drink on the table, and you couldn't have asked for anything better. Ivashko Zapechnik had some of everything and then told her, "I'm traveling, looking for a bride. If you would like to marry me, then come along with me."

The maiden agreed and gave him a golden ball, and they set off together. They walked and walked, and they came to the silver kingdom. Here they took the silver maiden along with them. They walked and walked some more; they came to the copper kingdom, and here too they took the maiden along. They all came to the hole they would have to climb out of, and the straps were hanging there. Meanwhile, the older brothers were already standing beside the hole: they were about to climb down and look for Ivashko.

So Ivashko set the maiden from the copper kingdom on the straps and shook one of the straps. His brothers pulled and lifted the maiden out, and they lowered the straps again. Ivashko set the maiden from the silver kingdom on them, and they pulled her out, too, and let the straps back down. Then he set the maiden from the golden kingdom, and they pulled that one out, and they let the straps down. Then Ivashko sat on them himself. His brothers started to lift him, too, pulled and pulled, but when they saw that it was Ivashko, they thought, "Maybe if we pull him out he won't give us any of the maidens!" So they cut the straps, and Ivashko fell back down.

There was nothing he could do; he cried a bit, he cried, and then he started walking straight ahead. He walked and walked, and he saw an old man sitting on a stump, short as a quart but with a beard to his elbow. He told the old man about everything that had happened to him and how. The old man told him to go along farther. "You'll come to a little house. In the house lies a long man from one corner to the other, and you can ask him how to get back out to Rus.'"

So Ivashko walked and walked, and he came to the little house. He dropped in and said, "Powerful Idol! Don't destroy me, but tell me how I can make my way to Rus.'"

"Fie, fie!" spoke up the Idol. "No one knew of the Russian bone, but it came here by itself. Well, set off and cross over thirty lakes. There's a little house there standing on a chicken leg, and in that house lives Yega[95] Baba. She has an eagle-bird, and it will carry you out."

So the good lad walked and walked, and he came to the little house. He stopped into the little house, and the Yega Baba started shouting, "Fie, fie, fie! Russian bone, why has it come here?"

Then Ivashko said, "Here's why, granny. The powerful Idol told me to come and ask you for a mighty eagle-bird, so it could carry me out to Rus'."

"You go along into the garden," said the Yega Baba. "There's a guard standing beside the doors, and you take the keys from him and go through seven doors. When you open the last door, then the eagle will start to beat its wings, and if you aren't frightened, you climb up on it and fly. Only take some beef with you, and every time it starts to look back you give it a piece of meat."

Ivashko did everything as the Yega Baba ordered. He climbed up on the eagle and flew off. He flew and flew; the eagle looked back, and Ivashko gave it a piece of meat. He flew and flew, and he often gave the eagle meat. He had already fed it everything he had, but there was still a ways to fly. The eagle looked back, but there was no meat, so the eagle snatched a piece of flesh out of Ivashko's shoulders. It ate the flesh and hauled him out of that same hole into Rus'.

When Ivashko got down off the eagle, the eagle spat out the piece of flesh and told him to press it against his shoulder. Ivashko pressed it there, and the piece grew back.

Ivashko came home, took the maiden from the golden kingdom from his brothers, and they began to live and exist, and they're still living. I was there, and I drank beer. That beer dripped down my mustache, but it didn't get into my mouth.

(Afanas'ev, no. 128)

The Tsar-Maiden

In a certain kingdom, in a certain state, there was once a merchant. His wife had died, and he had only one son, Ivan. He found his son a tutor, and after a certain time he himself married another wife. Since Ivan the merchant's son was already full grown and awfully good-looking, his stepmother fell in love with him.

Once Ivan the merchant's son and his tutor set off to sea on a little raft to fish. Suddenly they saw thirty ships sailing toward them. The Tsar-Maiden was on one of those ships with thirty other maidens, her foster sisters. When the ships reached the little raft, all thirty ships dropped anchor. They invited Ivan the merchant's son and his tutor onto the very best ship. There the Tsar-Maiden and the thirty maidens, her foster sisters, met them, and she told Ivan the merchant's son that she'd fallen deeply in love with him and had come to meet him. They exchanged rings on the spot and got engaged to be married.

The Tsar-Maiden told Ivan the merchant's son to come to the same place tomorrow at the same time. Then she said good-bye to him and sailed away.

Meanwhile, Ivan the merchant's son returned home, ate dinner, and lay down to sleep. The stepmother led his tutor into her room, plied him with drink, and started to ask him questions. Had anything happened while they were out fishing? The tutor told her everything.

She heard him out, gave him a pin, and said, "Tomorrow, when the ships start to sail close to you, stick this pin into Ivan the merchant's son's clothes."

The tutor promised he would do what she ordered.

In the morning, Ivan the merchant's son got up and set off to go fishing. As soon as the tutor spied the ships in the distance, he up and stuck the pin into Ivan's clothes.

"Ah, I'm so sleepy!" said the merchant's son. "Listen, uncle, I'll lie down and sleep a bit, but when the ships get close, then please wake me up."

"All right! Why wouldn't I wake you?"

Then the ships sailed up and dropped anchor. The Tsar-Maiden sent for Ivan the merchant's son and told him to come to her at once, but he was sleeping soundly-soundly. They tried to wake him, to disturb him, to jostle him, but no matter what they did they couldn't wake him, so they left him there.

The Tsar-Maiden told the tutor to have Ivan the merchant's son come again the next day, then she ordered the anchors raised and sails hoisted.

The moment the ships sailed away, the tutor yanked out the pin, and Ivan the merchant's son woke up, jumped up, and started to shout for the Tsar-Maiden to come back. No! She was already far away and didn't hear him. He went home sadly, full of grief.

The stepmother took the tutor into her room, got him drunk, asked him about everything that had happened, and ordered him to stick in the pin again the next day. The next day Ivan the merchant's son set off to fish; once again he slept the whole time, and he didn't see the Tsar-Maiden. She gave an order that he should be there one more time.

On the third day he and the tutor got ready to go fishing. They sailed up to the same place and saw the ships sailing from far away. Right away the tutor stuck in the pin, and Ivan the merchant's son fell sound asleep.

The ships sailed close and dropped anchor, and the Tsar-Maiden sent for her betrothed to come and see her on her ship. They started trying to wake him in every possible way, but no matter what they did they couldn't wake him up. The Tsar-Maiden understood the stepmother's wiles and the tutor's betrayal, and she wrote to Ivan the merchant's son that he must cut off the tutor's head. And if he loved his betrothed he must seek her beyond thrice-nine lands, in the thrice-tenth kingdom.

No sooner had the ships spread their sails and sailed off into the open sea than the tutor yanked the little pin out of Ivan the merchant's son's clothes. He woke up and began to shout loudly and call to the Tsar-Maiden. But she was far away and didn't hear anything!

The tutor handed him the letter from the Tsar-Maiden. Ivan the merchant's son read it, snatched out his sharp saber, and cut off the evil tutor's head. He himself quickly made for shore, went home, said good-bye to his father, and set off to look for the thrice-tenth kingdom.

He walked wherever his eyes led him, for a long time, for a short time: quickly may a tale be spun, but not so soon a deed is done. He came to a little house. The little house stood in an open field, turning around on chicken legs. He went into the little house, and there was a Baba Yaga, bony leg. "Fie, fie!" she said. "There was no sight or sound here of the Russian spirit, but now it's come by itself. By will or by compulsion, fine young man?"

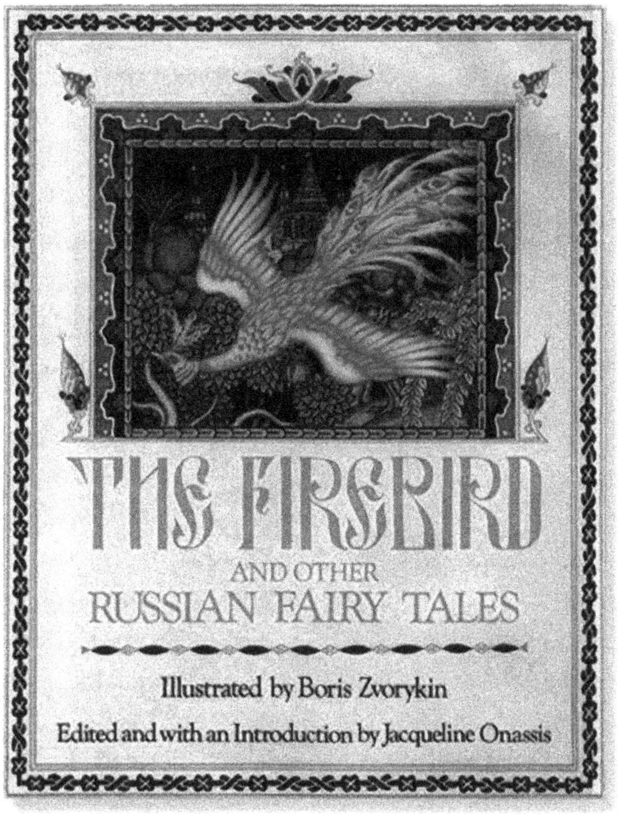

The Firebird and Other Russian Fairy Tales, edited by Jacqueline Onassis, illustrations by Boris Zvorykin. Of the volume's four tales, only "Maria Morevna" and "Vasilisa the Beautiful" (here, the Fair) feature Baba Yaga. Zvorykin's luxurious visuals compensate for the book's slimness, their sumptuous colors and jeweled textures making for a stunning Russ-Wonderland. *The Firebird and Other Russian Fairy Tales*, edited by Jacqueline Onassis, illustrations by Boris Zvorykin. Publisher: Studio, 1978.

"As much by will, but twice as much by compulsion! Do you happen to know, Baba Yaga, the thrice-tenth kingdom?"

"No, I don't!" said the yaga woman.[96] And she told him to go see her middle sister; perhaps that one would know.

Ivan the merchant's son thanked her and set off. He walked and walked, near or far, long or short, and he came to a little house of the same kind. He went into it, and there was a Baba Yaga. "Fie-fie!" she said, "There was no sight or sound of the Russian spirit here, but now it's come by itself. By free will or by compulsion, fine young man?"

"So much by free will, but twice as much by compulsion! Do you happen to know where the thrice-tenth kingdom is?"

"No, I don't!" answered the yaga woman, and she ordered him to go see her younger sister. Perhaps that one would know. "If she gets angry at you and wants to eat you, take three horns from her and ask to play on them. Play the first horn not too loudly, the second one louder, and the third one even louder."

Ivan the merchant's son thanked the yaga woman and went on.

He walked and walked, for a long time, for a short time, near or far. He finally saw the little house; it stood in an open field, spinning around on chicken shins. He went inside and there was a Baba Yaga. "Fie-fie! There was no sight or sound of the Russian smell here, but now it's come by itself!" said the yaga woman, and she ran to sharpen her teeth so she could eat up her uninvited guest.

Ivan the merchant's son asked her to give him the three horns. He played softly on the first one, louder on the second, and on the third even louder. Suddenly all kinds of birds flew in from all directions.

A Firebird came, too. "Climb up on me as quickly as you can," said the Firebird, "and we'll fly wherever you need to go. Otherwise, the Baba Yaga will eat you up!"

He just barely managed to climb up in time. Baba Yaga came running, grabbed the Firebird by the tail, and yanked out more than a few feathers.

The Firebird flew off with Ivan the merchant's son. For a long time it soared along through the sky, and finally it landed beside the wide sea. "Well, Ivan the merchant's son! The thrice-tenth kingdom lies over this sea. I don't have the strength to carry you over to the other side. Make your way across however you can!"

Ivan the merchant's son slid off the Firebird, thanked it, and started walking along the shore.

He walked and walked. There stood a little house, and he went inside it. An old, old woman met him. She gave him food and drink and started to ask him where he was going, why he was wandering.

He told her that he was going to the thrice-tenth kingdom, searching for the Tsar-Maiden, his intended.

"Ah!" said the old woman. "She's already fallen out of love with you. If she sets eyes on you, the Tsar-Maiden will tear you apart. Her love's hidden far away!"

"How can I get hold of it?"

"Wait a bit! My daughter lives with the Tsar-Maiden, and she promised to come see me for a while today. Perhaps she can find out for us."

Then the old woman turned Ivan the merchant's son into a pin and stuck it into the wall. In the evening her daughter flew in. The mother asked her: Did she happen to know where the Tsar-Maiden's love was hidden?

"I don't know," the daughter replied. She promised to find out that very thing from the Tsar-Maiden herself. The next day she came flying again and said to her mother, "On the other side of the ocean-sea there stands an oak tree. In the oak tree is a chest, in the chest a hare, in the hare a duck, in the duck an egg, and in that egg is the Tsar-Maiden's love!"

Ivan the merchant's son took some bread and set off for the place she had described. He found the oak tree, took down the chest down, pulled the hare out of it, the duck out of the hare, and the egg out of the duck, and he brought the little egg back to the old woman. Soon it was the old woman's name day.[97] She invited the Tsar-Maiden and the thirty other maidens, her foster sisters, as name-day guests. She baked the egg, and she dressed up Ivan the merchant's son in good clothes and hid him.

At midday the Tsar-Maiden and the thirty other maidens flew in all at once, sat down at the table, and began to eat lunch.

After the meal the old woman served each of them an ordinary egg. But she gave the Tsar-Maiden the very egg that Ivan the merchant's son had found. The Tsar-Maiden ate the egg, and that moment she fell deeply-deeply in love with Ivan the merchant's son. The old woman brought him out.

How many joys there were, what merriment! The Tsar-Maiden left together with her intended, the merchant's son, for her kingdom. They were married and began to live and thrive and store up riches.

(Afanas'ev, no. 232)

Vasilisa the Beautiful

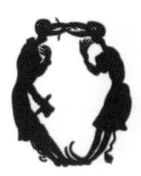

Once upon a time, in a certain kingdom, there lived a merchant. He lived with his wife for twelve years and had only one daughter, Vasilisa the Beautiful.

The girl was eight years old when her mother died. As she was dying, the merchant's wife called her daughter to her, pulled a doll out from under the blanket, gave it to her, and said, "Listen, my dear Vasilisa! Remember and carry out my final words. I'm dying, and along with my parental blessing I leave you this doll here. Always keep her with you and don't show her to anyone; if ever some grief happens to you, give her something to eat and ask her advice. She will eat and tell you what to do to help in your misfortune." Then the mother kissed her daughter and died.

After his wife's death the merchant grieved for a while, as is proper, and then he started to think about getting married again. He was a good man, and there were plenty of potential brides, but the one who pleased him most was a widow. She was already a certain age and had two daughters of her own, almost the same age as Vasilisa. He thought she must be an experienced housewife and mother.

The merchant married the widow, but he was disappointed in her and didn't gain a mother for his Vasilisa. Vasilisa was the prettiest girl in the village. Her stepmother and stepsisters envied her beauty and tormented her with all kinds of work, hoping she would get thin from the work and her skin would darken from the wind and sun. She had no kind of life at all!

Vasilisa bore it all without complaining. Every day she grew more plump and beautiful, while her stepmother and her daughters got skinnier and uglier from spite, even though they sat with their hands folded, like aristocratic young ladies.

And how could this be? Well, Vasilisa's little doll helped her. How could the girl have handled all the work without that!? But often Vasilisa herself would have nothing to eat; she would save the tastiest morsel for her doll.

Vasilisa and her Mother, detail by Forest Rogers. http://www.forestrogers.com/.

In the evening, once everyone had gone to bed, she would shut herself in the store-room where she lived and give the doll something to eat, saying, "Here, dolly, have a bite to eat, listen to my grief! I live in my father's house, but I see no joy. My evil stepmother is trying to drive me off the surface of the earth. Tell me, how should I act and live and what should I do?"

The dolly would have a bite and then give her advice and comfort in her grief, and in the morning she would do all kinds of work for Vasilisa. Vasilisa would just relax in the shade and pick flowers, while her rows of vegetables were already weeded, and the cabbage watered, and the water

A vivid lacquer box illustrating Vasilisa the Beautiful by the Mstera artist Anatolii Shirokov. It portrays not only Vasilisa, but also Baba Yaga, all three riders who serve her, as well as the famous hut and the forest creatures who do her bidding or aid protagonists as their magic helpers. Artist: Anatolii Shirokov, from the village of Mstera, http://www.russianlacquerart.com/gallery/Mstera/0050/002741.

carried, and the stove heated. The little doll also showed Vasilisa what herbs to use against sunburn. She had a good life with her doll.

Several years passed. Vasilisa grew up and was old enough to marry. All the young bachelors in the city had an eye on Vasilisa, but no one even looked at her stepmother's daughters. The stepmother grew even more spiteful and said to all the suitors, "I won't let the younger one marry before the older ones do!" After she saw the suitors out the door, she took out her angry feelings by beating Vasilisa.

One day the merchant had to leave on a long trip for business. The stepmother moved to another house, and that house stood next to a deep, dark forest. In a glade in the forest stood a little house, and a Baba Yaga lived in that little house. She didn't let anyone come near, and she ate people as if they were chickens. After they moved to the new place, the merchant's wife kept sending Vasilisa, who was so hateful to her, into the woods on some errand or other, but Vasilisa always came home safely. The little doll showed her the way and didn't let her get close to the Baba Yaga's house.

Autumn came. The stepmother gave all three girls evening tasks. She made one of them tat lace, the second one knit stockings, and Vasilisa spin, and she set them all to their lessons. She put out every light in the whole house, leaving only one candle where the girls were working, and she herself went to bed.

The White Horseman by Ivan Bilibin (1900). One of several illustrations in the renowned series of watercolors Bilibin supplied for the popular fairy tale of Vasilisa's visit to Baba Yaga, the visual references the heroine's encounter en route with the White Horseman. According to Baba Yaga, he is her "clear day"—an explanation that suggests Baba Yaga's command over the cycle of time. Illustration by Ivan Bilibin (1876–1942).

The girls worked. The candle started to smoke. One of the stepmother's daughters picked up the tongs to fix the wick, but instead of doing that she snuffed out the candle as if by accident, following her mother's orders.

"What can we do now?" the girls said. "There's no flame in the whole house, and we haven't finished our tasks. Someone has to run and get fire from the Baba Yaga!"

"I have light from my pins," said the one who was tatting lace, "I won't go."

"I won't go either," said the one who was knitting a stocking, "I have light from the needles!"

"You have to go get fire," they both shouted. "Go see Baba Yaga!" And they pushed Vasilisa out of the room.

Vasilisa went to her little store-room, put the dinner she had prepared in front of her doll, and said, "Here, dolly, have a bite to eat and listen to my grief. They're sending me to get fire from a Baba Yaga. The Baba Yaga will eat me up!"

The Red Horseman by Ivan Bilibin (1900). This illustration plays on the ambiguity of the Russian word "krasnyi," which earlier meant both "red" and "beautiful." The Red Horseman carrying a blazing torch is, Baba Yaga explains, her "beautiful/red sun," and logically should symbolize the hottest part of the day or the beautiful sunset of early evening, yet in the text he augurs sunrise. Illustration by Ivan Bilibin (1876–1942).

The doll had a bite to eat, and her eyes lit up like two candles. "Don't be afraid, dear Vasilisa!" she said. "Go where they're sending you, but always keep me with you. Nothing bad can happen to you at Baba Yaga's if I'm with you."

Vasilisa got ready, put her doll into her pocket, crossed herself, and set off into the deep, dark forest.

She walked along and trembled. Suddenly a horseman galloped past her. He himself was white and dressed in white. The horse he rode was white, and the harness on the horse was white. It began to get light in the woods.

As she walked along farther, another horseman galloped past. He himself was red, dressed in red and on a red steed. The sun began to rise.

Vasilisa walked all night and all day, and she didn't reach the clearing where Baba Yaga's house stood until evening. The fence around the house was made of human bones; human skulls with eyes were stuck on the fence. There were human leg-bones in the gate instead of posts, there were arm-

The Black Horseman by Ivan Bilibin (1900). Baba Yaga's "black night" as the Black Horseman, with the sinking sun in the background heralding the darkness of night. Like everything in her hut and sundry animals in her domain, all three horsemen are her servants. Illustration by Ivan Bilibin (1876–1942).

bones instead of doors, and a mouth with sharp teeth instead of a lock. Vasilisa felt faint with horror and stood there as if rooted to the spot. Suddenly another horseman rode by. He was black, dressed all in black, and on a black steed. He rode up to Baba Yaga's gate and disappeared as if the earth had swallowed him. Night had come.

But the darkness didn't last long: the eyes of all the skulls on the fence lit up, and the whole clearing became light as midday. Vasilisa was shaking with fear, but since she didn't know where to run she stayed where she was.

Soon a dreadful noise came from the forest. The trees cracked, the dry leaves rustled. Baba Yaga rode out of the forest; she was riding in a mortar, driving with a pestle, sweeping her tracks away with a broom. She rode up to the gate, stopped, sniffed all around her, and shouted, "Fie, fie! I smell a Russian smell! Who's there?"

Vasilisa went up to the old woman fearfully, bowed low, and said, "I'm here, granny! The stepmother's daughters sent me to get fire from you."

Baba Yaga Flying in Her Mortar by Ivan Bilibin (1900). In his portrayal of Baba Yaga, Bilibin combines shapes and colors that integrate her into the surroundings—streaming white hair and white broom that echo the white trunks of the birch trees, brownish-beige complexion, limbs, and pestle that blend with the vegetation—while the vivid pink and blue of her garments provide a strong contrast. After all, she is nature, but in anthropomorphic form. Moreover, ambivalence and ambiguity are her constitutive features. Illustration by Ivan Bilibin (1876–1942).

"All right," said the Yaga-Baba, "I know them. Live here for now and work for me, and then I'll give you some fire. If not, I'll eat you!" Then she turned to the gates and shouted, "Hey, unlock, my firm locks! Open up, my wide gate!"

The gate opened, and Baba Yaga rode in, whistling a tune. Vasilisa followed her, and then everything closed and locked back up. Once she got into the room, Baba Yaga stretched out and said to Vasilisa, "Serve up what's in the stove, I want to eat."

Vasilisa lit a splinter from the skulls on the fence and began getting food out of the stove and serving it to the Yaga. There was enough food ready there for ten people. She brought kvass, mead, beer, and wine up from the cellar.[98] The old woman ate and drank everything up. All she left for Vasilisa was a bit of cabbage soup, a crust of bread, and a little piece of ham.

Baba Yaga began to get ready for bed and said, "When I go out tomorrow, here's what I want you to do. Clean up the yard, sweep out the house, make dinner, get the laundry ready, and go into the granary, take a quarter measure of wheat and clean the wild peas out of it. And be sure to do everything. If you don't, I'll eat you!"

After she gave these orders, the Baba Yaga started snoring. But Vasilisa put the old woman's leftovers in front of the doll, burst into tears, and said, "Here, dolly, have a bite to eat and listen to my grief! Baba Yaga has given me hard work, and she says she'll eat me if I don't finish everything. Help me!"

The doll answered, "Don't fear, Vasilisa the Beautiful! Eat some dinner, say your prayers, and go to bed. Morning is wiser than the evening."

Vasilisa woke up early-early, but Baba Yaga was already up. She looked out the window. The eyes of the skulls were dimming. There the white rider passed, and it got completely light. Baba Yaga went out into the yard and whistled, and the mortar and pestle and the broom appeared before her. The red horseman flashed by, and the sun rose. Baba Yaga got in the mortar and rode out of the yard. She drove with the pestle and swept her tracks away with the broom.

Now Vasilisa was left alone. She looked around Baba Yaga's house, marveled at the abundance of everything, and stopped in thought. What task should she start first?

She looked, and all the work was already done—the doll was picking the last black grains out of the wheat. "Oh, you, you've saved me!" said Vasilisa to the doll. "You've rescued me from misfortune."

"All that's left for you to do is make the dinner," the doll answered, climbing into Vasilisa's pocket. "Good luck as you cook it, and then rest all you want!"

Toward evening, Vasilisa set the table and waited for Baba Yaga. It started to get dark. The black horseman flashed by outside the gate, and it got completely dark. Only the eyes of the skulls showed light. The trees began to crack, the leaves began to rustle; the Baba Yaga was coming. Vasilisa met her at the door.

"Is everything done?" asked Yaga.

"Be so good as to look for yourself, granny!" said Vasilisa.

Baba Yaga looked over everything, felt a bit disappointed that there was nothing to be angry about, and said, "All right!" Then she shouted, "My true servants, my heartfelt friends, grind the wheat for me!" Three pairs of hands appeared, picked up the wheat, and took it out of sight. Baba Yaga ate her fill, began to get ready for bed, and once again gave orders to Vasilisa. "Tomorrow do the same things you did today, and besides that take the poppy-seed from the granary and clean the dirt out of it, grain by grain. You see, someone mixed a lot of earth into it out of spite!"

The old woman finished speaking, turned to the wall, and started snoring, and Vasilisa started to feed her doll.

The doll ate a bit and told her the same thing as the night before. "Pray to God and go to bed. Morning's wiser than the evening. Everything will be done, Vasilisushka!"

In the morning Baba Yaga rode her mortar again out of the yard, and Vasilisa and the doll took care of all the work right away.

The old woman returned, looked everything over, and shouted, "My true servants, my heartfelt friends, press the oil out of the poppy-seed for me!" The three pairs of hands appeared, grabbed the poppy-seed, and took it away. Baba Yaga began to eat dinner. She ate, and Vasilisa stood there silently. "Why don't you say anything?" asked the Baba Yaga. "You stand there as if you're mute!"

"I didn't dare," answered Vasilisa. "But if you'll permit me, then I would like to ask you about a few things."

"Ask me. Only not every question leads to good. If you know too much, you'll soon get old!"

"I want to ask you, granny, only about what I saw. When I was coming here, a horseman on a white horse rode past me, all white and wearing white clothes. Who is he?"

"That's my clear day," answered Baba Yaga.

"Then another horseman passed me, on a red horse and all dressed in red. Who is that?"

"That's my beautiful sun!" answered Baba Yaga.[99]

"And what does the black horseman mean, granny, the one who passed me at your very gate?"

"That's my black night—they're all my faithful servants!"

Vasilisa remembered the three pairs of hands and said nothing.

"Why don't you ask me more?" asked Baba Yaga.

"That'll do for me. You said yourself, grandmother, that if I learn too much I'll get old."

Baba Yaga said, "It's good that you ask only about what you saw outside the yard, and not what's in the yard! I don't like to have dirty laundry brought out of my house, and I eat the ones who are too curious! Now I shall ask you. How do you manage to finish all the work I order you to do?"

"My mother's blessing helps me," answered Vasilisa.

Vasilisa the Beautiful, late nineteenth or early twentieth century, anonymous. Released after her doll has accomplished the three tasks set for Vasilisa, the girl returns to her stepmother and two stepsisters with the light she has obtained from Baba Yaga. The latter's hut behind her is illuminated by the skulls impaled on the surrounding fence—concrete evidence of Baba Yaga's association with death. Artist unknown, http://belialith.blogspot.com/2011/03/baba-yaga-black-goddess.html.

"So that's it! You get away from here, blessed daughter! I don't need anyone with a blessing."

She dragged Vasilisa out of the room and pushed her through the gate, took a skull with glowing eyes off the fence, stuck it on a stake, handed it to her, and said, "Here's the fire for the stepmother's daughters, take it. After all, that's why they sent you here."

Vasilisa set off homeward at a run with her skull, which stopped burning as soon as morning came. Finally, toward evening of the second day, she made it back to her own home.

As she came up to the gate, she wanted to throw the skull away. Surely they don't need the fire any more at home, she thought to herself. But suddenly she heard a dull voice out of the skull: "Don't throw me away! Take me to your stepmother."

Vasilisa Taking Home the Fire by Ivan Bilibin (1900). Her perilous mission accomplished, Vasilisa carries the light-bearing skull back home through the forest. The skull not only illuminates her path, but, in a gruesome way, ultimately solves her family problems. Illustration by Ivan Bilibin (1876–1942).

She glanced at her stepmother's house, saw no light in any of the windows, and made up her mind to take the skull in there.

For the very first time they welcomed her warmly, and they told her that ever since she had left there'd been no flame in the house. They couldn't strike one themselves and, no matter what fire they brought from the neighbors, it would go out as soon as they brought it into the room. "But perhaps your fire will last!" said her stepmother.

They brought the skull into the main room, and the eyes gave the stepmother and her daughters such a look from the skull that it just burned them! They tried to hide, but no matter where they ran, the eyes kept following them. Toward morning it had burned them entirely to ashes. Only Vasilisa was left untouched.

In the morning Vasilisa buried the skull in the earth, locked the house with a key, went into the city, and asked permission to live with an old woman who had no children. She lived very well there and waited for her father. Then one day she said to the old woman, "It's dull for me to sit with nothing to do, granny! Go and buy me some of the best flax. At least I can do some spinning."

The old woman bought her some of the very best flax. Vasilisa sat down to work. Her work went wonderfully, the thread came out thin and even as a hair. She collected a lot of thread; it was time to start weaving, but they couldn't find loom reeds to suit Vasilisa's thread. No one would agree to make them. Vasilisa tried asking her doll, and her doll said, "Bring me any old reed and an old shuttle and a horse's mane. I'll put everything together for you."

Vasilisa got everything necessary and lay down to sleep, while the doll prepared a wonderful loom for her overnight. Toward the end of winter the linen cloth was woven, and it was so fine that it could be put through a needle's eye in place of thread.

In the spring they bleached the cloth, and Vasilisa said to the old woman, "Granny, sell this cloth and take the money for yourself."

The old woman glanced at the stuff and gasped. "No, my child! No one may wear this kind of cloth except the tsar. I'll take it to the palace."

The old woman set off to the tsar's palace and walked back and forth under the windows. The tsar caught sight of her and said, "What do you need, old woman?"

"Your royal majesty," answered the old woman, "I have brought some wonderful goods. I don't want to show them to anyone but you."

The tsar ordered the old woman shown in to him, and as soon as he saw the cloth he marveled. "What do you want for it?" asked the tsar.

"It has no price, father tsar! I've brought it to you as a gift."

The tsar thanked the old woman and sent her home with presents.

They began to make the tsar shirts of that cloth. They cut them out, but they couldn't find a seamstress anywhere who would take it upon herself to make them. They looked for a long time. Finally the tsar summoned the old woman and said, "You knew how to spin and weave this kind of cloth, so you must know how to sew shirts from it."

"I'm not the one, lord, who spun and wove the cloth," said the old woman, "it's the work of my ward—a young woman."

"So then let her sew them!"

The old woman returned home and told Vasilisa about everything. Vasilisa said to her, "I knew this work would not pass by my hands." She shut herself up in her room and got to work. She sewed without resting, and soon a dozen shirts were ready.

This 6-kopek Soviet stamp issued in 1975 features Vasilisa leaving the notorious hut of Baba Yaga. As in the United States, the choice of visuals for stamps depends on the popularity of the persona or event represented, and this stamp corroborates Baba Yaga's status and the fairy tales in which she appears as central in Russian and Soviet culture.

The old woman took the shirts to the tsar, and Vasilisa washed her face, combed her hair, got dressed, and sat down under by the window. She sat there and waited to see what would happen. She saw the tsar's servant come into the old woman's yard.

He walked into the room and said, "The lord tsar wants to see the master who worked on the shirts for him, and to reward her from his own royal hands."

Vasilisa went and appeared before the tsar. The moment the tsar saw Vasilisa the Beautiful, he fell madly in love with her. "No," he said, "my beauty! I won't be separated from you. You're to be my wife."

Then the tsar took Vasilisa by her white hands and sat her down beside him, and they held the wedding then and there. Soon Vasilisa's father too returned, rejoiced at her fate, and stayed to live with his daughter. Vasilisa brought the old woman to live with her, and as long as Vasilisa lived she always carried the little doll in her pocket.

(Afanas'ev, no. 104)

Baba Yaga's Hut by Cynthia Ferguson. www.cindyferguson.com.

NOTES

FOREWORD

1. Gustav Henningsen, "'Ladies from the Outside': An Archaic Pattern of the Witches' Sabbath," in *Early Modern European Witchcraft: Centres and Peripheries*, ed. Ben Ankarloo and Gustav Henningsen (Oxford: Clarendon Press, 1990), 195.

PREFACE, ACKNOWLEDGMENTS, AND TRANSLATOR'S NOTE

1. Aleksandr Afanas'ev's *Narodnye russkie skazki* has been published in a number of editions, beginning in 1855; the most complete editions usually included three volumes and are edited by the foremost Russian folklorists of the day. The tales Afanas'ev collected are now also available on the FebWeb web site. Ivan Khudiakov's collection *Velikorusskie skazki* was first published in Moscow in 1860–1862, and they have also been reprinted more than once, though they never gained the fame of Afanas'ev's collection.
2. Robert Chandler, ed., *Russian Magic Tales from Pushkin to Platonov*, trans. Robert Chandler and Elizabeth Chandler, with Sibelan Forrester, Anna Gunin, and Olga Meerson (London: Penguin Books, 2012). The appendix, "Baba Yaga: The Wild Witch of the East," appears on pages 419–33.

INTRODUCTION

1. *Etimologicheskii slovar' russkogo jazyka* (Moscow: Izdatel'stvo "Progress," 1973), vol. IV, 542–43.
2. Fasmer points out that "yazi-baba" in Ukrainian means both 'witch' and . . . a hairy caterpillar.
3. The word for 'sea' in Russian is *more*, pronounced MORE-yeh. It is neuter in gender, not a man's name like the sources of most patronymics. Perhaps Mar'ia Morevna's father is the king of the sea; he is the heroine's father in some Russian wonder tales that do not feature Baba Yaga.
4. Joanna Hubbs, *Mother Russia: The Feminine Myth in Russian Culture* (Bloomington: Indiana University Press, 1988), 46.
5. Boris A. Rybakov, *Iazychestvo drevnei Rusi* (*The Pagan Religion of Old Rus'*) (Moscow: "Nauka," 1987).
6. The old calendar marked the changing seasons around February 1—Groundhog Day?—May 1, August 1, and November 1. Thus, Midsummer Night's Eve is called "midsummer" even though we now count the summer as beginning, rather than reaching its middle, on the solstice.
7. The length of the Russian term for a female cousin, *dvoiurodnaia sestra*, encourages speakers to abbreviate to its second half, *sestra*, which means just 'sister.'
8. Even modern Russian observes in a proverb that "God loves trinity."

9. Mistakes come in threes, too: Prince Ivan tries to rescue Mar'ia Morevna three times, even though Kashchei the Deathless has warned that he will kill him after the third time, and the kid in "Baba Yaga and the Kid" lets Baba Yaga provoke him into yelling three times even after his brothers, the cat and the bird, repeatedly warn him not to.
10. The shape of the wonder tale—the variety of folktales that begin once upon a time and end happily ever after—was brilliantly generalized by Vladimir Propp in *Morphology of the Folktale* (1928; English translation 1968), and by Joseph Campbell in *Hero with a Thousand Faces* (New York: Pantheon Books, 1949).
11. *Rus'* is the old name for the East Slavic land that was ruled from Kiev or Kyïv. The word is the root of "Russian" and also of "Ruthenia" and "Rusyn."
12. This is the case in one version of "The Feather of Finist, the Bright Falcon." The shift from Baba Yaga to helpful old woman minus chicken feet may be due to the rise of Orthodox religion as it displaced or "overwrote" pagan elements of traditional Russian folk culture.
13. The idea that dawn would be distinct from sunrise reflects an archaic worldview. The sun was the ruler but not the cause of the blue daytime sky. The sky grew pale long before the sun appeared and remained pale after the sun set, especially in northern latitudes, and in northern Russia in winter the sun might not rise at all.
14. The Russian word for "red," *krasnyi*, comes from the same root as the word for "beautiful," so the sun is at once red and beautiful.
15. Baba Yaga never seems to have a son, though she may have a grandson . . .
16. These powerful figures tend not to appear in great numbers in any one tale. They fulfill the same testing and rewarding function, or else one or two of them will suffice to signify the magical or ritual realm.
17. Even in the nineteenth century, hunting strongly shaped Russian experience: see Ivan Turgenev's first big literary success, *A Sportsman's Sketches* (1852), which presents both peasants and nobles as hunters.
18. See Natalie Kononenko, "Women as Performers of Oral Literature: A Re-examination of Epic and Lament," in *Women Writers in Russian Literature*, ed. Toby W. Clyman and Diana Greene (Westport, CT: Praeger, 1994), 17–33.
19. In the Russian wonder tales, characters are often torn apart—not only girls who fail to rescue the baby, but also Prince Ivan when he tries too often to take Mar'ia Morevna back from Kashchei. Prince Ivan is reconstituted and revived with dead water and living water. Death in a wonder tale is not always permanent.
20. The terrors of the forest were personified not only in Baba Yaga, but also in *leshii*, the nature spirit who was master of the forest, and a number of other nature spirits. For more about Russian nature spirits, see Linda Ivanits's book, *Russian Folk Belief* (Armonk, NY: M. E. Sharpe, 1989).
21. The sun itself might be seen as moving through a rapid cycle of birth and death as it rises and sets; the moon waxes and wanes more gradually, but its changing shape was often interpreted in ancient cultures as swelling with pregnant fertility, or as shrinking while it was devoured by a serpent or another monster.

22. Interestingly, the RuneQuest explanation of Baba Yaga and her daughters imagines her mating with men in dark places, rather than producing children by herself, "in the old way." See her page on Simon Phipp's RuneQuest/Gloriantha site, http://www.soltakss.com/babayaga.html.
23. Readers might be interested to learn that several of the tales in Afanas'ev's famous nineteenth-century collection were recorded in dialects of Belarusian or Ukrainian.
24. Some of the tales do seem to cry out for a Jungian reading: Mar'ia Morevna is an effective and terrifying war leader despite her feminine beauty until Prince Ivan lets Kashchei out of her closet. Then she appears to turn into a typical, passive fairy-tale princess. It is only after Ivan has rescued her that she receives the *bogatyr* horse that Kashchei once earned from Baba Yaga, which we know is not *quite* as good as Ivan's horse. Kashchei might be read as the critical or oppressive powers of her animus, and the horse as the autonomy that is returned to her once she and Ivan are finally united as equals. Nevertheless, the tale clearly focuses on Ivan's own development into full adulthood rather than Mar'ia Morevna's.
25. See Marija Gimbutas, *The Goddesses and Gods of Old Europe, 7000–3500 BC: Myths, Legends and Cult Images* (Berkeley and Los Angeles: University of California Press, 1974) and *The Civilization of the Goddess: The World of Old Europe* (San Francisco: HarperSanFrancisco, 1991), and Barbara G. Walker, *The Woman's Encyclopedia of Myths and Secrets* (San Francisco: Harper and Row, 1983).
26. Dubravka Ugrešić, *Baba Jaga je snijela jaje* (*Baba Yaga Laid an Egg*, translated into English by Ellen Elias-Bursać, Celia Hawkesworth, and Mark Thompson in 2009).

TALES OF BABA YAGA

1. The dialect word *zhikhar'* means a young man, but it is less formal than "young man." Translating it as "kid" is meant to suggest a combination of youth and energy. Norbert Guterman gives this tale the title "The Brave Youth."
2. The tale uses the regional word *ponuzhat*, which Afanas'ev glossed as *pogoniaet*, "drives."
3. *Zabazlal*—glossed as *gromko krichat'*, to shout loudly.
4. *Golbets*—"a wooden appendage/*pridelka* to the stove, above the passage to the cellar."
5. *Ladka*—a clay frying pan.
6. *Navolok*, literally the 'dragged over' or 'stretched over'; Afanas'ev notes its meaning as *pol*, floor.
7. *Tselo*—the upper part of a Russian stove.
8. *Zamoryshek*. Afanas'ev notes that some tellers use a different variant of this name, *Posledushek*, which also means "runt" or "the last little bit."
9. Afanas'ev lists this variant: the witch was tempted by the marvelous *bogatyr* horses and decided to kill the fine young men during the night. Runt took the garlands off her sleeping daughters, and the hats off his brothers; he put the garlands on his brothers, and the hats on the witch's daughters. The witch came and killed all of her daughters. Runt took a brush, a comb, and a towel from her, and with their help he saved them all as they ran away. When he threw down the brush a mountain rose up, when he threw down the comb

a forest grew up, and when he threw down the towel a deep river appeared.

10. The scarlet flower ties this tale to Konstantin Aksakov's "Little Scarlet Flower," 1858, which he wrote down from memory after hearing the tale many times from a beloved nanny. That detail shows the links of Finist to the Beast in "Beauty and the Beast," and to many other folklore animal grooms (and brides).
11. The word *zavetnyj* means something between "special" and "sacred": a thing that is *zavetnyi* comes with special conditions or even a covenant.
12. "When they sang '*Dostoino*,'" a prayer to Mary the Mother of God that begins "It is suitable to praise you . . ."
13. Afanas'ev cites this variant: inside she saw a Baba Yaga, bony leg, in a cast-iron mortar.
14. The Russian word "dukh" can mean "spirit," "breath," or "smell"—so "essence" might be a good translation, though that English word is from a higher stylistic register than most of the rest of this tale.
15. Variant: appears in real life.
16. Variant ending: Finist the bright falcon, after learning that the princess had sold him for diamonds and for gold, ordered his servants to drive her away from the palace; but he himself married the darling fair maiden. There's no need to say that it was merry at that wedding; there were many tsars and tsars' sons there, and kings and princes, and all kinds of Orthodox people. I myself was there, I drank mead and wine, it ran down my mustache, but it didn't go into my mouth.
17. Variant: He came to the shore of the sea and saw one gray duck swimming on the water.
18. Variant: "You knew how to get me, now marry me. I'm not a gray duck after all, I'm a king's daughter!"
19. Variant: two spirits.
20. Variant: on that island walks a golden-maned mare with nine foals.
21. Variant: let him send the musketeer to the edge of ruin, where Shmat-Razum lives.
22. Afanas'ev notes the word *kisa*, glossed as *meshok*, 'sack.'
23. The teller switches here from "king" to "tsar."
24. Variant: Urza-Murza.
25. Variant of the middle of the tale: The musketeer said good-bye to his wife, let the ball of thread roll before him, and set off after it. Close or else far, soon, or briefly, he came to an empty field, looked—and a little house was standing on a chicken's leg. He hid the ball of thread in his pocket and said, "Little house, little house! Stand with your front to me and your back to the woods." The house turned its front toward him. He stepped across the threshold and saw an old woman sitting in the house.

"Hello, granny!"

"Hello, good man! How has God brought you to our country—by your will or against your will?"

"Against my will, granny! The king sent me. 'Go,' he said, 'I don't know where, bring me back I don't know what.'"

"Well, lad, as long as I've been living in the world, I've never heard of that."

The musketeer took a pitcher of water, washed up from the road, took out his towel, and began to dry off. The old woman saw that and asked, "Listen, good man, where did you get hold of that towel? Why, that's the work of my niece."

"Of your niece, and of my God-given wife."

"Where is she, the dear?"
"She stayed at home, she's alive and well, she asked me to pass on her regards."
The old woman was overjoyed, gave him food and drink, and said, "Well, my friend! Come with me, I'll collect all my subjects for you and ask them. Perhaps, if your fate is happy, one of them will know where and why the king has sent you."
They went out into the yard. The old woman called out in a loud voice and gave a manly whistle, and all the birds came flying to her. As many as there are in the whole white world, [The Russian expression "the white world" suggests every place where the sunlight shines.] all of them came flying. "Flying birds! Whoever among you knows, tell me how to get to I don't know where, to bring back I don't know what." None of the birds had heard of it.
The musketeer walked farther, and he stopped by another old woman's house. That one gathered the beasts and asked them. The beasts didn't know anything either.
The musketeer continued on his way, stopped by the house of a third old woman, and told her his grief. The old woman went out into her yard, shouted in a loud voice, and gave a manly whistle, and all the reptiles of every name came crawling, both the hissing snakes and the jumping frogs. So many of them came that there was nowhere to step! Not one of the reptiles knew where and why the king had sent the good lad.
Then the old woman took the list of names and began to call the roll—was everyone in place? All the reptiles were there in their places; only one frog was missing. They sent runners right away to find her. Not even an hour had passed before they came, dragging a frog with three legs. "Where did you get to, you rascal?"
"It's my fault, my lady! I hurried with all my strength, but I had an accident on the road. A peasant was driving a wagon; the wheel rolled over me and crushed off my leg. I could hardly make my way to your mercy."
"Do you know how to go I don't know where and to bring back I don't know what?"
"Perhaps I could show the way, only it's whoooo!—ever so far! There's no way I could jump all the way there."
The musketeer took the frog, wrapped it in a kerchief, and carried it in his hand. He walked along, and the frog told him the way. He walked and walked; he came to the blue sea, crossed on a boat to the other side, and saw a palace standing there. He went inside and hid behind the stove.
Right at midnight twelve handsome lads came into the palace. The leader stepped up and shouted, "Hey, Gulbrey!"
An invisible creature answered, "What are your orders?"
"Serve dinner and wine for twelve people, and let there be a choir of musicians."
At once everything appeared: the music began to roar and the party got started! . . . (The musketeer lures the invisible creature away with him and sets out on the way back.) He came up to the sea and saw that the boat was nowhere to be found. "Hey, Gulbrey! How could we get to the other side?"
"Here's a burned stump. Sit down on it and hold on tight."
The musketeer put the frog inside his shirt, sat down on the burned stump and grabbed it tightly with both hands. Suddenly the stump rose up into the air and flew all the way across the sea . . .

26. Variant: One merchant pulled out a snuff-box. The moment he lifted the lid, that moment a big city spread out. The other merchant got out an axe. He tapped with the blade on the ground, and at once a palace appeared; he struck with the butt on the back corner, and the palace was gone! And the third merchant showed him a needle case: he just opened it, and out rode an army with both cavalry and infantry.
27. *Moklak*, glossed by Afanas'ev as *bessovestnyj chelovek*, 'man without a conscience,' and *poproshajka*, 'cadger.'
28. The Russian name Ol'ga is pronounced with a very soft "l" sound, spelled by the "soft sign." The name comes from a word connected to magic.
29. Variant: Prince Ivan looked—and there was a dragon with twelve heads, with twelve snouts hanging on iron hooks, and blood was flowing from its wounds. The dragon said to Prince Ivan, "Ah, good man! Dip your finger in my blood and breathe on me. For your service I'll save you three times from death." Ivan Tsarevich dipped his finger in the blood and blew on the dragon; the dragon leapt up, broke the hooks and flew away.
30. Variant: "Leave us your golden ring. We'll look at it and think of you. If the ring's bright, that will mean you're alive and well, but if it gets dull we'll know right away that some misfortune has overtaken you." Prince Ivan left his gold ring and set off for the dragon kingdom.
31. Variant: full of pies.
32. Variant: Eagle Eagleson flew to the sea and called the strong winds. The sea got rough and threw the barrel out onto the shore. Falcon Falconson grabbed the barrel in his talons, flew with it high up above the clouds, and threw it from there onto the earth, and the barrel fell and broke into pieces. Raven Ravenson brought healing water and living water and sprayed it onto Prince Ivan. After that all three of them lifted him up and took him over thrice-nine lands, to the thrice-tenth kingdom. They brought him to the thrice-tenth kingdom and said, "Go to the blue sea; a marvelous mare is strolling there. Ahead of her twelve mowers are mowing hay and twelve rakers are raking it; she follows them and eats it all up. When the mare starts drinking water, the blue sea gets rough, and leaves fall from the trees. When she starts scratching herself on the hundred-year-old oaks, those oak trees fall over on the ground, as if they were sheaves of oats. Every month she bears one foal. Twelve wolves walk around after her, and they devour those foals. Choose the moment, and as soon as the mare has borne a foal with a star on its forehead pick it up right away, and take it away from the wolves. That will be your *bogatyr* horse! With it, Koshchei the Deathless won't be able to catch you." Prince Ivan did everything his brothers-in-law had told him to . . .
33. Variant: Instead of the beehive, according to another recording, Prince Ivan meets a crab.
34. Variant: "How could we help coming back? Crabs came crawling from the whole sea, they started to grab onto us and pinch us with their claws—we'd have been glad to run until we came to the end of the world!"
35. Of course the reader remembers that Mar'ia Morevna has already seen Prince Ivan since he was brought back to life: she gave him the magic handkerchief and told him to get a horse from Baba Yaga. Perhaps the transfer of her joy and relief from that scene to this one reflects the possible dangers of his visit

to Baba Yaga, who could have torn him apart just as Koshchei did.

36. Variant: "And can we catch them?" "If we set off now, then perhaps we'll catch them. Prince Ivan has a new horse, my younger brother." Koshchei chased after Prince Ivan, and he was about to catch up to him. "Ah, brother," said Prince Ivan's horse to Koshchei's horse. "Why are you serving such an unclean monster? Throw him off and kick him!" The horse obeyed, threw Koshchei off, and kicked him to death.

37. Moon and Star would be very unusual names for girls in Russia: the names could be rendered as Luna and Stella, but the names "Mesiats" and "Zvezda" are the everyday names for the astronomical objects.

38. *Vanechka* is a diminutive form of Ivan—an affectionate nickname.

39. Saying a charm to work magic is often described with very simple language, with the charm or spell called simply "a word" or "the words."

40. Khudiakov's note: "Written down by me in the Nizhegorod *guberniia* in Ardatnovskii *uezd* in the village of Kotovko from the old woman Ol'ga Stepanovna Kotysheva, née in the village Nuchi of the same *uezd*."

41. "Govorila" means 'said' or 'was talking,' but it is the feminine verb form that would be used for a woman, not a man (like Prince Danila).

42. Variant: *Polyak Belyi Kolpak*, 'The Polish Man White Cap'; *Polyanin* means 'man who lives in the fields' or 'lowlander.'

43. Variant: He walked and walked. Smithies were standing there, and in those smithies they were heating iron and beating it with hammers. With every blow of the hammer, a soldier would be ready, with a rifle, with a saber, in full field ammunition, ready to go to war this minute!

Prince Ivan asked, "Blacksmiths, blacksmiths! Who are you making all these soldiers for?"

"For Baba Yaga, golden leg. She's been fighting with Beloy Polyanin for thirty years, but she still can't defeat him."

... He walked and walked. Some huts were standing there, and fair maidens sat in those huts, working at looms. The moment they made the loom-reed boom, all at once a soldier would leap out, with a rifle, with a saber, with the whole field ammunition, ready to go to war this moment! ...

44. In another recording the story ends differently: Beloy Polyanin hauled out the fair maiden with the cable, but feared that Prince Ivan would take away his bride, and thought of killing him. Prince Ivan guessed what was going on and wanted to test ahead of time whether Beloy Polyanin was true to him. He took a big stone and fastened it to the cable. Beloy Polyanin pulled and pulled, pulled it halfway up and then cut the cable, and the stone fell and shattered into fine dust. A huge eagle carried Prince Ivan from the other world (as in the tale "*Norka-zver*'" / "The Mink-Beast"). As soon as Beloy Polyanin saw him, he was mighty frightened, fell to his feet, and began begging for forgiveness. "Well, brother," said Prince Ivan, "I wouldn't forgive you for anything, if not for your young wife. I feel sorry for her. Thanks to her I forgive you!" After that Prince Ivan rides off to the dragon kingdom ...

45. Afanas'ev notes: "This word, *medved'*, is pronounced *vedmet'* in the local dialect."

46. Just as Ivan is the most common name for a fairy-tale hero, Mar'ia is a very common name for a heroine. There is

a Russian flower called *Ivan-da-Mar'ia*, 'Ivan and Mar'ia'; this tale is not the only place where the names are found together.

47. Variant: a raven.

48. Variant: The Bear Tsar ran off to get food, and Prince Ivan and Princess Mar'ia stood there and cried. Out of nowhere a good horse appeared. "Climb up on me," it said. "I'll take you to the blue sea." The moment they had climbed up, the good horse leapt with them over the standing trees, under the passing clouds. The bear saw and started chasing.

"Ah, good horse! The bear's chasing behind us!"

"No matter, Prince Ivan! Take the splinter out of my left ear and throw it behind you."

Prince Ivan pulled out the splinter and threw it, and all at once it became a deep, dark forest—you couldn't walk or ride through it! While the Bear Tsar was fighting his way through the grove, they rode off very far away. The bear came running in pursuit; he was already getting close!

"Ah, good horse! The bear is running up behind us."

"It's no matter, Prince Ivan! Take the little vial out of my right ear and spray behind you."

Prince Ivan did that, and right away it made a deep blue sea. The bear ran up to the blue sea, looked and gazed, and then ran off into the dark forests.

The good horse began to say good-bye to Prince Ivan and Princess Mar'ia. They were sorry to part with him, but there was nothing to be done. They said good-bye, and the prince and princess set off in one direction, while the horse went the other. Prince Ivan found an empty hut and settled there with his sister . . .

49. Variant: "Live in this house," said the little bullock, "and slaughter me. Eat the meat, and put the bones together in one place and water that place with the water you washed the cups and spoons in. Those bones will grow up into two dogs."

50. The name Duginya suggests a bow, *duga*.

51. *Soska*—like the other *bogatyr* names—is not an actual Russian name. It seems to be an affectionate diminutive from the word for a pine tree, *sosna*, so it would mean something like "Piney." The word *soska* also means 'nipple' in Russian, so the story may have a bawdy undercurrent.

52. Gorynya suggests the word root *gor-*, associated with fire, and perhaps reminding the listener of the serpent *Zmei Gorynych* in Russian folklore.

53. *Usynya* from *us*, mustache.

54. Afanas'ev summarizes the ending of this variant: *bogatyr* Soska fell. He was brought out into Rus' by a huge bird. He married Baba Yaga's daughter, but his *bogatyr* comrades scattered in fear to various foreign lands.

55. Khudiakov notes that this variety of beetle is called *rogach*, "horny one."

56. Variant 1: Once there lived a tsar named Dolmat. He gathered an army of three thousand, and all of them were soldiers' children, sixteen years old. He found them all places in the palace regiments. Some ten years went by, and the soldiers' children had risen in the ranks. Some had become officers, some were colonels, and some were generals! Only one of all the comrades, Semyon Erofeev, had remained an ordinary soldier. He began complaining to the tsar. "It's like this and like that," he said.

"I couldn't serve my way to any kind of little rank. There's happiness for other people, but I don't seem to count for anything!"

Tsar Dolmat ordered them to let Semyon retire and gave him three acres of land. Semyon hired a workman, plowed and sowed the land with wheat. The wheat grew up marvelously! One day he went out to his field and took a look. A tenth of it was completely trampled, and there wasn't a single sprout standing: all you could see was the black soil. He felt terribly sorry to have suffered such a loss. Right away he armed some peasant guards and gave them strict instructions not to sleep all night, but to guard the grain.

The men went out into the field and started to stand guard, but right at midnight, just as it struck twelve, not a one of them could resist falling asleep. Each one fell down right where he'd been standing. A sound, heavy sleep came over them, and they slept right through until broad daylight. In the morning, what do you know—another tenth was trampled. Semyon armed even more guards than before, both on horse and on foot, and he himself went into the field with them. "So, brothers!" he said. "Let's form two groups. Let half stand guard from evening to midnight, and the other half from midnight to dawn." And so they did. As midnight began to draw closer, the first guards began to be overcome by sleep; they woke up the new ones to take their shift, and then they fell right over and went to sleep. But the new guards themselves could barely resist, sleep was pushing at them from all sides! Semyon Erofeev saw that things were looking bad, and he ordered them to hit one another on the ear and shout "Listen!" The peasants started hitting one another on the ear. This was the only way they could drive off sleep. Suddenly a powerful storm blew up. A huge chariot came rolling, with twelve horses pulling it. The horses writhed just like snakes, and behind them came twelve wolves, and just as many bears shackled with iron chains. The chariot quickly passed over the field. Where the wheat had been growing green, there was nothing but black soil, and not a single sprout was left!

Semyon leapt onto his horse and raced off after the chariot. Eleven men broke into a gallop after him. They rode for a long time or a short time, and then they rode up to an enormous castle. There they went into the white-stone chambers and saw a table spread. Twelve places were set on the table, and all kinds of wines and snacks were prepared in plenty. They had something to eat and drink and were getting ready to go back, but no matter where they turned they couldn't find any doors.

An ancient old woman came in and said to them, "Why are you trying so hard for nothing? Coming in to see us is easy, but getting out is hard. The gates into here are wide, but the ones going out are narrow. Soon twelve she-bears will come in, they'll eat dinner and then leave again. But they aren't she-bears, they're enchanted fair maidens. Eleven are boyars' daughters, and the twelfth is a princess. If you spend three nights here, then you'll rescue all of them and win good fortune for yourselves!"

Variant 2: Once there lived a rich merchant, he died and left a young son behind. Grief and longing fell upon him, and he got the idea of going to the tavern to have a good time among good people. He came to the tavern, and there sat a tavern barfly [Afanas'ev notes: in the Russian, *yaryga*] singing songs. The merchant's son asked him, "Tell me, why are you so cheerful?"

"And what reason do I have to be sorrowful? I just drank a measure of wine, and that cheers me up."

"Can that be true?"

"Try it, you'll find out yourself!"

The merchant's son drank a glass, and another, and he began to feel more cheerful. "Let me try some more!" He emptied half a carafe, got drunk, and started up a song.

"Why should we just sit here like this?" asked the tavern drunk. "Let's try our luck at cards."

"If you want to!"

They sat down to play cards. In a short time the merchant's son had lost all his money. He said, "I have nothing more to play for!"

"There's not only money, you can play for your house and your shops!" answered the tavern drunk. "Perhaps you'll make up for all your losses!"

Before even half an hour had passed, the merchant's son was left with nothing. His house, his shops—he'd lost everything. He woke up in the morning poor as a church mouse! [In Russian, *gol kak sokol*, literally 'naked as a falcon.'] What could he do now?

He went from grief to enlist as a soldier. The soldier's fate isn't an easy one; you answer with your back for everything and everyone! And so he decided to run away. He ran off into a thick, deep forest, walked up into a clearing, and sat down to rest . . . Three doves came flying out of nowhere, with three snakes chasing after them. They flew into that clearing and started to fight.

"Soldier! Help us," said the snakes. "We'll give you a lot of money."

"No, soldier! Better help *us*," said the doves. "We'll come in handy to you!"

The merchant's son bared his sharp sword and slashed at the three snakes until they were dead, and the little doves flapped their wings and flew away. The merchant's son rested and went along on his way, following his nose. He walked and walked and came to a dugout house. He went inside. In the dugout house stood a table, and on the table three places were set with dishes. He took a piece from each place and ate it, crawled under the bed, and lay there, keeping very still. Suddenly the three doves flew in, struck against the damp ground, and turned into fair maidens.

"Ah!" they said, "some guest has visited us, and it seems to have been a good man: he offended no one but took a piece from each plate."

The merchant's son heard these words, crawled out from under the bed and said, "Hello, fair maidens!"

"Ah, you fine young man! You did us one good turn—you killed the three snakes. Now do another as well—stay here for three nights! No matter what happens around you, even if thunder rumbles, winds whistle, and horrors try to frighten you, stand firm, don't fear, and read this book here . . ."

57. A pood is a traditional Russian weight, slightly more than sixteen kilograms—a bit more than thirty-six pounds.

58. Baba Yaga does not appear by name in this tale, yet it is clear that the three old women who welcome the heroine are very close to her.

59. In Russian traditional culture, strangers may address each other with kinship terms, especially when the speaker is a child: "auntie" or "uncle" for younger adults, and "granny" or "granddad" for older ones. The word for grandmother,

babuhska, is the affectionate diminutive form of the first part of Baba Yaga's name.

60. In the original *ne po kostiam*, 'don't suit my bones.'
61. Khudiakov noted: "Written down by me from a man born in the village of Selin, in the Venev *uezd* of Tula *guberniia*."
62. "Haiduk" is a word used in Central Europe with various meanings; here it suggests dashing uniformed guards.
63. An *arshin* is an old Russian measurement, about seventy centimeters or roughly two feet.
64. Afanas'ev notes: "A *lubok* (woodcut) edition from 1847; it is given here in abbreviated form."
65. *Terem* in Russian means 'women's quarters'; the word suggests the Muscovite period.
66. Variant: a cuckoo. While the swan is known for its beauty, in Russian culture the cuckoo is associated with lamentation (as in the chant of the dolls in the tale "Prince Danila-Govorila").
67. Variant: He came up to the sea: the shores were made of custard, the water was flowing milk! Here he ate his fill, drank his fill, and gathered his strength . . .
68. Variant: The prince went into the little house, and there was a Baba Yaga, bony leg, lying from corner to corner. She was as hungry as could be.
69. Variant 1: "Ah, I know!" said Baba Yaga. "Wait, soon she'll come flying to me to search my head. As soon as you see her, grab her right away. Vasilisa the Wise will start to turn into various shapes. Watch her and don't be afraid, hold her tight! When she turns into a spindle, you break her in two pieces. Throw them behind you and say: this was a spindle, but now grow behind me as a white birch tree, and turn into a dear fair maiden in front of me!" Prince Ivan did just that: a white birch tree grew up behind him, and in front of him stood Vasilisa the Wise.

    Variant 2: "Eh," said Baba Yaga, "if you had come sooner, then you'd have found her here, but now you'll have to wait for her until tomorrow." Early in the morning the Yaga woke Prince Ivan and said, "Go out in the green meadow and hide behind a bush. A white swan will fly past; it will hover there over you. Don't miss your chance: take hold of her and hold on tight. It's Vasilisa the Wise! If you let go, you'll never find her again." Prince Ivan went out into the green meadow and caught the white swan. No matter how much she struggled or tried to tear loose, she couldn't get loose. Vasilisa the Wise said to him, "Let go, my dear friend! You've crumpled my little wings all up. You knew how to find me, so now I'll be yours forever."
70. In Khudiakov's collection this tale follows another (that lacks Baba Yaga) about a stepmother and stepdaughter, and so its title there is "Again the Stepmother and the Stepmother's Daughter."
71. Khudiakov noted: "Recorded by me in the city of Kazan."
72. Variant: The two older brothers rode and rode and came to a fiery river. They didn't know how to go farther, so they set up tents to one side and started to live in the empty field, to spend their time in revelry. But the younger brother set out on the road to Baba Yaga. She gave him a towel and said, "With this you can ride across the fiery river. Wave the towel to the right and a bridge will appear, wave it to the left and the bridge will vanish."
73. Note from Afanas'ev: Another recording says that a dragon is curled all around the garden with the apples of youth and the springs of the water of

life and of death—his head and tail come together in one place. The Baba Yaga tells the prince, "You strike that dragon in the head. From that *bogatyr* blow he'll sleep for three days. During that time you'll manage to do everything! And here's a dry twig for you. When you go into the garden, run right away to all the springs and dip this twig into the water. The spring that makes it put out leaves and flowers—that one, it means, has living water flowing in it."

74. She gave him a *stezh*, glossed by Afanas'ev as *udar prutom ili plet'ju*, 'a blow with a stick or a lash.'
75. According to the formation of Russian patronymics, a *yagishna* must be the child of a Baba Yaga, though she seems to behave exactly like a Baba Yaga herself.
76. The word in Russian is *chezhelko*.
77. The word in Russian is *navokhrili*, glossed by Afanas'ev as *nakolotili*, 'hammered a lot.'
78. Bast shoes are made from an inner layer of birch or linden bark; they were worn by Russian peasants who could not afford shoes of leather.
79. A lovely dialect word for clothing, *lopot'*.
80. Like Beloy Polyanin, Bel Belyanin's name tells us that he is white—perhaps silver-haired—with age.
81. Zlatokos means literally "Goldenhair"—almost "Goldilocks."
82. The Russian verbs for hearing and smelling are the same, perhaps reflecting that hearing and smell are more passive senses than sight, touch, and taste.
83. The dialect word *diuzhe*, glossed as *ochen'*.
84. The Russian saying in this case means "the old woman said yes and no," a reminder of old women's role in fortune-telling.
85. "Through," not "around," suggesting that the teller thought of the world as flat.
86. From here to the end the tale follows the version that Afanas'ev offers as a variant on tale no. 129, because his primary variant does not involve Baba Yaga.
87. Variant: He saw a golden ring; the prince took the ring, and as soon as he put it on his finger two black men appeared at once and said, "What is your will, Prince Ivan?"
88. *Chereviki*.
89. *Zalët* means 'drop-in' or 'fly-by.'
90. *Misha Kosolapoy*, 'Misha Crooked-Paw' or 'Misha Clumsy-Paw,' was a typical name for bears in Russian animal tales.
91. *Zapechnik* means 'Behind the Stove.'
92. Ivashko is the diminutive form of Ivas', not the same name as Ivan. Perhaps the first "Ivan" in this tale was a mistake—the person recording it was so used to the third brother being named Ivan that he or she heard it wrong the first time it was mentioned.
93. "Bread and salt" is the typical Russian expression for hospitality.
94. See note 92 above.
95. Like the hero's name "Ivashko," rather than the more typical Russian "Ivan," the spelling 'Yega' suggests that this tale was collected in a western part of the Russian empire.
96. Here and in some other places later in this story the word Yaga is turned into an adjective, *yagaia*.
97. Russians traditionally did not celebrate birthdays, but instead the feast day of the saint a person was named after. In this tale, we see a name day although we never learn the old woman's name.
98. *Kvass* is a slightly sweet, slightly alcoholic, traditional Russian drink made from fermented rye bread and sometimes raisins or other fruit.
99. As noted before, the Russian word *krasnyi* means both 'red' and 'beautiful.'

INDEX

CPSIA information can be obtained
at www.ICGtesting.com
Printed in the USA
BVHW010412230123
656660BV00001B/2

9 781617 035968